MW00366369

LIVING UNDERWATER

KATI VAN DER HOEVEN
AS TOLD TO SARAH TUN

Kati van der Hoeven © Copyright 2019

The right of Kati van der Hoeven to be identified as the author of this work has been asserted by her in accordance with the Copyright, Designs and Patents Act 1998.

All rights reserved. No reproduction, copy or transmission of this publication may be made without express prior written permission. No paragraph of this publication may be reproduced, copied or transmitted except with express prior written permission or in accordance with the provisions of the Copyright Act 1956 (as amended). Any person who commits any unauthorised act in relation to this publication may be liable to criminal prosecution and civil claims for damage.

Although every effort has been made to ensure the accuracy of the information contained in this book, as of the date of publication, nothing herein should be construed as giving advice. The opinions expressed herein are those of the author.

Some names and identifying details have been changed to protect the privacy of individuals.

Published by Goldcrest Books International Ltd
www.goldcrestbooks.com
publish@goldcrestbooks.com

ISBN: 978-1-911505-63-1 (paperback)
ISBN: 978-1-911505-64-8 (ebook)

'All the adversity I've had in my life, all the trouble and obstacles, have strengthened me... You may not realise it when it happens, but a kick in the teeth may be the best thing in the world for you.'

Walt Disney

Kati 1994

CONTENTS

Part 3: Learning to Float

Part 4: Riding the Tide

FOREWORD

Surrender is a most difficult part of life. We are born with a freedom and a will to create our own world and to direct our circumstances. Witness any baby's cry. He may not have the words to express his needs, but he makes himself heard. A young child may be limited in her vocabulary, but she expresses herself when she is happy, sad, frustrated, injured or hungry. We all know what we want from a very early age, and self-determination develops and thrives, as we are encouraged to live according to our values, our desires and our goals.

Imagine then, if you are perfectly clear-headed one day, and the next, just as clear but are no longer able to move or speak. What do you do with the self-determination now?

I have met a woman who has learnt to make the best out of a bad situation, and in fact, to have recognised that she is the better person for her misfortune. Because Kati Lepistö van der Hoeven knows something few others do: she has learnt to surrender to her circumstances and she has thrived.

In a much loved book of the late twentieth century called *The Road Less Travelled* by Dr Scott Peck, he writes: "Life is difficult... Once we truly know that life is difficult – once we truly understand and accept it – then life is no longer difficult."[1]

As a young woman in my life's journey, I read that book as I was searching for relief from a string of broken romantic relationships. It helped me a lot. Dr Peck is no longer with us on earth, but I am certain he would have smiled if he had met Kati, for she is a woman who personifies the living of a difficult life.

Kati embodies one who lives a full life in spite of – and she would even say because of – the difficulties she has had to face. She is as bold, as feisty and as determined as she was as a child, to fulfil her goals and to live out her purpose.

Join me as we discover Kati, this resilient woman who is living an amazing life because of her incredible attitude, wisdom and love of life. I have had the privilege to meet her and now will share with you her journey. This is Kati's story.

Sarah Tun
Writing Coach and Author

---

1. Peck, Dr M. Scott, *The Road Less Travelled*, (New York: Simon and Schuster, 1978)

PROLOGUE

Once upon a time there was an island with a very advanced civilisation. The surrounding ocean level was rising rapidly and the island would soon be underwater.

The government leaders of this island took swift and strategic action. They went to the academics for guidance. How could they save their country and their lives?

The scholars consulted and agreed that the best course of action would be to build a wall around the island, and hope that it would be high enough, and strong enough, to keep the water out.

But the governors were not content with this advice and so they went to the retired intellectuals, who had more life experience, and asked for their advice.

The intellectuals proposed they build a holy place where everyone on the island could come together to pray for God's mercy, and hope that the island would be spared.

Needless to say, the governors were not completely assured by this proposal either. So, they went to the country's wise old man for his advice.

The wise old man told them, "Learn to live underwater". Sometimes in life, you cannot change your circumstances. Instead you need to learn to live inside them.

Part 1: On the Water

'We learn best by living'

Kati van der Hoeven

CHAPTER 1

In the Beginning is Family

I grew up in a family of four: my father, or *isa* in Finnish, is Risto Lepistö; my mother, or äiti, is Marjatta Appelqvist Lepistö; my brother, Jukka, who is three years older than me, and me.

Äiti is a lioness. She watches over her family, and nobody had better mess with any of us, or they'll have to answer to her. She is strong but gentle, and very loving, and it is because of her that I became a model. Not because she told me to, but because she allowed me the freedom to make my choices, and I did.

About me:

I was born on 25 June 1974. My mother had been carrying me for over nine months, and my designated birthdate arrived but I didn't. She waited a while, but I remained in her belly. Eventually, she went to the hospital in Mikkeli and said, "I'm overdue."

She was told to go home.

"I'm more than ten days overdue. I'm not going home."

Such is the determination of my mother, something I definitely inherited. I was born by caesarean section on 25 June. There were no complications.

Although I was a healthy, happy little girl, I was prone to throat infections, and so sometime when I was school aged, I had my tonsils removed.

I moved to Los Angeles to build up my modelling career when I was eighteen. It was great, but I hadn't accounted for the smog; it was a killer on my throat and I had frequent infections. Shades of the old school days while I was growing up, I guess. My mother wonders, did the throat infection I'd picked up before 9 January 1995 have anything to do with the stroke? You see, I'm a tetraplegic because when I was twenty I had an undiagnosed stroke. Over a twenty-four-hour period, during which I was conscious, my faculties gradually deteriorated and by 11 January I was no longer able to move or speak. Did an infection running through my body finally land and destroy a part of my brainstem forever? If my mother could have done more in the hospital on the night of 9 January, she would have.

About Äiti:

Let me tell you about my mother, a lioness who watches over her cubs.

My first contact with a doctor that I can remember happened when I was twelve years old.

Every year, all children would have a regular check-up with the old school nurse. This particular year though, the year I was twelve, the nurse wanted to see me a second time to repeat all the usual tests. She got the same results, which showed that my eye sight had worsened and, as well, that my growth had suddenly stopped. She was alarmed, so she made an appointment for me to visit the doctor. Äiti came with me.

When your eyesight deteriorates it does so gradually, so that you don't really notice. When you're a child, you don't even realise what you're supposed to be able to see; you don't know what's normal.

I remember sitting in the waiting room just a couple of metres away from the doctor's door, where his name was posted in big letters. Jokingly, Äiti asked me to read his name out loud.

"I can't see it," I said, and she was shocked.

When we got called into the office, the doctor repeated the eye tests again. A week later we were summoned back to his office.

This doctor was a man of few words, and his room was as dark and unfriendly as his mood and character. The room smelled like old cigarettes. I remember his dark brown glasses were constantly slipping down his nose, as he was going through my result papers in silence. The only sounds he made were loud sighs. We watched while he read. Eventually the doctor asked my mom, "Have you noticed anything?"

"What?" she said. I could tell her voice was full of worry and fear. He was so ominous, she was thinking I must have had something growing in my brain.

He didn't seem to notice her fear. After a long pause, and with tension mounting inside my mother with every one of his sighs, he finally said, "There really seems to be nothing wrong." And he closed the file.

"What? That's it?"

Äiti was so furious at him for making her worry, I thought she was going to hit him! He was totally unaware though. She grabbed my hand immediately, and pulled me out of the office. He had frightened her, ignored my bad eyesight, and was totally oblivious to both problems he had created.

Eventually, we realised the old school nurse had written down the eye test results incorrectly, so the vision problem had been completely overlooked. I would eventually end up with glasses, but it took a while. Äiti would not go back to any doctor, not even for glasses. I understood why. Even at my young age of twelve, I understood that doctors need to be sensitive to people, not only clinical. When they are studying to be doctors, some education in bedside manner is necessary too. Looking back to that time, it should have been a signal to us of how disregarded patients are in Mikkeli.

My mother is not one for letting go or giving up easily. I don't know when she learnt that, but since the stroke she has hung on to me and would not let me go, even when I wanted to give up all hope. Truly, if it had not been for her, I'm not sure I would be with you now, telling this story.

About Isa (Finnish for Dad):

Now to my father. Isa is loyal, quiet and strong. He doesn't say much, but he thinks deeply – I suppose I get that from him. When he does speak, everybody listens, because he only says what he thinks is very important to say. He's interesting to listen to, even when people disagree, because he's always willing to discuss his point of view, and share what's on his mind, once he starts to open up. It just takes a lot to get him started.

He doesn't pay compliments, but he shows his love in other ways. When I was young he took me fishing for hours, because I wanted to catch a fish. He rowed and rowed for a week, just to give me a chance. His love makes me a stronger person; not because he says gushy things, but because he says what I need to hear. Sometimes he's very blunt. When I was little, he would come right up to my face and tell me what he thought, even when it wasn't a very nice thought. It was something I needed to hear, to learn.

Twelve must have been a particularly memorable year of childhood for me. It was the summer when I was twelve that I went rock climbing with my brother and fell.

As with every summer, our family spent time camping up in Lapland, and out on our boat, to experience nature. Always it was Isa, Äiti, Jukka and Kati. Jukka would get me to do all kinds of adventurous things, more suitable to teenage boys like him than a pre-teen girl like me. But we were both fit. He'd always encourage me to go along with him, and I always did.

On one particular day, we were on an island and he had me rock climbing.

"Come on, Kalle," (that's what he calls me – the boy's version of Kati) he'd say.

But I fell. It was only a couple or three metres (maybe a ten-foot drop), but I landed on rocks and I screamed when I did – the landing hurt!

Isa was on his boat and heard me scream. He came and found me, carried me to the boat, patched me up, and assured me, without great ceremony or drama, that I would be fine.

My dad gave me no lecture (not Jukka either), cleaned me up and let me run off when I was up to it again. No big deal said, but I knew he'd always stick by me, no matter what. That's my dad. While my mom is a robust person, with plenty to say, my dad is an anchor, keeping the family steady. They are good for each other and great parents too.

About Jukka:

Jukka and I love each other a lot. We always have. But we've also always fought like cat and dog.

Once we had a scrap and punched a hole in our bathroom door. I don't remember which of us did it. We both wanted Grandpa's belt buckle. I'm into fashion and I could accessorise with it. Jukka was a young man and wanted his grandpa's belt. He won, but he shared it with me. Yeah, we fight but we love each other a lot.

Growing up he called me Kalle, because that's the name my parents would have called me if I'd been a boy. He is amazing: gorgeous, smart and adventurous. He would always challenge me to follow him wherever he went, which drove my parents crazy. Sometimes he would climb high or explore far, and say, "Come on, Kalle." I always did and sometimes got mildly hurt, by falling or getting a scrape. In exchange, I watched out for him, including who he dated. We grew up to be very close. He even let me screen his girlfriends, in case any were bad news.

I think the first time a girl came and I opened the door, she asked me if Jukka could come out to play. I was five. She looked all right, so I said, "Yes." I called him and he went off with this girl.

But then when I was six or seven maybe, some girl came and she was not okay. I knew her from school and she was a girl who used to tease other girls who weren't very pretty. So, when she asked if Jukka was home, I said, "No." Well, he was, but he wasn't home for her.

Sure, she was pretty, with big eyes and long, flowing hair, but I knew she wasn't nice, so I said no to her, and closed the door.

When Jukka asked who was at the door, I told him some girl who makes fun of other girls.

"You don't want to play with her," I said.

"No, I guess not," he said, and that was the first time I screened a girl away from him. It wouldn't be the last.

Now he's with Anu. She's perfect for him. They've been together for a very long time, and she is as much a part of the family now as any of us. Whereas Jukka is a bit of a tease but doesn't show his real feelings, Anu is serious, down to earth and observant.

Both are athletic. Anu was going to enter for Olympic dressage (horse riding) before she met Jukka. She was the top rider in Finland. I've seen a lot of girls change direction when they meet their future husbands. Anu is an example of that.

Me to Anu years ago: "So, you like my brother?"

Anu to me: "Yes."

Years later she tells me, "The day I met him I immediately felt at home."

Jukka has always been into outdoor activities for fun. Well, he's like most Finnish boys. He is level-headed and very calm. In fact they are both calm. Very different from me, but perfect for each other. They say that opposites attract. In their case this is true: Jukka is hearty and intense, and Anu is elegant, poised and very calm. I've never heard her even raise her voice. On the other hand, Jukka and their daughter, Sofia, laugh up a storm, making fun and teasing Anu for how slowly she eats. Does she mind? No. She's got it together.

Anu seems delicate, but she is strong. She gives the sense that, while having a cup of coffee at home, even if an avalanche struck, she'd quietly sip her coffee until she finished. I lived through an earthquake once and it totally freaked me out. I think about Anu, and I bet she would have sat, waiting for it to pass. She wears beautiful clothes, has a tidy and beautiful home, and always there is a sense of calm confidence about her. She rarely says what's on her mind, but don't think she isn't 100 per cent aware. She's the quietest person I know, she's also the most observant.

As for Jukka, while he acts distant and quite tough, inside he's actually gentle. He told me once the worst thing that could happen to him is if Sofia got really sick, or injured, and died. Yeah, he's hardy and aloof, but Anu is perfect for him. She's patient when he keeps his feelings in and available when he wants to talk.

But I'm supposed to be talking about when we were little...

People always compete with someone: siblings, friends, or even ourselves. But I never competed with Jukka. In fact, we looked after each other, keeping each other occupied so much so that our parents rarely had to look out for us.

Me again:

In school, I don't remember ever feeling the need to compete with anybody else, probably because I was so confident and always seemed to know what I wanted, and how to achieve it. I guess I have always been very independent, not wanting or letting anybody help me. My mother tells a story of when I was under three, trying to put on a pair of thick pantyhose. She wanted to help me but it goes without saying, I didn't accept help. I bet it was a very funny sight, me struggling with pantyhose, Äiti offering to help, but me shouting, "no!" and getting all twisted up in them.

My favourite memory of growing up was our summer boat trips. All of them. For about ten years, every summer the whole family rode on our ten-metre boat that went really slowly along the huge Lake Saimaa.

It was an easy and relaxing way to travel, our family alone, sometimes with some cousins, eating and sleeping on the boat, miles from any other people. My cousin Annika and I would play with Barbies, swim, and walk in the forest; we'd pick berries, watch animals and learn their behaviours. I discovered a lot about plants and animals on those trips. We spent hours looking around us, laughing, and being together. They were simple times, wonderful times, with my family.

I don't remember many arguments with my family, but I do remember my mother paying me to stop talking when she was teaching me maths. I used to get so mad when I got the wrong answers in my homework (which wasn't too often, fortunately), and I didn't want anybody to teach me except Äiti, with that payment system. That was the year I was twelve.

The thing is, I had a very happy childhood. Both parents worked. Jukka and I got along really well. I was always a good pupil – often helping teachers in the classroom. Such are my roots.

I've always been independent, wanting to work out everything for myself. I *had* to do everything on my own. Looking at me now, it's pretty ironic if you think about it.

The truth is, I've always hated asking for things. I got a bank account when I was five and learnt early how to manage my purchases. At age six, I made my first fashion purchase. My first part-time job came when I was fourteen, working full time during the summer. All of this was, of course, so that I could be as independent as possible, buying the fashion magazines and clothes I liked, all so I could be prepared for modelling whenever I was ready to leave home – which would be very, very soon...

CHAPTER 2

Growing Years' Snapshots

A mother's point of view:
"I will tie my shoes, I will buy my own boots and I *will* have long hair!"

"Yes, you will have long hair because it will grow! But for now it is short," said Marjatta, Kati's mother.

Kati was crying. She'd just had one of those obligatory haircuts little girls get. At six she already knew what she wanted to do with her life.

"I'm going to be a model when I grow up." And to her mind, all models had long hair, and if they didn't, they certainly should.

*

"I want those pale blue boots, Äiti."

"The ones we saw last week?"

"Yes."

"Well, you can go to the bank with your isa and you can take out enough money from your account to buy them. Do you remember how much they cost?"

"Yes."

"Good. You can go, and get Isa to take you."

"Thanks, Äiti."

And off she went. She was six.

My Kati has always been Little Miss Independent. When she was less than two years old, and still wearing diapers, it was very difficult to change her, because she wanted to do it herself. Imagine me, her äiti, changing her, with her little fingers getting in the way because she wanted to do it herself. Who changes their own diaper? But Kati tried!

"Isa, I have been saving money. I need to go to the bank to get some money for boots."

He nods. They go in the car. She gets her money and they go to the store. They come home.

"Marjatta." Isa kisses me. "Look!" Kati's put on the boots and we all smile.

"I especially like the tassels," says Kati.

*

"Auntie, I have never been on a plane. This is wonderful! What's it like in Italy?"

"Warm, sunny and very old."

"Oh, old?"

"Yes, very. But the buildings are beautiful and I think you'll like it. There are a lot of amazing clothes. So many designs come from Italy."

"I'm going to like it! You're only thirteen once, you know!"

"Yes."

But although the take-off was great, and I loved going to Italy, it ended kind of abruptly.

"Look out!" But it was too late. My dear auntie was run over by a moped. Fortunately, passers-by called an ambulance. I watched from the side of the road as my auntie was put onto a stretcher and taken to hospital – no room for a ward like me.

I didn't speak a word of Italian. Not even of English. But this resourceful girl got back to the hotel, packed her things and got herself to the airport and onto a plane to get home.

Although that first travel experience abroad was pretty dramatic, it didn't put me off. Not only have I been to Italy since, I plan to make many long-distance destinations in my modelling career.

And my aunt recovered.

*

"What will you be when you grow up, Irina?"

"I dunno, Kati. But I know who I like."

"Erik?"

"How did you know? I never told you." She punched me gently.

We're lying on my bed, just talking, like we usually do.

"I can tell. You talk about him enough. And you stare at him at school."

"I do not!"

"You do. And I can prove it. What colour are his eyes?"

"Blue."

"You sure?"

"Yeah."

"How are you sure?"

"Because I look at him..."

"You stare. Admit it. Right?"

"Yeah, okay. Who do you like? I can't tell."

"Aw, I don't have time to think about it. There's school and working, and I'm gonna be a model, so I have to work at it and not think about Miikka."

"So, you like him?"

"Yeah, no, I don't know. I don't have time to think about him. I'm going to be a model and I have a lot to do to be ready. You know, you can never dream too big."

But Irina wouldn't give up.

"What colour are his eyes... Hmm? I bet you know..."

"Yeah, deep sea blue."

Then we burst out laughing.

And I guess she did get me thinking about him. Maybe the conversation was carried along in the air because it wasn't very long before Miikka asked me to be his girlfriend.

"Ah, yes," I said, but not too dreamy-eyed.

In movies you see these teenagers googly eyed over each other. I thought he was cute, and nice, but I never dreamt about him and it didn't last.

"I'm sorry, Miikka, but I've got too much to do, so I can't have a boyfriend."

That was it. My first boyfriend lasted for two weeks. We held hands and talked sometimes, but a busy fourteen-year-old with modelling plans really doesn't have time for a boyfriend.

Life ought to be uncomplicated when you're fourteen.

*

"Name?"

I'm standing in front of this gorgeous guy, but he doesn't even notice me. Why not? Because the room is full of beautiful models, and I'm just a kid among all these women.

"Kati Lepistö."

"Age?"

"Fourteen."

"Height?"

"Five feet, nine inches."

"Hair – brown. Eyes – green. Weight?"

"Thirty-five kilos."

It's a crowded room, but I manage to find a place in a quiet corner, so I don't have to talk to anybody, until...

"Hi, I'm Inka."

"Hi. Kati."

"Have you ever done a hair show before?"

"Nope. This is my first one. But it won't be my last."

"Me too. I wonder how long this will take. My äiti made me come. I don't mind, I guess, but I'm not really interested."

"Hmm."

"So, what about you?"

"I just need to concentrate and do the best I can. So, I'll see you later. Good luck."

"Ah, okay. Bye."

She may not be interested, but this is what I've been waiting for forever. I can't get distracted. This is serious!

It takes hours, or it seems like it. Finally...

"Kati Lepistö."

I've been watching, looking to see what the other girls do, and following to see what happens next.

I go to the platform, stand, smile, flip my hair around, throw it to the back, to the side. I've always loved being the centre of attention – and for three minutes, I am. Funny though, I don't like having my picture taken. I have to force myself to like it. Otherwise, I wouldn't make it in modelling now would I?

"Thank you."

That was it. Three minutes exactly. Don't call us, we'll call you. But I'm starting and nothing's gonna hold me back. Nothing!

*

I'm standing in my local magazine shop.

"Are the new ones in yet?"

"Yes, Kati, for you, anything."

I buy *Elle* and *Vogue*. I save all my money for magazines and clothes. I love *Harper's Bazaar* but my favourite is, of course, *Glamour*. It's funny sometimes.

Anything with up-to-date fashion really will do. I study the poses, the looks. I must develop attitude.

Do all these girls love what they're doing? Underneath the poses and the cool stares, I wonder who these women are. Are they as excited to model as I am? I'm discovering that it's hard work, and we don't do it *just for fun!*

I smile at the man behind the counter. He smiles back. I'm practising on him, to get him to like me, but still it is a sincere smile. So is his.

I pay for the magazines. "Well, gotta go," I say, and I'm out the door.

*

Dancing. When I was a little girl I used to love ballet. Now, it's whatever style will teach me the newest ways to move. I think I've tried every possible dance there is, since the ability to move helps a lot as a model.

I love working hard and getting up a sweat. It feels great. And everything is geared to getting myself up on the platform and keeping eyes on me. As I've said before, I have always liked to be the centre of attention. I suppose that's why I've chosen to become a professional model.

*

Another hair show. It's sort of a job this time, but not exactly. I'll explain.

It's more organised than the first casting, and I'm a bit more in the know. I contacted them and I was specifically chosen for the show, so I know my time will not be wasted.

It's eight in the morning and I'll be here until at least ten tonight. I might leave here a redhead, who knows?

It's been an hour and a half, but finally:

"Kati Lepistö?"

Nope. Blonde, with just a trim. I smile at the hairdresser, who looks as nervous as I feel.

"You new?" she asks me. I nod. "Me too," she says.

So many people on trial, all the time. We learn and aim to shine.

"Go mad!" I tell her. Why not? So she curls and flips and I love it!

"They should give you a gown for this hairdo." And they do.

I'm driven to the venue along with a few other girls. Everybody is jabbering away, except me. I'm thinking: *how can I stand out in this group?* I saw somebody shove another girl once, to get into the centre of the lens. I'm not going to stoop so low. Wait, I know...

We pile out of the van, and I let everyone else out first. At the door I pause, just for a moment.

"Girls, this way?" A steward leads the other girls. I'm about to fall behind.

"Oh, there you are," says some guy walking towards me. "Thought we were one short. Come on. Hmm. I've got just the dress for you, pretty lady."

Ruffles to go with my hair. Fantastic. All because I was patient.

We're given lunch, which consists of raw veggies, diet soda and a bit of fruit. Doesn't anyone here like meat or bread?

Again there's some waiting around.

"No dancing today, girls, just a parade in stilettos. Look smart!"

I'd heard about choreography practice, which could take several hours, depending on how complicated the dance might be. Thankfully, we're sent straight to make-up and will get to dress soon.

I'm looking forward to it. This *is* the best dress imaginable for me. Long low waist, with a knee-length ruffled skirt. Fun and sexy too.

It's a crowded changing room, but all the girls are giggling with excitement. You're not here unless you like getting your hair done and you like stylish clothes.

Earlier today they were playing the same music over and over again, and then they stopped. It's been quiet for a while. But all of a sudden, the music has started up again. Will we be called soon? We think so. We're all holding our breath.

"I've got butterflies," someone whispers, and we all laugh nervously.

"Shush," the stage manager whispers.

"Grrgle," says someone's stomach. We all stifle laughter. But honestly, that veggie lunch was five hours ago.

The music begins to swell, and one after another, we're given our cue.

Don't trip, glide, I tell myself. I bet every other girl backstage is saying the same thing. These stilettos are five inches high at least!

But we all glide, we slither, we're cool and although we quiver inside, we don't show nerves one bit.

And then the show ends.

Backstage, we have to undress super-fast because all the outfits have to be checked, accounted for and sorted by

Costumes before any of us are allowed out of the door. That includes the shoes.

And when everything is over, we don't get paid in money, and we're not going to get a cheque in the mail. What we're looking forward to is the great package of hair products. And the organisers don't disappoint us.

*

Contests come and contests go. Once or twice Irina and I do a fashion show. She likes the fabrics on her skin; I like the practice for serious work. Her interest wanes, but mine only gets stronger and I keep pursuing my dream, one casting, one contest at a time.

"Sorry you didn't win, Kati!"

"It doesn't matter, Irina. That's not the point."

"Yeah, you always say that."

"It's okay, really. Sure, winning's great. But I made the finals the first time. What did that get me?"

Irina shrugs.

"Seen. It got me *seen*. And I learnt a lot! That's what really matters. I can win and then stop, or I can keep going until I get to the top. And guess what?"

"What?" she asks.

"I got my first modelling job!"

"Really?"

We kind of squeal. It's a bit loud I guess, because Äiti yells from downstairs:

"What's going on?"

"Nothing. I just told Irina about the job." Then I tell Irina some details.

"You know Sokos Department Store?"

"Yeah. Wait – they've hired you?"

I nod. "Fashion show."

"Kati Lepistö – on the runway!" she announces.

"Amazing. Now I can say, 'I know Kati Lepistö' and everyone will be impressed."

"Yeah, not really. I mean, this is Mikkeli. Everyone knows me, everyone knows everyone, practically. It's no big deal. But it's a job and I'll have pictures and..."

"Yeah, I know. You'll get seen, you'll learn lots and you'll build up your portfolio."

"You got it, chick!"

"Cluck, cluck, you're a duck."

Girl talk.

"Remember when I hated to be in front of the camera?"

"Yeah, Kati, that was weird. 'I'm gonna be a model,' one second and then, 'No, no, don't take my picture'."

Irina knows me best of all.

"Yeah, good thing I got over that, sort of."

"No kidding. And not totally."

We laugh.

"I think I was uncomfortable because I didn't really know what to do. Now, I do. I know how to sell myself, and look – somebody's buying." I present a confident pose.

"Yeah, Sokos Department Store!" she says enthusiastically.

"Yeah!"

I'm surrounded by people who help me to believe in myself.

*

My first big wake-up call comes at the professional course I first see advertised in a magazine.

"Äiti! I don't believe it. Look!"

"What is it?" My mom looks up from her cooking.

"Look! They're coming here!"

"Who?"

In Mikkeli. I almost can't believe my luck. A course is being offered here!

It'd cost me extra – tons – if I had to study away from home, but the course comes to *me* in Mikkeli.

"I almost can't believe it!" I shout. But when you're working to do what you're meant to be doing, things work out.

I call the number and they give me the details. At barely seventeen, I'm old enough. And they run contests and have information for other courses too.

"How much?" She has to tell me twice. It's expensive but I know it's only a quarter of the cost for the same thing in Helsinki. And I have enough. I've been working in a clothing shop part-time (full time during the summers), so I can pay for the course.

Äiti and Isa decide to drive me to the classes. Teamwork. That's my family. I will always be grateful.

I see lots of girls my age taking their parents for granted, but I don't want to. If mine didn't take me to all these castings, what would be the point of the course? So, I'm grateful.

"Thanks," I say, as I hop in, or out of, the car.

"Thanks again." I'm loving this!

Sometimes even Jukka drives me around. I'll get my licence soon, and then I can make my own way.

*

On this course, Don, the photographer, gives me the best tip of my entire life.

"What do you mean, you hate having your picture taken?"

"Well, yeah. I know it doesn't make any sense."

"It sure doesn't, Kati. Come here."

The modelling world can be pretty harsh. But in the early days I meet Don, who becomes a friend. We'll stay connected for years.

"Come on." He is standing next to a full-length mirror, and waving me towards him.

"Stand here," he says.

I do.

"Now, look."

I'm gazing at myself in front of the mirror. It's unavoidable; I can't escape.

"I'm going to load some film. I've got a couple other girls I can shoot first. Stand here, and don't move your feet. Got it?"

I glare at him. What's he talking about?

"Kati, make faces, lots of faces, and learn how your face works. Don't move, just look. Got it?"

"Okay." I shrug, but I watch, like he's just told me to do, and I see how my face has gone into a grimace, then a smile. Gosh, flexible or what? And I see, at that thought, my eyebrows rise and fall gently. Gee, he's onto something.

I must have been in front of that mirror for an hour, because he shot two other girls before he came back. But it felt like two minutes.

"Your turn, Kati. Let's see what you've got to give me."

Don shoots me a warm smile, and I feel my cheeks glow as I smile back. It's different this time, in front of the camera. He's put on some background music and it happens to be my favourite artist – Prince. I feel my face moving and widening, opening to the camera. I'm so busy feeling my wonderful feeling when he says,

"Brilliant, wrap!" I'm thinking really? Already?

I shoot him a kiss through my hand. Wow! I'm feeling

great! No nerves and I didn't mind him taking my picture, not at all.

"Thanks, Don. That was amazing!" He's my photography hero.

"So were you, Kati. See ya next time."

No successful person makes it on their own. We have to be grateful to the people we meet. Sometimes people are nice, and sometimes they're not. But each encounter happens to help us to become better at what we're meant to be doing.

I met some great girls too; some will make it and some won't. I will, of course, because I want to. Only there was that one thing – I hated having my picture taken. But Don has helped me through and I'll always be grateful.

*

Graduation from the modelling course is nothing fancy, just an opportunity to receive proof we've taken the course.

"We like your work, Kati. You've got promise."

I smile inside, but I project a *warm-yet-aloof* attitude that I'm perfecting, on the outside. I nod a little so the coach knows I've heard her.

"Congratulations. The course is finished. You've got a great portfolio and the world awaits."

Two sentences and a certificate, an attitude and a lot of pictures. Was it worth the price? You betcha!

*

From 1990–91 it's busy; learning, going to castings, entering contests. I've gone from a modelling course to fashion shows and castings. Sometimes I feel nervous, but everything I do is leading me towards fulfilling my dream. I'm getting more confident, and the thought of the international scene is hardly scary now. I think it's going to be a reality soon.

At seventeen, I've been in contests, done jobs and a recent trip to Helsinki got me some excellent photos. Everything I do builds my confidence.

It's the summer holidays, and time to take a break.

*

"Äiti, I am going to Italy with Linda during the summer holidays. I've saved up and I have enough money."

Linda is my friend from the clothing store. She's a lot of fun.

"Italy? Just two girls?"

"I have the money. Why not?"

My äiti thought about it. "For how long will you go?"

"Three weeks."

She nodded.

My mother is the best mother. She knows I can do things on my own. Ever since I was thirteen when I was travelling with my auntie and she got knocked down by a moped, and I had to make my way back to Finland on my own. My mother knows I can manage well on my own, even travelling. And I won't be on my own. I will be with Linda. Well, for most of the time. Then I will be with Luigi. He makes me smile, and laugh, and I am in love.

*

"Kati, this is *so* great! How did you convince your parents to come with me?"

"I didn't have to. They know I love travelling, and they know I can do it. I've done it before."

"On your own. How? You're only seventeen."

"Yes, well, my mother calls me 'Little Miss Independent' for a good reason."

The flight is packed, and Linda and I can't stop talking all the way to Rimini where we land.

"So, how do you know Luigi?"

I smile. I'm going to spend a week alone with Luigi after years of letters. I can almost scream I'm so excited. But first, Linda and I will see some sights together – Firenze, San Marino.

"Well," I begin, "I never told you about Luigi?"

"A bit. Only that you know this hot guy you're going to meet after we have our two-week vacation," says Linda.

"Yeah. Riccione here we come!"

"So, are you going to tell me about this guy?"

"Yeah. Okay. I met Luigi two years ago, when I was going to Germany by boat with my school. Luigi's a little bit older than me. He was in Finland to see Finnish architecture by Alvar Aalto. He was planning to be an architect – and now he is one!"

"Good job!"

"Yeah, I think he really loves it. He also loves driving rally, so he liked going to Finland to visit where the famous Finnish drivers come from. Anyway, he was on this boat, where we met.

So, I was on the boat with my best class friend on the school trip, and we were in the elevator. The doors opened and we stepped out – and there he was!

I have to tell you as soon as I saw him, it was crazy. Luigi's eyes locked with mine. I remember he was sitting on the hallway floor, just across from the elevator. I don't even remember how we ended up talking, but we did. I guess you'd say Luigi and I had an electric connection. We spent the whole night talking and kissing. We found some corridor somewhere, where we could be alone."

"That's pretty romantic."

"Yeah, and the next morning we exchanged addresses. But it was not goodbye."

"No, obviously." She smiles and raises her eyebrows. We laugh.

"You know the first thing I did when I got home after that boat trip? When I got home from Germany, I sent him a package. I found a small rally car, wrapped it up and put a letter with it, and sent it to him."

"That's so sweet."

I smile. "He's sweet too. We've been writing to each other now for two years. Every time I get a letter from him, I'm so excited."

"What's he say?"

"He writes really nice stuff, and tells me about his school and work. I know he's excited too. He's an architect now. Just like he planned. I guess we're a lot alike. I've got plans too."

"Yeah, modelling."

"And guess where he lives?"

"I think you told me. Milan?"

"Fashion capital of the world."

"You've got it sorted, Kati."

"Yeah. I guess. You never can dream too big. Maybe I'll marry Luigi and live in the fashion capital of the world for the rest of my life."

"Want that?"

"Yeah, maybe. I'll see how the week goes."

"Yeah, that makes sense."

*

Italy with Linda is so much fun. But the whole time I'm thinking of Luigi too. What will it be like to see him again? Will it be electric like that night we met? I know it will be.

*

And then I see him. Finally, after all these months, and all our letters, he is standing in front of me, waiting for me as I come from the hotel.

It doesn't even take two seconds and we are kissing, the longest kiss in the world, and I nearly collapse, I'm so happy.

I've never made love before and we don't even talk about it, but he takes me to his place and almost immediately we are in each other's pants. He's so gorgeous and so gentle, and so perfect.

I'm in love and this is the most wonderful thing in the world, even better than dancing.

It is the best week of my life. I can't imagine anything more perfect.

Saying goodbye is horrible. We both cry. But we love each other and promise...

"Do you promise me you'll keep writing to me?" he asks me.

"Forever, I will, I promise. Will you?"

"I'll never stop loving you. I'll never stop."

We kiss one last time and I have to get on the plane.

Oh, life is so wonderful. But sad sometimes too.

CHAPTER 3

Secure to Fly

Back in Mikkeli, I can't help but think about Luigi. Ah, but what's the point? He's too far away and will move on with his life. I'm starting my career, he's already into his and he's going to be moving around, so we just have to carry on. I think of him a lot, still write to him, but with each passing day I know there is no chance for us. We must move on.

The music is pumping and I'm having a great time with some friends. Dancing is my life, after modelling, and as I come out of the nightclub warehouse, who do I bump into but Mr Gorgeous? Practically the most incredibly good-looking Finn I've ever seen.

"Hi," he says.

Our eyes lock. "Excuse me," I say, but the doorway is narrow and our bodies touch as we try to squeeze past each other. I'm leaving, he's arriving at the venue.

"Jukka," he says, recognising my brother who's come to pick me up. "Who's this lady?"

"My sister," says Jukka.

"Will you introduce us?" I ask him, but then I don't wait. "So, you're a friend of Jukka's? I'm Kati. Hi."

"Hi." He smiles and his smile lights up the whole doorway this evening.

We're jostled by people coming and going.

He says, "I'll call you tomorrow, Jukka?" I don't even know his name yet, but I'll never forget that smile.

"Yeah, yeah," says my brother, looking at me as we walk back to the car.

"Who's that?" I ask as casually as I can.

"Jari. He's all right."

And it's good to get my brother's approval. I nod, and expect something exciting to happen. And it does. The next day he calls my brother, then me.

It's the start of a perfect romance. He loves sailing and I know I could spend my life with him.

So, after a month I end it, because I know I *could* spend my life with him, and that is out of the question.

"All my life I've dreamt about moving abroad and pursuing my modelling career, Jari, and I can't let *us* ruin my plans."

"Yes, Kati. Are you sure?" He kisses me.

I kiss him back, but then I have to pull myself away and say, "Yes, I'm sure."

He has his sailing, which will take him around the world. He understands passion – not just love, passion, but passion for other things in life, and he lets me go, at least for now.

*

It's a busy year in the romance department, and one day, not too long after ending it with Jari, I meet DJ.

DJ is a professional DJ. He's five years older than I am. We meet at a hair show; me with my brunette cascade and him with his blonde dreadlocks.

He's a working man, who is sensible and down to earth. He organises techno parties, which of course I attend. Dancing is my fave pastime and DJ and I are a perfect fit.

You might think it's because of the music, or even the dancing, from dusk until dawn at warehouses in and around Mikkeli. But it isn't the dancing, although we have a fabulous time, every time. What I like most about us is the fact that we can just sit and talk for hours, about anything. He's a best friend as much as a lover, and even saying goodbye is pretty easy because of it.

"So, pretty woman, you're going to Milan tomorrow. This is only the beginning, I know. You have a plan and everything you dream of will happen, because you make things happen. That's something I love about you."

It's our last night together before Milan, and one I'll always remember. He isn't the man for the rest of my life, but he is the man that has taught me a lot about being a woman.

DJ is my first real relationship. He'll always have a place in my heart, as a good friend and the man who taught me that love and friendship go together, like salt and pepper, and macaroni and cheese.

I'm quieter than usual, maybe because I don't want to be sentimental.

He drives me home and we kiss outside my parents' house.

"I won't forget us," I tell him.

He's been with me all year. Now I'm bound for Milan, and Rome.

Milan will take me into the international modelling world, and where I'll make a bittersweet discovery.

"I'll only be gone a few months," I tell him.

"Kati, I don't think you'll come back the same girl." He brushes my hair from my face and kisses me for the last time.

DJ knows I won't change, but I won't be in Mikkeli forever either.

Milan: Fashion capital. My hopes are pinned on this opportunity. I don't know exactly where it will lead, but I'm heading in the right direction. Being seen, getting known; Milan is the just the beginning.

The contest in Milan will also take me to Rome – one of the most romantic destinations in the world. Rome: the finals for *New Model Today*. I love Italy. I'm so excited!

I hop out of the car and DJ pulls away slowly as I go into the house.

For the *New Model Today* contest there will be other girls from around the world to represent the same agency. Girls working for the same model agency support one another. It's true, the world of modelling can be harsh and cold, where girls can be so competitive, sometimes trying to destroy your spirit so they will shine brighter than you do. But girls who work for the same agent make good friends with each other. Sure, we have to be independent to keep ourselves in shape and on top of our careers, but we can be friendly too. Being in their company is going to be a nice break from the independent life I've led so far.

Alone in my little bedroom, my quiet haven from the otherwise hectic pace I live, I'm reflecting on how everything is falling into place. Options are now opening up.

The Finnish agent called me this week: "Kati, they said they like you very much. The shots were great. They want you in LA now."

"LA. Wow! Absolutely. That's great. Only not this year. I have to finish school first."

"What? Are you crazy? You can't keep them waiting. This is a once-in-a-lifetime opportunity."

"I'm seventeen. They'll have to wait. School then modelling, for the rest of my life."

We argue back and forth and finally I say, "If they really like me that much, then they'll wait for me. One year."

Originally, I had this plan to finish college. I'm not sure what I'd study, but I figured I needed a back-up plan, in case things didn't go as planned in the modelling scene. Well, if work is coming, then I can skip college, but to leave before finishing high school? Naw, that's just too soon and not too smart.

My agent isn't pleased, but gets back to me saying, "LA says they'll wait." Even if they hadn't agreed to wait I don't think I'd have gone yet. Too soon. Timing is important.

I didn't give up LA, I just put it on hold. And then, as though confirming I made the right decision, another option comes up: the competition in Milan under the Italian Why Not agency. When I met the sweetest agent on earth, Giovani, I was thrilled. And of course I said yes. How could I not work with him?

I'm going for this competition, but much more too. Milan has opportunity after opportunity for me. It's going to be my introduction to the international scene: castings, jobs, different photographers, and preparation for the world. While LA waits, I can only get better. I know I'm gonna love Milan!

I have most of my things packed, with just the last bits to organise before heading out for what will be a few months. I've already been given a place to live, where there will be other models from the agency too. We'll share space and food. Five models from around the world converging on Milan, Italy, to kick-start our careers. Cool. My life starts for real now. My modelling life. My adult life. My career. What I've always wanted, what I've been waiting for – it's here. It's my time. And I'm ready.

How crazy-sweet is my life! It just goes to show you, when you want something bad enough, and you work hard, really hard, your dream can come true. I'm prepared for disappointments too. That's part of life. But I expect it, and I'm ready, even for occasional setbacks.

If I think about my career plan, Milan – or some other place, nameless but foreign – has always been in my sights. A few weeks ago, I took photos to a magazine contest. I knew somehow that the beautiful *Anna Magazine*'s contest would make something happen. It was so important; I took the photos to them personally. I can't know for sure, but I wonder if that made a difference?

I didn't win the contest, but that's how agents found me, including Giovani, the sweetest man on earth, who wants a Finnish representative for the Why Not modelling agency, and their New Model Now competition. So, he's entered me into a worldwide contest in Milan. I didn't win the magazine contest, but so much more came out of it that, in a way, I did win.

I stand looking in my mirror. I know it's *the* golden moment in Kati Lepistö's history: LA is waiting for me, Why Not and New Model Now have me. Milan is my step into the international modelling world of work and a professional life – the life I've always wanted more than anything else in the world. When you dream and you work for it, the dream can happen!

Thoughts of DJ drift into my mind. The furthest he's going is maybe to Helsinki one day, and everybody knows the modelling capital of the world is not Helsinki. And even if it were, would I stay in Finland: cold, positively freezing Finland, land of ice and snow with no sun? Never. I hate the cold, dreary, frost-glistening winters. I'd go to any other modelling capital. There are several, and I'll choose one with lots and lots of warm, wonderful sunshine.

CHAPTER 4

From Milan to LA

Guess how hard it is to get an agent? It takes a lot of photos, a lot of practice, and a lot of running around, along with quite a bit of persuading too. That's expensive, but it's fun.

For my look, I first have to develop the attitude that's right for me. I have to recreate it every time I get a photo. Deep inside me, I have to pull this same attitude out of me every time. It's not just my face that matters, not even just the eyes, but what's going on behind that look that transcends the clothes and make-up. It's what agents want to see over and over again. So, I have to create it over and over again, with different hair and different clothes. I have to admit, I haven't got it perfected yet, I'm still a work in progress. But it's enough for my stepping stone: Milan.

"This agent, what's he like?"

Irina has always stuck by me, and she has some experience of modelling too. We did a few fashion shows together, only she wasn't serious about it like I was. We had fun and now when I talk about Milan she has some real idea about what I'm talking about.

"He's the sweetest man on the planet. Quite old, but very kind. His name's Giovani."

"Nice."

"Yes. So, I'm going to represent Lapland for their New Model Today contest."

We both giggle.

"Lapland?"

"Yeah. Turns out they've already got a girl to represent Finland, so they're creating a category just for me!"

"A whole nation in fact."

"Yeah."

"A cold one. That's funny."

"Yeah, me representing Santa country. Crazy. If they only knew..."

"...how much you hate the cold."

"Yeah, but..."

Together: "We're not gonna tell them!"

We burst out laughing.

"And not just for a contest. I'm going to live there, for a while, if school lets me go."

"They will."

There's a pause. Life really is going to change.

"Come on. Let's go shopping to celebrate."

I can't remember which one of us suggested it. What does it matter?

*

It's fall of 1992. I'm eighteen with one more year of high school. One year. Then I'm going 100 per cent into the professional modelling world.

First, Äiti helps me out by speaking to the school principal.

"Yes, she has an invitation to compete in Milan. She'll be gone for three months, or maybe just two." But it isn't just my mom's permission and persuasion. It's my reputation that sets me free.

"She is a good student. She will have to study while she is away..." But they agree to let me go, with my text books. Along with Italian, while I'm there I will work on all my school subjects. I'll take my books to castings, which are sometimes long days with a lot of nothing to do. I'll get on that plane to Milan, with my suitcase and my schoolbooks.

"That's bizarre!" Irina laughs.

"Isn't it?" I say. Ha ha. They should give me a photo shoot in *Harper's Bazaar*! Get it?

Seriously, it's a good thing I always studied hard. They trust me and give me my first set of wings.

What I'm flying into is a schedule of castings, several a day, just to see if a client wants me. At castings the room is always full of beautiful girls, sometimes hundreds of them. They're looking for something special that you have, that no one else has. They're super-picky, but usually they don't really know what they're looking for until they see it.

Have you ever had a job interview? Imagine attending five interviews per day, every single day. Well, that's what I'm going into, eyes more or less wide open, excited and smiling a big grin. This is the real beginning of the rest of my life. It sounds clichéd, but it's the truth. I've been waiting, working and planning this and now I'm leaving home to find my life.

"I don't care what you say anymore, this is my life..." pops into my head. It's an old Billy Joel lyric. It makes me smile. Prince is my idol though, and I put on my headphones and relax into his music.

The flight to Milan is cool. I'm excited but I keep my head, and as I look from the plane over the landscape that is Italy, I think of Luigi. I don't rest my thoughts there though. He's working in Paris now, and I won't be seeing him. Some things just aren't meant to be.

Why Not – it's the best agency there is and I'm going to be competing for them. New Model Today will start photo shoots here, and then we'll go to Rome for the finals. Oooooh, keeping my cool is hard.

The hotel for the models has only two floors and smells of Asian food. It's not so nice, but it will do. Meeting the other girls is easy. There are "Hi's" all around, and we're all a little bit nervous. There are five of us, all young contestants for New Model Today.

"I'm Kati, and I'm Finnish. I'm representing Lapland, land of reindeer and snow, snow, snow." I smile through my pretend shiver. Everybody laughs. I have a room-mate, who is the Finnish contestant. They put us together, maybe so we could talk to each other. That's nice. But our English is pretty good anyway. There are three other girls, all English-speaking.

One is really quiet and just says, "Hi, I'm Chantelle."

Later I learn she's only fifteen. She looks a bit overwhelmed. Well, why not? She's so young. She's from the US and beautiful, but her personality doesn't stand out.

"I remember what it was like when I started out. I was fourteen." I'm trying to help her relax.

We are all talking at once, a little bit about ourselves to melt the ice. Chantelle doesn't say much. The rest of us are older and have more life experience, I guess, so we're more at ease with each other. It doesn't take long for us to get to know each other. The other three girls in the hotel will be upstairs sharing a room. First Chantelle, and next there's the party-girl, Linda, from Australia.

"Anyone for a smoke?" she says. And it isn't tobacco. I'm not interested, never have been, and never will be. There's more important stuff to spend my money and attention on than pot. Last of the three is Stephanie from New Zealand. We hit it off immediately. She's so funny, and we share the same crazy-ass sense of humour.

At first we girls really stick together. Whenever we're outdoors, I become the leader, because I'm learning Italian as a hobby. I'm also a pretty good map-reader, an essential skill for models because we have to find castings in this unfamiliar city.

Once I find Stephanie alone at the corner just down from the hotel.

"Stephanie, what are you doing here?"

"Eating the only thing I can."

I look at her. "What, breadsticks and coke? What do you mean, the only thing you can eat?"

"I don't know how to buy food. I don't know any Italian. So I do my shopping here."

It's a little corner shop with junk food, cigarettes and booze.

"You crazy girl! You can't live on breadsticks and coke. Come on!"

"Where?"

"To the grocery store."

"Really? How?"

"Come on. I'll speak for you. I have a map. You came all the way from New Zealand and you can't buy groceries?"

"You're a lifesaver, Kati."

"Yeah, just... buy me an apple."

"Gladly."

The girl was going to live for weeks on breadsticks and coke? Crazee!

Steph is the first of us to get a Milan shoot. We all go to several castings every day, but she's the only one to get a job of her own. No one knows their way around Milan, and castings and shoots are all over the city, so the agency sends us with a driver every time. After Steph's job the rest of us hop in a taxi to pick her up from the shoot.

I don't smoke, but everyone else does, like chimneys. We're sitting in the air-con car and the other girls are smoking while we wait for Steph.

When Stephanie shows up and gets in the car, she says, "You're killing Kati with your cigarettes, ladies." But then she lights up too.

"The shoot was smokin'," she says, and gives me a wink.

I just know right then, with her crazy sense of humour, we'll be friends for life.

*

"Anybody up here?" I climb to the other girls' room after a long day out on my own. They have a little stovetop and they're all gathered around it right now.

"So, who's got the fork? Whip it up," orders Stephanie. She's getting everyone involved in making her 'model bread'.

This is so bad for models it's funny – bread soaked in milk and an egg, cooked New Zealand style in oil and eaten with tons of butter. Yummy!

"Ah, give me some – I'm starving!" I plead. We all share, all for one and one for all, like the Musketeers.

So here we are, me, Kati, the brunette green-eyed girl from Lapland; quiet Chantelle, with long blonde hair, big blue eyes and sparkling white teeth, from America; party-girl Linda, the fun-loving, blue-eyed blonde from Australia and my best model friend, Stephanie, the quick-witted shorthaired brunette from New Zealand. The other Finnish model, Jenni, prefers to keep to herself.

*

"I'll get this one, you get that one."

Yes, we all buy the magazines together and share them out. There's just too little money and too much expense for us to get everything on our own. As starving models, we spend most of our money on clothes and fashion magazines, to study new poses. Sometimes an old, disgusting male client, who only has one thing on his mind, invites one or two of us for dinner. That's good news because it means we get food.

Life is great in Milan, but expensive. Money has to go towards film and photo sessions with photographers who want to shoot us. The model has to pay for the film and development. (It's 1992, before the cheaper, digital way to create photos.) When we meet a photographer who wants to shoot us, and we like his portfolio too, we set up a shoot with him. There are a few female photographers but most are men. Our expenses include the photos and also a make-up artist and hair stylist. We have to bring our own clothes too. Usually we'll shoot five different looks at once. The photographer shoots one roll of film for each look. It all adds up. Sometimes while I'm in Milan I have to ask my parents to send me some money. I don't like to, but it's necessary. They never say no. Thanks, Äiti and Isa!

Then there are the castings. Some days with five, some days with even ten castings in a day, I go back and forth around town, carrying my school books too, so I can read or study while I'm waiting for hours to show my portfolio. For some of these castings, we have to dance too. Until now, I've loved dancing, but not here. Somehow it's creepy. Gradually I do get over the ugly feeling, because I have to. Milan is tough, beautiful, fun, exhausting, and a great training ground for me. Eventually the day arrives to go to the New Model Today competition. By the time we have to set off for the competition, we are ready. The competition is taking twelve girls from Milan to... the Bahamas! Land of sun, sand and heat. I am ready for it. We are shooting videos for Italian television. The first videos will be shown around the world to promote the contest. Then the contest will be broadcast live in Rome.

After all our hard work and near-starvation in Milan, I have to say it's paying off. When we get to the Bahamas we're offered limousines to take us to our fancy hotel.

Stephanie and I share a room.

"Ooooh, this is fantastic!" coos Stephanie. It's easy to get her going.

"Too bad we're only here for one night. Shall we make it count?"

"Definitely!"

The first thing we do is to take a swim in the big hotel pool. It's already late; swimming in the moonlight feels so relaxing after the hectic and stressful pace of Milan. The warm water and air feel like velvet on our skin. I'm in paradise! Then, I sleep like a log. In the morning, we go for breakfast where all us girls feel like we've died and gone to heaven.

"Oh my god," we're saying over and over again. Our shrieks of delight are hard to contain.

There are long counters full of amazing food, with all kinds of delicacies from all around the world. People say models don't eat? Well, given the chance we can, and this morning we do.

After breakfast it's time to check out of our amazing hotel. We're off to the airport again, this time to fly to Eleuthera, a stunning island of white sandy beaches surrounded by crystal clear sea. We're treated like celebrities, getting the star treatment again, in limos to and from the airport.

It feels like we're the only tourists on the island.

One of the best things about modelling is that whenever you travel, you always see the best of the best, that is to say, the best locations in the best regions. It's necessary for the shoots to have incredibly beautiful locations. This island is definitely a *best* in the Caribbean.

The hotel is small and cosy, and the models and team are the only guests. The girls will share rooms again and three of us share a spacious bungalow: Stephanie, me again (we always insist on being together), and a girl from Argentina. The girl is beautiful, but her story is practically tragic. Steph and I figure she's had a lot of work done on herself. She's seventeen for crying out loud, and she tells us she's had a nose job and something done to her cheeks. She tells us it's her face cheeks, but we figure her butt cheeks have had some work too. OMG!

All the girls have to do their own hair and make-up, so being sociable has paid off – we're friends and we want the best for each other and help each other out. It's great weather and beautiful surroundings, but still we have to work very hard. First, we have to find the perfect swimsuit for every girl. Waiting your turn is never easy, and this process is very slow. Next we have to memorise the words to the old song, 'Feeling hot, hot, hot,' and learn a dance to go with it.

"Again," we're told, and then, "again."

I think we've tried this one a hundred times, every take with a great big smile, as we sing and dance this song, in thirty-degree weather. Yeah, it certainly is "hot, hot, hot!" To top it off, we have to stay looking fresh and beautiful. It ain't easy under these conditions.

To be a model we obviously have to be in good shape physically, because it's our bodies that get us the work, but actually, even more important believe it or not, is that we have to be in excellent mental shape, to keep us going in the tough, tough times. Pressure? Let me put it this way, as soon as anyone forgets a word or a step, we have to film the whole sequence all over again. Hundred-times easy, like I said.

"Come on, girls," the director, Piccio, calls. "Again." But we don't moan. It's fun in the sun and we all want to win. That's what's going on inside every single pretty head on that beach. We just have to keep on going till we get everything right.

Piccio and I are already good friends. He's older, in his fifties, and very professional. He is not trying to get into anyone's pants. Stephanie's become good friends with one of the cameramen. Even though we didn't make these friends intentionally – we just really like the company – it is good for any model to have friends in the crew. A director who likes you will give you the best parts, and a cameraman will show you in the best lighting. In modelling, diamonds aren't a girl's best friend, but lighting is.

Next morning it's time to get our evening dresses.

Steph and I pick ours up. They are first class.

"Oh my god. This is gorgeous."

"Kati. Yours and mine are so alike."

"Complementary," we both say and give high fives.

Was it luck, or having friends in high places? Sure, our dresses are two of the nicest, that's for sure.

The day is long and hot. We shoot on location among the colourful neighbourhood houses, and we keep the dresses on even in the evening, when we film our introductions for the competition. Steph and I look and feel amazing.

Piccio plays one of my favourite songs the next day on the shoot – 'Drive' by The Cars. It's work, work, work but it never feels like it, because the people are so nice.

Another day we're filmed riding bikes around in the sand and by the end of the day I'm ready to smash that bike into pieces, I'm so sick of it.

"I hear you like belly dancing?" Piccio asks me one evening. It seems we both like Arabic music.

It isn't enough to be pretty, you have to be sociable too, to find ways to connect with people so that they want to work with you. This is an isolating business and you have to both survive on your own but get along with other people, so you can fit in. Constantly, we're finding things in common with others, to keep the conversation light and pleasant, which makes the days go smoothly. I know I'll keep in touch with Piccio. He's smart, and nice and very supportive.

Our time on the island can't last forever, and anyway Rome is next, where we'll see the sights in between shootings, and maybe even some of the shoots will be in ancient ruins. That'd be so cool!

As well as models, the flight is full of tourists. What will we see in Rome? I'm so excited.

But it turns out I've been naive. As soon as we land in Rome, we're met by the contacts from the model agency and swept away to the hotel. I see glimpses of the sights on my way. Little do I realise that's the most I'll see of Rome.

We work, work, work, from 7.00 a.m. to 11.00 p.m., at a movie studio far away from anything amazing. Lunch is not in some gorgeous ancient plaza but in the studio cafeteria. Rome? I go from hotel to venue and back to the hotel. We eat at the hotel café. Nothing fancy, but food that sustains us.

"I don't want to go pee, Steph."

"Yeah, no kidding."

"Did you see it? They can't call it a toilet. It's disgusting; it's nothing but a hole in the ground."

"Well, they don't call it 'Ancient Rome' for nothing," and Steph and I laugh it off.

The only sights we see are through the car window as we drive past to the venue. Eight days of transporting, shooting, eating and sleeping. Well, at least the shoots produce good photos.

Lesson learnt: in the modelling world, sometimes you can go to great destinations and see nothing but inside a studio. Never pin your expectations on extracurricular activities because there may not be any. Don't choose modelling for the places you'll see or the glamour you'll experience. Sometimes you will have those things, but sometimes not.

And you know what? To top off the frustration at missing Rome's sights, at the end of the schedule we are told, in no uncertain terms, that the winner of the contest has already been chosen.

"What a bummer!" says Steph.

"Yeah, well. At least we got to see Rome." We burst out laughing.

"Hey, girl," Steph says to me, "You got to wear *that dress.*"

And she's not just talking about any dress. *That dress* was a significant experience! At a press meeting, I was one of only two girls who got to wear a beautiful Italian haute couture evening dress. It was really unbelievable. I never imagined that a piece of clothing could make me feel *so* beautiful, and I wasn't even wearing any make-up.

My dress, for a few hours, was a two-piece, dark blue, narrow-but-layered chiffon skirt and a silver steel bra full of dark blue and silver gems. I'll never forget it, even though I don't have a decent picture – can you imagine?

Milan has given me some great friends, incredible photos and... opportunities. No, I didn't win New Model Today, but offers rolled in from Milan, Paris, Cape Town, and of course the agent from Los Angeles is still interested.

Which place is the sunniest? Naw, just joking. Which is the best place to go? Considering the competition, I choose LA, and the agent who's been waiting for me. Nice to be wanted and anyway, I think there won't be so many European girls from these ancient cities, all competing with each other and with me. But my information is limited. Although I choose LA for good reasons, I make assumptions that are not really based on all the facts.

CHAPTER 5

Juggling

"Hey, Kati, how was Rome?"
"Great, Irina, for the modelling. But I didn't actually get to see anything outside the photo studios."
"What? No art, no Coliseum?"
"Nope."
"Hmm."
"Well." I shrug. "I can't complain, because I got lots of pictures." Pictures, pictures and always more pictures. I shoot her a *big* smile, and add a roll of my eyes. She gets me.
She rolls her eyes and we have a good laugh.
"It'll all pay off, Kati."
"Yes it will. In fact it already has. You know that offer to go to LA?"
"Yes?"
"I'm gonna take it!"
Shrieks! It's great to share and Irina is 100 per cent supportive.
From Milan to home. Now I have to finish high school and get my driving licence. Then I'll move to LA.

But I hit a potential roadblock. Isa doesn't like the US and Äiti is worried about me driving.

"You can't get a car!"

"It is not possible to tell Kati what to do," my brother says. He's so right.

"Look, you saw the letter from the agent. I have to have a car in LA, there's no choice. But I'll get a safe one. Bye!" And I'm off.

It's crazy-exciting – I'm so lucky and I know it.

I need a car as soon as I get to LA. Judith, my agent, has set me up in a house with two other models, both men, Dale and Chad. The place is pricey and in Van Nuys, which might as well be a million miles away from anything related to the business of modelling.

Well, with some cash I brought from Finland, I get my dream car. A pearl green Cadillac. It'll get me around.

However, my mom goes ballistic!

"No, you don't drive, Kati. Absolutely not!" says Isa.

I've had my licence for three weeks and I got that in little Mikkeli. But they don't understand. There aren't any trains. Buses will not get me anywhere. I have casting after casting and I have to have a car. Everyone has a car. That's why the smog is so bad.

Judith starts to set me up for some castings, but there is a hitch with my work permit.

"What? I don't have a work permit? I thought it was all sorted before I got here."

I was supposed to bring some certain paperwork. I thought I was just supposed to prove I had some money. Shit! Now what? I'm in a daze.

Mandy, Chad's girlfriend, comes over to console me. She's great.

"Well, I do know somebody who wants to meet you – my colleague."

"Yeah, sure. But what about the work permit?"

"One thing at a time. It'll be okay."

So, before I know it, we're on our way to meet the #1 salesman at her workplace, which happens to be a Porsche dealership.

"His name is Warren, and ever since I told him about you he's been begging me to introduce you," she says.

I don't know what to expect but it's always good to meet people.

"Hey, babe. Mandy's been telling me all about you."

Wow! I didn't expect this. Warren is hot. He's probably the best looking man I've ever seen, and in modelling I've met a lot of good-looking men. Tall, fit, dark wispy hair, torn jeans, deep voice – the perfect surfer look. And he *is* a surfer, which is very sexy.

He doesn't invite us into his place, even though he's cooking dinner.

"Let's all go to Malibu for a bite." And he chucks the spaghetti he's been making.

We have a great dinner, good talk and then it's home for me. But it isn't long before we end up together again, Warren and me, this time one afternoon at an amusement park. It's our second date, our first alone. We talk and drink wine and talk, and he takes my mind off all my work permit worries. Mandy must have known we were made for each other. Thanks, Mandy!

I've spent my life making plans. I can't remember when I didn't have my plan for my modelling future. Now I've finally started to live the dream. Until now, I've put off real romance. Anything that wasn't modelling was shoved in the corner. Well, now that I've met a real man then maybe, just maybe, it's time I let myself live a little more, now that the plan is in action.

A few weeks pass, with a few more dates with Warren. It doesn't take us very long to work out that without a work permit it's hard for me to make money, and that expensive house all the way in Van Nuys isn't affordable or sensible. When Warren pops the question I'm all for it.

"Move in with you? Ah," I say, and I throw my arms around him.

Life just can't get any better than this, can it?

There are two things that are important in life: career and love. Although career has always been my focus, adults have needs and desires, which living isolated from the world won't satisfy. I've decided that now that I'm in LA I ought to find a balance, to make some room for a private life. I'm thousands of miles from my family. What's the point of success if you're all alone to celebrate?

It takes ages for the work permit to be sorted out. It costs 800 bucks right away and another 450 a few weeks later. It still doesn't come through and so I'm severely limited in what castings I can take. Fortunately not everybody insists on a work permit.

So, now I'm in a relationship, living with a wonderful guy, waiting for my agent to book me into castings. I'm almost living my LA dream!

Even before the work permit there are some opportunities available to me without a work permit. When I get to my first casting call, and the possibilities start to look promising, I'm nervously excited. It's a hair shoot for L'Oréal and I flip my long brunette locks and get a callback. But I don't get to the third level. Downer. For every casting there are fifty girls at least. The competition is tough. There are a lot of jobs and a lot of girls to take those jobs. I realise pretty quickly that getting jobs might be a bit tougher than I expected. No worries. I'll work hard.

I meet Renee, a Colorado girl chasing her dream just like me. She's been here a while and we learn that hanging out together at castings makes the days go better.

"Let's go in my car," she says one day. Her little white car always blasts out Big Audio Dynamite. We have a lot of fun together.

Some castings, however, are pretty discouraging, while others are really the pits. The worst is one with a sleazy photographer. He interviews me, twice. He wants me, and not just my face. I grit my teeth through a couple of meetings, and then I say,

"No," which is basically unheard of.

I'm glad when I get away from that creepy photographer. I do report the guy to the agency, but I don't suppose it'll do much good. Some girls are willing to sleep their way to getting good pics. For me, that's a no-no.

It's already been one month of no offers, and while I won't sell myself out, I also know I can't be too picky. I've been to so many castings, up to five a day, five days a week, with, "don't call us, we'll call you," over and over again. It's nothing personal, I know, but that amount of rejection would drive me crazy if I wasn't so tough on the outside. And it is inevitable that, with that much exposure, eventually something has to come my way. And it does.

Today's my first job. Finally. It's nothing too special, just some print photos for a local department store, with another girl and a guy model, but it's fun. We do a few shots and everything's going smoothly. The last shoot is just the guy and me. He's good looking, of course, but also he's a nice enough guy. I have to act as his girlfriend. It's always a bit awkward at first, playing a bit of intimacy, but we get along well and it all comes together. The client's happy, and I'm getting paid (at last!) so I'm happy too.

I think for a second about one of the other castings I had, with that sleazy photographer I would *not* have wanted to work with, and I'm even happier about the work today. Some things *do* work out and this week turned out okay. With the first job under my belt, I'm off and running now. Things will progress slowly but steadily, with portfolio shoots, castings and some paid gigs.

There is only one other situation that comes along that turns out to be really trashy and best forgotten, except that it makes me appreciate what I've got. The worst casting ever, in the City of Angels, with the most obscene arrangement I've ever seen before or since, was a body painting casting. I'll never forget it. There were about fifty girls before my turn came round. One girl at a time would go into casting room, and then very soon after, she'd come out, looking pretty shaken up. Everyone was pretty young, like me.

At first I couldn't figure out why some of the other girls were upset.

"What's going on?" I heard someone ask.

The girl who had just come out of the casting room was crying.

"They made me... lift up my top. That's it!" she said.

Shit. Am I gonna stay?

Immediately my name was called. With no more time to think, I went into the casting room, a very big room, where there were three men, each of them standing behind a small table.

Usually the castings are pretty civilised. There's someone to take your name, maybe ask you a few questions. But not this time. I had to stand about sixty feet away from the tables, lift up my shirt and show my boobs to these three perfectly unfamiliar men. And that was it! Shirt down. "Next."

And let me make this perfectly plain – there were no bras! I felt so dirty and used. I suppose it helped a little that I had developed a modelling attitude by the time I got to LA. Some of the girls at that casting were pretty broken up by it. I think I might have been too, if I hadn't been perfecting the tough exterior.

To be a model you need to have a modelling attitude. It is a must. You cannot be a model without it. But it is just that: your modelling attitude. You do not have to become it 24/7. It is just in your eyes, when the light and cameras are on you. It helps you to be prepared, it makes you push yourself to the limit, because sometimes modelling requires sweat and tears to get the job done. The modelling world is totally cut-throat, a very cold and harsh environment.

Fortunately, the rest of my castings this year are good ones. One of them even makes me feel really special. To start, they give some clues as to what they're actually looking for. Then they provide a huge mirror, where we even get to practise our poses. And at the end of my audition, they smile at me and say, "thanks, pet," before someone shouts, "Next!"

I still don't have my permit and the jobs without a permit don't pay too well, and aren't very regular. Expenses for photos are high, and so financially things are really tight. Just when I'm thinking about how I'm going to pay my next rent, I get side-swiped on the road. Jeez! The damage to my car is pretty ugly.

I call my dad.

"Isa, I'm okay but my car's been hit."

"Kati, didn't I tell you not to drive?"

"Sure, but I had to."

"But you're okay?"

"Yeah, of course, but the car needs fixing."

"What about the insurance."

"Ah, insurance?"

Silence.

Yeah, it's expensive to drive in LA without insurance, and illegal of course Models starting out should always research everything before purchasing tickets, a car, signing rental agreements etc. I was really freaking out at the time.

The good news is I'm busy. I'm going to the gym every morning at seven o'clock and I take some ballet classes too. I love the feeling of burning sweat. Even though I have to travel back and forth across town, do I care? No. Because I'm doing the castings, one by one, getting some work, and the permit's on its way.

I know it takes time, effort, commitment, perseverance and patience to become a successful model. I know success isn't going to happen overnight. Ultimately it's all up to me. Oh, I have Judith, but modelling is a business, and I am my own business. I'm my own boss and if I'm going to make it, I have to do it for myself. I'm my manager, I'm my employer and I'm my own secretary. So I'll never make the excuse I don't have a work permit. I just have to get around the problem until the permit comes through. I won't give up.

It takes a few months, but when the permit *finally* comes through, I'm really in the groove.

"Whee! Come on, Warren, let's dance!"

"Yeah, all right. Just a minute."

"I love this. Do you feel the beat?"

"Yeah. Let's ... let's – here, babe." He kisses me. It's good.

"Aw, you're so smooth. Come on. Dance."

"Come here."

Well, we didn't dance for long, and we didn't go out that night, but we had fun anyway.

"Ah, dreamboat, you're perfect," I tell him. But I think to myself I really ought to go on the pill.

The next morning I almost wake up too late. I've got to get to the crazy casting. First I grab my bag, my big black attaché bag with my portfolio and make-up, which I take everywhere – it's like an appendage. I'm all set for the usual day of gym, across town to a casting, and across again to another one. I eat light because it's cheaper, and I save my money for my portfolio.

Slipping out the door even before Warren wakes up, I'm off to the gym first. I like the gym at 7.00 a.m. There's hardly anybody there and I can get my workout done and get on with my day. Oh, the shower feels good afterwards.

Next are the castings. It's a waiting game; I don't get seen for hours. But it's all part of the plan. I'm loving LA, and life couldn't be better. I don't miss Mikkeli, although sometimes I think about Mom and Dad. Jukka's probably cosy with Anu and it's good for them. But not for me. Not dark, cold Finland. It's never been right for me. I love Christmas there, then after I visit I can escape back to the Californian sun. It's taking some time, but the LA sun has given me a natural tan and I'm glowing inside and out. I'm here. I'm living my dream. How many eighteen-year-olds can say that?

Before I came to LA I had to finish school, of course. I was surprised at the good results I got, considering how much school I missed. I did even better than Jukka, even though he spent his whole school life in Mikkeli. And all the time I'm in LA I keep writing to Piccio from Milan, and Jari, Irina, Luigi, and of course my parents. Sometimes I even talk to them on the phone. At first I cried when I had to hang up after talking to my mom, but I got used to saying goodbye after a while. It's just what I have to do to make it.

When I'm not dancing with Warren, or writing letters, I'm running around LA in my car to castings, a few every day. And then there are the days I get a shoot, which pays me to do what I love. That's the icing on the cake.

But I have to tell the truth, it's not all wonderful. The world-renowned LA smog irritates my throat, but I've always had throat infections so I can live with that. And life here can be stressful, sometimes horrible. I walk around town in my shades most of the time because the drug pushers might nab me if they see my face. Photo shoots in LA take some getting used to.

There are two types of shoot: my own for my portfolio, and the ones that pay. During photo shoots, usually the public stare at you because jobs are often in a public place. It can be very tense and uncomfortable when it's a paying job, because the clients will criticise. But when it's my own portfolio shoot, just with me and the photographer, it's nice, because we usually put on my favourite music in the background, which helps me to enjoy my time, relax and move more easily too. Regardless of the circumstance or reason for the shoot, the model is the centre of attention, which is what any model loves. We have to get used to whatever situation we're in. And we do.

One thing I will probably never get used to is the weight issue. The first time anyone said anything to me was before I went to Milan.

"You should lose a few centimetres off your rear, dear," I was told by one agent.

I'm sorry, but where would it come off? I pull down my pants to just below my hip bones, so she can see them protruding.

"These are typical female, child-bearing hips. I can't *do* anything about them, or my butt. I can't lose anything off bone, can I?"

"Hmm." She inspected me. Got right up close, looking at my bones. "No, that's true."

"Sheesh!" Believe me it wasn't big then, and it still isn't. But here in LA, for the first time, I'm told to go on a diet. Crazy! It's very hard to lose weight when you're already exercising, eating very little, and only weigh thirty-four kilos (seventy-five pounds). I'm five feet ten for crying out loud. It's impossible. Sigh! But it's true that there is no shortage of stick-thin beauties here, so yeah, I have to diet. No more of Stephanie's model bread for me, that's for sure!

Now, it does not take a genius to be a model. It also isn't a usual, nine-to-five, all-week-long job either. It's long days of waiting and being ready, and shining at all the right moments. What it takes is hard work, a certain tough and determined attitude to do it, and always with a smile on your face.

You also have to make decisions, because being a model is like running a business. You are both the business and the brand. Everything that has to be done has to be done by you. If you can't do everything, you have to decide what to ignore. Choosing wisely what to do, and what to leave behind, is pressure.

And of course there's the party scene to consider too. For example, there's drugs, alcohol, and the sexual-social climb to the top. I choose to stay home. I'm here to work, not party, and anyway, it's too exhausting to live like that on top of everything else. There's not a moment to spare. That's my crazy life, here in the City of Angels.

CHAPTER 6

Romance Adrift

"Hi, Jamie." Warren's good friend, and now mine, lives a few doors down from us. Some mornings or evenings we bump into each other.

"Oh no. Where's my car? It's not here. It's not where I left it. It's gone!"

"Is this where you usually park it?" he asks.

"Sometimes. Why?"

"Because there's a no parking sign over here. You, um, ever get a ticket?"

"Sometimes."

"Oh boy, Kati. Do you pay them?"

"Naw, no one does, right? I mean, I try to park where I'm allowed but sometimes it just isn't possible."

"I think I can guess where your car is."

"Really? Oh that's great. I mean, how do you know?"

"I think it's probably been impounded, Kati."

"What do you mean, impounded?" He's just staring at me. "Jamie?"

"Oh boy. It's like it's been taken to jail and you can't get it back without paying your fines."

"Fines? You mean my parking fines?"

"For starters, yeah. But there's more. Because they had to tow it from here to the pound, you'll have that fee too. And storage."

"Jeez."

"It's okay, Kati. I'll take you there. We'll stop at the bank along the way."

Oh, man, our choices really matter. I guess I should have paid those parking fines.

The guy at the car pound is grumpy.

"Yeah, yeah, I'll get your car. Where's the money first?" He adds up what I owe, and then gives me the invoice. It isn't pretty.

"Here." I stuff the money in his hand.

He looks at Jamie. "Pretty in the head but shite for brains, eh?" Then to me he says, "Didn't nobody tell ya to pay your fines, what?"

"Hey," Jamie says. He's about to defend me, but I don't want to get into an argument.

"It's okay, Jamie. He's right, isn't he? I mean, I should have paid my tickets."

"You're a pretty one. An actress, I betcha? Another wannabe eh? If you take those sun specs off I can see if you look familiar."

I almost always wear sunglasses. It's a habit I picked up when I moved here. I was told when I'm in LA to hide my eyes. Druggies try to get the look-in to size you up. This guy's no dealer, but still I'm not going to give him the satisfaction of doing what he asks me to do.

"I'm a fashion model, if you must know."

"Bein' a model, is a doddle." He chuckles at his little rhyme. "Car's in section B, just over there." He points.

"What do you mean, a doddle?" I ask him.

"Where I come from, madam, a doddle is a cinch, an easy ride, something simple for simple minds, like. You know?"

"What planet are you from?" I ask. "I've never heard of a doddle before. Have you Jamie?" Neither has Jamie. (Turns out he's English.)

"You listen here," I start. "How would you like every day to be a new job, starting from scratch? You go to agencies where they may or may not like you. You take around a big black book full of photos to prove you've got what it takes. Then, if that agent doesn't want you, or even if he does, you go across town to another agent and do the whole thing again. After about three or four of these visits, you might have a parking fine, because you didn't know the free places to park. You might have time for a smoothie or a piece of fruit, and then you spend the afternoon doing the same thing all over again."

He glares at Jamie and back at me.

"I don't think you could manage it, dude. You have to be the perfect candidate each time, looking and sounding fresh and confident. Being cheery even if you've got a stinking headache or a bad cold. Gotta be fresh-faced and friendly, and hit the pose every time, every day. And you've gotta connect with each client and give them a positive impression so they'll think well of you, and remember you. Just like I'm connecting with you right now... only positive."

"Horses for courses, madam. Horses for courses. You take your pick and live it."

"I'm not sure you'd be up to that. Every day, all day, being charming to your customers. Do you think you could do that?"

His jaw is open. He says nothing.

"Naw. I didn't think so."

"Come on, Kati. Let's get you back home." Jamie chuckles,

collects the keys from the pound man, and gently but firmly steers me by the elbow, escorting me to my car.

"I guess you gave it to him, eh?" Jamie says. He smiles.

I smile too. "Yeah, I guess. Well...."

"Ah, he deserved it. He had it coming. Actually, it gives me an idea."

"What?"

"Nothing fazes you does it?"

"What do you mean?"

"You can take just about anybody on. I wonder if you'd like to speak to some high school kids."

"High school? That's easy. Sure. Oh, you mean, some of *your* kids?" Jamie does guest appearances at schools. He was in prison or something, but he got clean, so he does these motivational talks for the kids, about career, life choices and avoiding drugs and booze. He was a user, a con, who's completely changed. Now he does his bit to try to help other kids to avoid his mistakes. Pretty neat, I think.

"Yeah, I could do that."

"Yup, I think you could. Let's plan it."

I look in the back of my car as usual, before I get in.

"What are you doing?" Jamie asks me.

"Oh, it's a habit. I always check the back seat, just in case there's somebody hiding. A girl can't be too careful."

"You are one sharp cookie, Kati Lepistö," Jamie says to me, as I get into my car.

Jamie's become like a big brother to me. No one can replace Jukka, but Jamie's like twenty years older than me, and Warren asked him a long time ago to look out for me, because Warren works such long hours. Sometimes Jamie has taken me to castings or shoots when he was free. Driving in LA can be intimidating! Now I can return the favour.

Not long after the car pound, I'm going to one of Jamie's speaking gigs. I'm tagging along to talk about coming over to America to fulfil my modelling dream. America – the land of opportunity. I'm all set. He's asked me to present it in a few languages since I'm multi-lingual. That's quite cool. I bet a lot of the kids will understand Spanish, but I don't speak it. Maybe a few will have Italian backgrounds, which I do.

We drive up to the school. Oh, wow! This is different from my high school. It's got a high fence all around it, topped off with – believe it or not – barbed wire. I'm not kidding. And the kids have to pass an armed guard at the gate, who's checking everyone's book-bags. Jeez.

Jamie's told me that most of the kids have already been expelled from other schools. Some are juvies. But this is *really* intense!

We get into the auditorium and the kids sort of gawk at me, but at least they aren't swearing at me. Most of them are boys, and man, they are tough looking. But when Jamie talks, absolutely everybody listens. Then he introduces me, and they whistle, until Jamie gives them a look, and they stop immediately.

He wants me to help the kids get an idea of career development through hard work. I can feel their eyes on me, and some of them are jealous girls, but most are image conscious guys and some super-intense girls, all listening to me talk about what it takes to succeed in your dream career: determination, fitness, healthy eating, not using drugs or anything else to get ahead, and not letting myself get scared of the huge competition within the modelling industry. They listen. I tell it in English first, so they know what I'm saying. I tell them about my long-term dream, show them my portfolio (I just hold up the bag, I don't take out the photos), and tell them what I had to do to get here, and stay here. Then I tell them I'm from Finland and say everything all over again in Finnish, then in Italian (even though I haven't done my exams yet) and finally in German. Some of the kids laugh, because, let's face it, foreign languages can sound funny. They make me laugh and we have a good time over it. I end everything by saying, "anything is possible, if you work hard and stick to it."

They clap when I'm done. It's kind of a kick. A couple of guys try to get me to go out with them. Jeez, I'm only nineteen myself, so who can blame them? But of course I'm not interested. Thankfully, big bro steps in.

"Gentlemen, she's our guest speaker. Let's keep it cool," he says.

"Yes, sir." The boys back off.

I'm having the adventure of a lifetime in LA. Turning nineteen is fun and the career is progressing. It seems everything is perfect.

Ah, until the predictably impossible happens that literally shakes my world. January 1994. The first notable date is my mom's birthday.

"Hi, Äiti. Happy birthday! Did you have a nice day?" (Her day is done, my time is ten hours behind hers.)

We talk for a while and goodbyes don't make us cry anymore. We're used to it.

"So, I want to come home soon to visit. Maybe I can get a job over here that will pay for the ticket."

Then, on 17 January my whole world is shaken. It's 4.30 a.m., just a little before dawn, when Warren and I are woken up by a horrible shaking.

"What's happening?" I ask Warren. "What's going on?" I'm clinging to him, practically on top of him.

"Oh God, it's an earthquake. Stay put till it passes!"

But it doesn't pass. It seems to go on forever, and stuff is crashing down from the cupboards, even the dresser itself tips over and everything falls out of the drawers. Then it's pitch black; all the street lights have gone out.

"Get dressed," he yells over the sound of rattling windows and shaking walls. But I can't find my jeans in all the mess.

Then it stops. I grab some clothes and put them on. On the wall above the bed there are fish mounted on big hooks. How did they not manage to crash down on top of us?

Creeping around, we can make out that the house is a war zone. The kitchen floor is covered in food from the cupboards and fridge, and broken dishes. Ah, I can get those dishes I really like now. Bizarre, the things you can think of during a disaster.

The living room floor is covered with broken furniture and the upturned TV. The walls are seriously cracked where they used to be perfect. Forget getting into the bathroom; the floor is covered in spilled pills from broken bottles, and everything else you can imagine that would fill our bathroom cupboards.

We live in a two-storey apartment building. I don't want to imagine what the state of the high rises might be. We run down the stairs and outside. Santa Monica looks very bad. There's dust everywhere. A big brick wall that used to be behind our building has come down, and gas and water pipes are spitting and spluttering.

Outside the lawn is full of people. It's funny how disasters bring people together. Even in this small building, where we have never talked with our neighbours, everybody has gathered in small groups, as though we're all the best of friends. Well, that's a good thing in this otherwise total mess.

Warren has grabbed his shotgun. "Looting, probably," he says, as if he's experienced this sort of thing before. He's also grabbed a six-pack of beer. What? In a crisis you grab beer? Who else on earth would think of beer first in a life-threatening situation for crying out loud!

We hop into Warren's old black Thunderbird and go to check on his parents, who live just a couple blocks away in a similar small apartment building. We run up the stairs where his French mother, Julia, and Yugoslavian father, Andrei live. No wonder my Warren is a little hot-tempered, I think. Actually, he's cool and calm right now, when it's important. The apartment is pitch black. Just like our place, the kitchen cupboards have spilled out their contents, leaving broken china everywhere.

"Mom, Dad," Warren calls, but we get no answer. I can see cool Warren is beginning to panic. "Dad! Mom!" He shouts extra hard, the frustration and terror creeping into his voice.

After searching the whole apartment, we go back outside looking for them. It's hard to spot certain people in a dark space full of strangers. Eventually though, we do find them, in the schoolyard next to the apartment building. A lot of locals seem to have congregated there. Christine and her neighbour are in shock, so while Warren talks to his dad, I'm trying to calm the women down. Ironic – I've only been here a few months and I'm calming them down.

A little later, sure his parents are safe, Warren and I go back to our apartment. We pause outside the building though, not really wanting to go inside. It's too scary! Around us gas pipes are blowing up, and there's rubble everywhere. What else can happen? The power lines? Finally, we decide we gotta go in.

I want to call my parents, to let them know I'm okay. Luckily the phone line is working.

"Hi, it's Kati. I'm still alive! Did you hear about the earthquake?"

"Yeah," my dad says, "We heard there was a quake in Santa Monica and LA. Was it bad? The news didn't say much. They have earthquakes all the time though, right?"

"No, and anyway, not like this. Ever!"

My parents want to talk to Warren, to find out how serious it is, since I've never been through it before.

"No, she's right, this one was bad. It's finished now though," Warren says. "There will be some aftershocks today or tomorrow, but there won't be much more damage. The damage has been done already. And yeah, man, there's a lot of damage."

People in Finland don't have the slightest idea how terrifying it is to live through an earthquake. To think that the ground from underneath you can just vanish at any given moment. Finnish people complain about the snow. Sheesh! Have I got things in perspective now. It's good they didn't really know how bad it was before I called them. My parents would have been so worried.

Not much will be going on around us the day after the quake, I guess. There's a lot of cleaning up to do. The news tells us what's happened. The quake was ten seconds. What? It seemed like a lot longer than that! Ten terrifying seconds that shook my world. They're calling it the Northridge Earthquake, the most serious quake since 1933. The main line, Santa Monica Freeway, is toast. It's a mess. There'll be no work today. People are just too shaken and it'll take hours for cops to work out how to re-route traffic. But still, it isn't until later, when I'm driving down the Santa Monica Boulevard, that I realise the full impact of the quake. Highways near us have simply snapped and crumbled like crackers. The city literally looks like a war zone. Big buildings have been blown apart like some big bomb has exploded.

In the afternoon, while I'm at home tidying up, it starts again. "Oh my god! It's coming again," I hear myself scream. But it isn't another quake. It's a huge aftershock. All I can do is scream. In fact, today is even worse than the actual earthquake itself. There are 200 aftershocks! I'm trying to clean up the apartment, but by the end of the day, I'm shaking so badly, and I'm so emotionally drained, that I just burst out crying. My muscles have been on high alert all day, aching and ready to run. By nightfall, I'm too terrified to go to sleep. But eventually, I just crash out on the sofa. When I wake up later, I realise I fell asleep because I was so tired from cleaning up all day.

It's going to take forever to clean up the mess everywhere. To top it off, the streets of the City of Angels have become filled with moving trucks. It seems like anybody who's able to work somewhere else has ditched this city just like that. I think if I could, I would leave in a heartbeat. But it's business as usual in the modelling world. For a while, I sleep in my clothes. After a couple of weeks, I relax a little, and keep a set of clothes and sneakers next to my bed. The romance of living in LA has definitely worn off. What a crazy living nightmare.

The disaster is all over the news. Thousands out of their homes, infrastructure demolished. Billions of dollars lost. What next? But Warren is a California guy. He's lived here all his life. He says it's just the way it is.

"They felt the tremors in Las Vegas for crying out loud, over 200 miles away!" I say.

"Yeah, it was bad," he says, "but it's over now."

About sixty people are dead.

"That's not so bad," Warren says.

"Tell that to their families, Warren." I'm so mad at him.

Eventually, life returns to normal, more or less. I'll keep

a set of clothes permanently in my car, one way of coping with the stress. At least I ought to be able to change my underwear no matter what. Well, hey, life has stress, right? The threat of an earthquake is just one source.

Actually, I have another stressful thing to admit. I've got time to think and there is something serious on my mind. I have to face it. While I'm at home alone this evening, 'cause Warren is working late, I finally admit what's been bugging me all week. I'm late. I can't deny this anymore. I've missed my period. I don't want to think the worst, but I have to find out.

I drive to the pharmacy, purchase a test, and drive back home. What if I'm pregnant? If I am, I'm going to have to tell Warren. And what then?

The pregnancy test is in my hand. I look in the bathroom mirror. How did I get here? Holding the pregnancy kit, I can feel my heart pounding just thinking about it. I can't see myself having an abortion...

I pull the kit out of the box and read the instructions. My hands are shaking. It's a one-minute test, one minute to tell my future. I can't believe I'm doing this. Jeez! This is *not* in the plan. I'm staring at this thing. I'm praying – well if there's a God, maybe he'll pay attention.

My whole life is before me. Could I marry Warren? I remember before I got the work permit we thought about getting married then, just so I could stay in the US and work. But we waited for the permit instead, and managed. I'm too young to get married.

So I pee and I wait. And wait. I never realised how l-o-n-g a minute actually is. Tick tock... It's beginning to colour... It's... I'm okay. Ah! It's okay. I'm not pregnant!

Okay, I gotta do something about this, to make sure I don't have to do this ever again.

Now Warren walks in the door.

"Hey, babe," he slurs. Why does he have to drink so much?

I've always believed in love. I learnt from my parents that you stick out the hard times and it all comes right. A relationship is for keeps and I'm all in, for keeps.

"Marry me, babe," he says, in his drunken stupor.

But why would I marry him? I'm nineteen years old. Like I said, I'm too young for marriage.

*

A few days later, there's a fantastic shoot in Death Valley. It's outstanding, and I like the pictures a lot. I've picked out my fave pic to include in my portfolio. I'm looking at the wispy scarf and my penetrating green eyes. This might just be the look that sells me. There are some great opportunities in LA. Nothing like this in Finland.

The next day a letter comes in the mail for me, from Piccio.

"Warren, look!" It's a video of the shoot we did when I was in Italy. He's always sending me cards and letters, just to keep in touch. It makes me think of Milan and that great time with crazy Stephanie, the excellent shoot in Eleuthera, and our un-sightseeing tour of Rome.

"No sales, no frigging sales at all this week. Shit!"

"Come on, this was a great shoot. It'll cheer you up!"

"I can't fucking do this, babe. This is trash. I'm tired, man, I don't wanna go frickin' dancin' with you. Stay with me, babe. You're mine."

"I just thought it'd be nice, Warren. Please let's go. We don't need to drink. Let's just feel the beat. We can get Jamie to come, or Mandy. Yeah, they'll come."

But Warren slides into bed, and urges me to follow.

Well, life is full of ups and downs, and that includes in relationships. We have some differences, but I guess we just have to work them out.

*

Time has a way of flying by when you're busy and working hard. All of a sudden I'm twenty and summer is here and gone. Well, in LA it always feels like summer. Work is good. Life isn't so perfect, however.

"Babe, quit naggin' me, will ya. Shit. I just want another drink."

Life should be good. I'm getting more and more work. But it seems like the better things go for me the worse it gets for Warren. Sales have been down, so he's down, way down. I don't know what to do.

Another evening, Warren is still out and I go to bed. I've got another early morning and they don't call it beauty sleep for nothing. I wake up in the night when I feel Warren crawl in beside me.

"Warren, where have you been?" He's crawled into bed but his breath is stale with the smell of booze. I roll over and find there's blood all over the sheets.

"Warren, what have you done?" Has he cut himself?

Then I see his chest is sliced.

"Who did this to you, Warren?"

But he's passed out.

When I take a close look, I can see the wound isn't deep, but what am I supposed to do? It isn't the first time he's bled. I know he didn't get in a fight, unless you call self-mutilation a fight. He tears at his skin with his nails, I've seen him do it. But this time I think he's used a knife to cut himself.

"Oh God, what am I supposed to do?"

I don't sleep too well.

Come to think of it, actually, LA is not everything I expected. It's golden sunshine and some really nice people, but I thought the competition would be less than in Europe. Wrong! For every square yard there are about ten beautiful women all looking for modelling and acting jobs. So, the competition is a lot tougher than I thought it was going to be. I've been here about eighteen months, and almost from the start Warren was in the picture. But I'm too young to be committed to someone for the rest of my life. He's dreamy. But he's also drunk most of the time. And he's always on my case about work. I'm here for work. If it wasn't for modelling I wouldn't be here at all. He doesn't seem to get that. So, what am I supposed to do? I was brought up never to give up. If you're in a relationship, you stick with it. But maybe this was a big mistake.

Milan has been asking for me for months. And I think I could break into Florida. Helena Hirvela is a friend and we've both been talking about getting into the Florida books for ages. Helena and I have a lead. Why shouldn't we follow it?

I look through my portfolio. I love the newest pic, the Death Valley look. This girl is confident; this girl knows where she's going and how to get there; this might just be the look that sells me big time. LA is not all I expected. The earthquake is not something I ever want to live through again. I carry a change of clothes with me in the back of my car now, in case my house collapses. What kind of a life is THAT?

Being totally honest, I don't think Warren fits into this picture. Warren wants me with him whenever he's not working. But I can't do that and build my career. Staying in LA with Warren is not what's best for me. It's hard moving on, but I think, somehow, I have to.

*

Another couple of weeks pass.

"Hey, babe, let's go out. I sold a car today. Let's celebrate."

"Oh, dreamboat. Yeah, let's."

Jamie joins us.

"But Warren's drinking so much, Jamie, and I don't know what I'm supposed to do."

"Let me talk to him."

Warren comes back from the can and I go to the ladies' room. When I get back, Warren glares at me.

"Let's get outta here," he says, and grabs my hand.

"Jamie?"

"Look, Warren, I think you'd better let me drive, okay?"

"Yeah, okay." Warren sulks in the back seat and we take off for home. "I'm going jogging" Warren takes off as soon as we get home.

Jamie comes in for coffee.

"How's work going?" he asks me.

"It's really good, Jamie." I hesitate. Shall I tell him a little about my plans? "And I'm looking around at other cities. You know, where I can grow and get some new bookings."

It isn't just that I'm confused about Warren. Travelling is a regular part of international modelling. We have to go to different places for location shoots. We also need to meet different agents and clients from all over the world. Sometimes they come to where you are, but mostly we have to go to them.

"I've always believed that you stick at a relationship through the hard times, no matter what. But I have to build my career too."

Jamie nods.

"Success does not happen overnight. Even if it isn't overseas travel for jobs, we need different locations for shoots to build our portfolios. Some clients have great imaginations, but most don't. They need to see you in a shot that's almost exactly the situation they're looking for, in order to hire you."

"You do that, Kati. You do whatever you need to do. You deserve the best." Then he stares at me. I can see he's thinking.

"What is it?" I ask him.

"This is only my opinion, but I've never seen anyone with the determination to succeed that you have. You're obviously beautiful, but there's a lot more to you than that. You're down to earth, approachable – not stuck-up like some models can be. And you're smart. You don't try to take the easy way up. You're going to make it in this profession. You have so much to offer and you're special. Go for it! Don't let anything hold you back. That's what I think."

"Wow. Thanks. Wow! Well, I *am* going back to Finland for a while. I've got some bookings over there. It's just what I have to do."

Jamie kisses my forehead on his way out. "You're full of life, Kati. Don't let anyone or anything hold you back."

Warren still isn't back and I have to get to bed. I'd like to cry myself to sleep, but if I do that, I think I'd never stop. Warren is the nicest man alive, when he's sober, but that's less and less often. I think maybe it's time to go.

Warren gets home a couple of hours later. He's sober and he's calm. He must have been running because he takes a shower before he crawls into bed.

"Hey, babe, I'm sorry."

And we make the best love, like we used to, and fall asleep in each other's arms. He's such a hunk and a dreamboat. He just needs to stay sober.

I've just booked my flight home. "I told you I had those bookings in Finland, Warren. Gloria and Florella have both booked me, so I have to go. I'll only be gone a few weeks. I'll stay there a while with my parents too, to make it worth the trip."

"Yeah, right. You gotta. Everything's always about you. Your career. Your photos. Your success. What about me?"

"We'll connect on fax every day. And sometimes we can phone."

He just shrugs his shoulders, like a little kid.

I hate fighting like this.

"Warren, let's go. You know, let's…"

"Ah, babe."

And we make mad passionate love. It'll have to keep us going while I'm gone. And while I'm in Finland, I'm definitely going to see a doctor for a prescription.

When I land at Helsinki, I'm treated like a princess by the paparazzi. It's my homeland, and photographers gather around me to take my picture. I'm the star, like small-town-Cinderella-made-good-in-LA. It's great publicity, and it's fun. It's nice to be in Finland in the summer. It's warm and the air is clean too.

"Äiti, I might move to Florida. Milan wants me back too."

My mom just smiles.

Another day we're just shopping.

"Äiti, I'm going to go on the pill."

"I thought you already were."

I shrug. "Yeah, I guess I should have been by now." No matter what happens with Warren, it won't end right away. I'm going to be safe from now on, rather than sorry later.

The next day Warren and I have an argument over the phone. He's mad because I haven't faxed him often enough. Jeez! I can't help it. I'm not there because I'm working here.

"Äiti, I'm not sure what's happening with me and Warren."

My mom sits down to listen, but I don't talk. We don't keep secrets, but I don't know what to say. I don't tell her about him slashing himself. I think that's just too much for her to have to hear, but I have admitted things aren't too good between us. She looks worried.

CHAPTER 7

Florida Bound

The doctor only asks me one question.

"Are you sexually active now?"

"Yes, I'm in a relationship."

He gives me the prescription. He doesn't say anything else. Well, why should he? I'm a healthy, red-blooded woman and I don't want to make babies right now. Someday, but not right now. There's nothing else to talk about. Femoden will ensure I don't get another pregnancy scare.

Warren calls me in the evening. He's crying.

"Oh, babe, I need you. When are you coming home?"

He's drunk, I think. Mom overhears us talking.

"Yeah, sometimes he drinks too much, Äiti, and I'm not sure what to do. He loves me. We love each other." She doesn't say anything.

"I know I'm going to have to make up my mind about us." I have to work my way towards making a decision – do I stay with Warren or move to Miami? It should be easy, but it's not.

My friend Helena Hirvela, another Finn in LA, is a little older than I am and more experienced; she's ahead of me in the modelling biz. Maybe it's finally time for us to actually try Florida. We could at least fly over to meet the agent we've been connected to. Bo, at the Michele Pommier agency, is really keen to meet us.

Alone, relaxing on my own little bed in Mikkeli, I'm thinking, just like I used to do before I started out. Florida or Milan – which is better? Why Not have not forgotten me. They keep asking me, "When are you coming back?" That feels good. I think after Florida with Helena and making some good connections there, I could base myself in Milan once and for all. It's something I'll have to tell Warren about sooner or later.

Jeez, I can't believe he's sore at me again. Isn't it okay sometimes to have a break in communication? Is love supposed to be so complicated all the time?

I've always been determined about modelling. Nothing could break my spirit. Some other models try to mess with their competition by saying stupid derogatory remarks, like: "Oh, didn't you know you're supposed to wear something pink today?" or "That pimple is hardly noticeable. Great make-up."

They're trying to eliminate the competition. It's so obvious. But it's never worked on me. What do I care what the competition thinks?

Then there are the girls who think they can make it by sleeping with influential photographers or others who'll give them a leg-up. And there are the partygoers, fitting in to get their way ahead. But I'm not like either of those; I'm not afraid of hard work and long hours. But when I'm done for the day, I'm a homegirl, ready to curl up with the TV and my man. However, lately my man isn't into cuddling. Deciding about him is so different than planning my career. Maybe I just need to be brave and say goodbye to the most gorgeous guy I've ever met.

What's wrong with me? There are Miami opportunities, and the best agency in the state is willing to meet with Helena and me. Why Not is still asking for me in Milan. So, why not?

What could hold me back? Nothing. Not a man who's crazy for me, or just plain crazy.

*

"Irina, what should I do?"

"Kati, I've never heard you ask anyone what to do. If this guy has you messed up in the head, he's no good for you."

"Yeah, you're right. Jeez, I had to come all the way back to Finland to hear sense."

She smiles. "You'll be fine, girl. Your life awaits."

I smile a little. It'll be good to get back to America and of course I'll take that meeting in Florida.

*

"Äiti." We're driving into the city to go shopping. I'm reading this book about positive thinking. It's great. Only, I want to tell my mother something. "If something ever happens to me and I end up in the hospital, on life support, don't pull the plug, okay?"

"Okay," she answers.

*

Warren isn't pleased because I come back with news that I have castings on the East Coast. I don't tell him it's to change agents. He just thinks it's for a job, and it is, partly.

I keep taking the pill though. Life with Warren is still good, sometimes. I just don't know what to do about the other times.

I'm tired. I've got a headache, which isn't usual for me. It must be a combination of the jet lag and the tension between Warren and me. I'll sleep it off and call Helena tomorrow, to make sure she's still up for Florida. And then, we'll book our flights.

Florida awaits!

*

It's been a hectic day, with a shoot and a job, but it's invigorating as usual. Tonight we're flying to Florida. I can hardly wait. Warren comes home early from work. I think he wants to see me off, maybe even take me to the airport.

"Kati, it's summer, it should be a busy car time, but I'm doing shit. Don't go and leave me here. You just got back," he whines.

"It's only two weeks. Maybe you'll make some sales while I'm gone."

"You're my inspiration, babe. I need you here."

Warren doesn't like it, but this is my work and I've gotta do it.

*

Miami!

With changes of clothes packed and portfolios practically glued to our hands, Helena Hirvela and I sit together on the flight, jabbering in Finnish for a change. It's nice. Ever since we met on a shoot a few months ago, we've managed to have some good times together. Tonight we share our portfolios. Even though we're both Finnish, the similarities almost stop there. We get along really well, but our look is so different. Our body types are not the same, and while you can always change hair colour and style, you can't really change your body.

"These pictures really show off your personality, Helena. The rough-and-ready tomboy look suits your broad shoulders perfectly."

Helena is a very unusual model. She isn't typically stunning, she's unique. When the make-up and hair are complete, she looks completely different from her day-to-day look. I guess you could say she's versatile, because depending on what she wears, or how she's made up, she will look totally different. That's special in a model.

"Thanks, Kati. And your feminine clothes really suit you, totally. Glamorous but not cold, always sexy but homey too – you're classic. It's so important to accentuate what works naturally, isn't it?"

She's totally right. A model's portfolio is incredibly important. It includes pictures and past work. It's the first thing the casting agency will look at, and they'll want the brand managers and designers to be able to determine immediately whether or not they want to work with us. Our books are perfect. This can make or break getting into Florida, and Florida can make or break our careers.

"There's so much in here," we say to each other. We're excited, and we laugh like little girls on the way to Disneyworld.

When we started out, our books were so thin. But especially since being in LA, both of ours have expanded so much. The sunny climate allows outdoor pics all through the year, and outdoor shots are so easy to light. The lighting is the most important thing, and our pics have to be just right. No shadows on the photos is maybe *the* most important thing.

Since being in LA, I've submitted to a lot of other agencies around the States. Getting an appointment with the Michele Pommier agency has been a big breakthrough, and don't I know it.

Some people have to submit to every single agency with their portfolio, in person. If they prepare well, their book includes a few headshots, just showing their face from a few different angles. They'll have smiling shots for the commercial modelling and some others showing themselves straight-faced. Then they'll have some full-length shots too, as dressed in swimwear is absolutely essential if you want to be considered for glamorous work.

We're ready to roll as the plane hits the tarmac in Florida, the Sunshine State.

We only have two weeks in Miami, but Helena and I will have a few castings and do some shoots with photographers. The agency will want to test us out, and we've got an appointment with one of their agents, Bo. We get to Michele Pommier and introduce ourselves. Bo is a very relaxed guy. Even his name sounds laid-back.

"So, these are the Finnish twins. You don't look much alike. Are you sure you're Finnish? You're not even blonde."

Helena laughs. "Naw, we're not twins, although we are inseparable. I guess you could say we're like Siamese twins."

"I can be blonde, but I prefer me this way," I say. "We are definitely Finnish."

"I may not be blonde, but I am versatile. Kati says so, and she must be right," Helena says.

We all laugh, and we pore over our portfolios with Bo, so he can see the range we have.

Helena is twenty-seven and a lot more experienced than I am. I'm really lucky to have her company. As we settle into our hotel room, we talk for a while.

"Can you see yourself living here, Kati?"

"On Ocean Drive, you bet. You?"

"Yes, but Craig and I are pretty stuck on each other. I don't think I'll be leaving LA anytime soon. You?"

"I dunno. Maybe. Probably."

*

I sign a contract with Bo.

On one of the castings I meet a Korean scout.

"Come to Korea," he says.

Really? Wow! Coming to Florida has really opened my eyes to possibilities. Well, actually I guess it's put me where people are, and I open their eyes. It's really exciting.

Helena and I do some work together, and separately, of course. One day I'm on my own to meet with Rico, a fantastic photographer that the agency has recommended. We work together so I can get some new shots.

"Look left. Right. How do you like the music?"

"It's perfect. How did you know Prince is my fave?"

"I didn't."

Spending the whole day with one photographer is very unusual, but we click really well, and he just wants to keep going.

"When do you think the pics'll be ready?" I ask before I leave.

"Can you give me a couple of days? I'll send them to this lab." He hands me a piece of paper with a name and address on.

"Of course. And thanks. It was a great day!"

"You're not too tired, I hope?" Rico asks. He looks a little concerned.

"No, not at all. It was fantastic, wasn't it?" Actually, I have had a bit of a headache, but I brush it off.

He relaxes. "I don't like to work anybody too hard, but we were really in the groove, so I didn't want to stop. Fantastic? Absolutely, pretty lady. One of the best days I've had in a while. I think we got some great shots."

A couple of days later, I go to the lab to collect the pictures and look through them quickly. When I get back to the hotel, I open the envelope, and look at the photos carefully, one by one. They are such good photos. Then I notice there is one photo that Rico's attached a note to. It's a great shot.

'Kati, you are a very special model, beautiful, fun and smart. You take direction so well. You should go where the models are.'

Wow!

Instantly I think about Milan. They keep contacting me to ask, "When are you coming back?" Spring, I decide. I'll move back there in the spring.

*

As always, Warren and I have a great reunion. He meets me at the airport and we go straight back to our place. He puts on soft music and it's an evening just like when we first met.

*

The next morning, as usual, I'm up at dawn to start my day. Unfortunately, I've got a tiny headache, which is odd, but life is great. I'm gonna have to talk to Warren about future plans though. Modelling is my number one priority, and he has to understand that. It always has been and it always will be. I'm moving up. It's so exciting! I wish Warren could be happier for me, but when I try to tell him about it, he's not really paying attention. He was drinking last night again, so he's not very perky this morning.

"Have a good day," he says.

It's a quiet day ahead, so after the gym Jamie and I meet up and go for a bike ride to Venice Beach. Then we cycle to our favourite stop for potato soup. He's interested in what I did in Florida.

"Kati, you've got the determination and common sense needed to achieve all your goals."

"I'm just not sure how long I can stay in LA. I tried to talk to Warren. Rico in Florida's message has really struck home. There are better places to be than LA if I'm going to succeed."

"What's that?" Jamie asks me, as I pop an Advil.

"Advil."

"Headache?"

"Yeah. I never used to get headaches, and lately I can't seem to shake this."

"Well, when you go for gold, I guess sometimes you'll get stress. But seriously, you have everything it takes to make it. So, although I know you won't relax – it's not your style – I hope you won't worry. You've got everything going for you – the look you need, which goes without saying. But your business is a lot more than looks. You're warm towards people, and you're clean. And you've got the work ethic to boot. Seriously, you've got the world at your feet. Enjoy, be yourself and don't look back."

Jamie's got me thinking. Yeah, I am clean. I've never taken drugs and I hardly even drink. And I've had a really happy home life. But I've got my weak points too. I could have messed up. I could have been pregnant that day I took the test, and that would have really changed my life. I've learnt from Jamie – like the things he says to his kids at the motivational talks he gives – that we've got to be careful about the things we do, and make good choices. I'm glad I'm on the pill now. At least I won't make that mistake again.

"Thanks, Jamie. It's always good talking to you."

*

At home it's time to break the news to Warren – I've got another trip.

"Warren, I don't want to argue, but I've got a gig in Helsinki again. Imagine, they want me. Only me. They didn't even advertise. It's a job in the Canary Islands at Christmastime. I'll get to spend time at my mom and dad's and I don't have to pay for it. They're flying me over there!"

"Yeah, sure, whatever. Christmas in Finland." He just gets up and goes to the fridge for a beer. I watch him down it. At least he doesn't put up an argument, which is good, but I can see he's not pleased.

When I'm in Finland, I'll make a clear decision about what to do about us. I don't think I can stay with Warren anymore. He's a great guy in so many ways, but we fight so much. I figured when we started out it wouldn't be perfect forever. Relationships need adjustments and we have to work at it. But it isn't getting any better. If anything, it's getting worse. And I do have to think about my career.

Being home means Äiti's great food, friends like Irina, and maybe I'll even see Jari over Christmas. Sometimes he writes me out here in LA. It'd be nice to see him.

I can't be worrying all the time about Warren.

The shoot in the Canaries will be nice too. Guaranteed.

*

I don't sleep very well and when 7.00 a.m. comes, I'm wide awake, ready to go.

It's so peaceful at the gym. After a great workout I head for the shower, and I'm thinking about having a little breakfast.

Suddenly I'm really dizzy. My head's spinning and I feel woozy. I step out of the hot water to put my head down. Thankfully, the dizziness passes. I step back into the shower, but the wooziness comes back again in waves, big waves. I have to hold on to the wall to keep from collapsing, and I barely manage to turn off the hot water with my other hand. Now the black tiles are beginning to spin, like some ballerina picking up speed with every twirl. Jeez, I should have had more sleep last night. I'm clinging to the wall for dear life, afraid I'm gonna pass out on these hard tiles, and there's nobody here to catch me. There's nobody here to call out to; not sure I could if there was. Suddenly, all the power leaves my body, and I want to drop. I know I've got to hold on, this will pass. Is this what it's like to faint? I'm desperate, nearly keeling over.

I'm trying to see around me, but things are blurry and moving. It makes me want to throw up. All the time I think I'm going to fall because the strength is just leaving my body. There's nobody here, which makes me start to panic. I'm just gripping the wall, the railing, for dear life. Head down, I think I'm panting, gasping almost. I'm trying to breathe, deep and long. It's helping. Somehow, the powerless feeling is going, and I don't feel weak or dizzy anymore, thank God. I'm sweating and exhausted, but I'm okay. I sit down on the shower floor. Jeez! I guess I'd better eat something.

I'm thinking: has life been more crazy than usual? Yeah, maybe. I guess it has. I've been dieting and travelling.

Eventually, I reach up and turn on the water again, cool not hot, and let the water wash over me. I stare at the floor. Thank God I never fell down completely. I could have really hurt myself going down on those tiles.

The headache seems to be gone and the rest of the day and the week pass without incident. On the weekend, I phone my mom like I usually do, and tell her about the fainting spell in the shower.

"It was so weird, Äiti. It just came on me so fast, and then it went again."

"What do you think caused this?" she asks me. I can hear she's worried.

"I don't know. I guess I just worked out too hard on an empty stomach. I should have eaten something before that hot shower."

"Has it happened before?"

"Nope, never."

From now on I'll be sure to eat a piece of fruit before my workouts, not just drink a coffee.

I do try to keep a little food in my stomach after that shower episode, but sometimes the dizziness comes back. It's random. There's one other time when I nearly pass out, at home when I'm alone, relaxing over some mags. The phone rings and I jump up, but as soon as I do, I get that woozy feeling again, like I'm going to pass out. I answer the phone, and soon I realise the wooziness has gone. I drink some water and get on with the day. I won't mention it to my mom again, because she sounded really worried the first time. Really, I just have to slow down.

The dull headache never seems to go away. Could there be some connection? The Advil are practically useless, so I've abandoned them. I guess it's time to go home to Finland, for some good home cooking, and I can spend time with everyone. I don't have to run around. Except for the one big job in the fabulous Canaries, I can relax.

*

The day to fly home arrives.

"Yes, I promise, Warren. I'll fax you when I get there. I can call you too, soon."

His parting kiss at the airport is luscious. I will miss him.

*

December 1994, and I'm heading out from Los Angeles, California. Apart from that earthquake, which is now history, everything's great. I need to sort out what to do about Warren, and whether to stay in LA. I don't want to hurt him. I love him. But I have to keep building my modelling career too. Only God knows where I got the crazy idea to become an international model from.

Here's me, living on the other side of the world from Finland, in the City of Angels, meeting celebrities like they're ordinary people. Working for big international campaigns. Making music videos. Doing fashion shows. You name it. Yeah, it's a crazy, hectic time, and so wonderful. Oh yeah, I gotta keep clear of those headaches and dizzy spells. Water, food, rest. I'll get all of the above at my parents' in Finland.

I loved meeting Bjorn Borg. I was casually strolling along Third Street Promenade near my place in Santa Monica, with a colleague of Warren's who had sold him his Porsche, and we were introduced. And Michael Jordan; I met him while I was going through some paperwork with a client. My agents knew him; I guess he was going to do some product representation or something. Then there was the Arab prince who wanted to marry me – major problem, he already has a harem. And some TV celebrities; one or two wanting a date from me, others just really friendly. It's fascinating to see how natural, ordinary and down to earth they are. Except for the prince.

I'm in my seat bound for Finland, and I'm thinking it's nice to go home for Christmas, but would I seriously change my life for anything else in the world?

CHAPTER 8

Crash

I'm so looking forward to going home. And that's so rare for me. It's winter and I'm going to Finland and looking forward to it? Crazy.

The fresh air will cool my head. I'm never sick, but for the past four months I've just not been feeling 100 per cent. This damn headache won't go away and about two months ago I started to get dizzy spells. Go to a doctor? Never. And especially not in LA – it would cost a fortune.

Anyway, here with Äiti and Isa I'll have great food and the fresh air will take my headache away for good. I'm sure of it. It's just time for a break, some Christmas food and rest. And to top off a great visit I've got the shoot right after Christmas, in the warm and beautiful Canary Islands, to look forward to.

"Kati, you seem tired. What are you doing in LA?"

"Yeah, I'm a bit tired. Too much working out and not enough of your great cooking, Mom." It's funny saying 'Mom' to her, but it makes her smile. She likes it when I speak 'Americano' to her.

It's wonderful to be at my parents' house. Jukka and Anu visit, Anu and I go shopping together. But I still don't feel myself.

"Are you tired?" she asks me.

"You too? Everybody's asking me that."

Being back in Finland in the winter, so dark and depressing, is hard. There isn't even any snow this year to brighten it up. How can I find any energy after living in super-sunny California?

Warren gets sore and complains via fax every day. When he doesn't hear from me, he thinks I'm avoiding him. Or if I don't reply five times a day, he starts accusing me of not loving him. Jeez, I'm just trying to live. That, and the fact that some moments I feel like my head is a ton of bricks, get me down.

Just before Christmas, my mother insists on taking me to the doctor. I know what he'll say, but I figure it will make her happy, so I agree to go. Sitting at the health centre, waiting for some test results, I look at a fashion magazine. I'm in it! Oh, yeah, it's from the summer shoot. Humph. I'm sure I didn't have the headache then.

"The laboratory tests don't show anything. There's nothing to worry about. It's just a bad cold," says the doctor. Naw, it's actually a throat infection. I used to get those when I was a kid, and living in smoggy LA triggers them. I'm so used to it, I don't even notice. Nothing serious, nothing I'm not used to living with, nothing to worry about.

Christmas Day arrives, the day I can cheat – or excuse myself – to eat all the usual special Finnish Christmas yummies that Äiti makes. Today though, I'm not very hungry. I nibble a little, but nothing tastes delicious like it usually does. Mom's staring at me out of the corner of her eye, so I try to eat some more of her delicious snacks, but it's kind of like forcing myself to eat, which is very unusual for me. I don't feel much like socialising either. Looking around the living room, I'm sure my relatives think I'm too stuck-up to talk, as if I think I'm a big shot or something. But it isn't that. I'm really just not feeling talkative.

"Kati?"

"Mom, I'm just not hungry. Nothing tastes like anything. I'm just going to lie down."

And that's Christmas 1994. Totally forgettable, unfortunately.

*

Two days before I leave for my shoot in the Canaries, I'm feeling better. I've got errands and Äiti comes with me. We head for the pharmacy, for shampoo and a prescription renewal.

"I don't know what to do about Warren, Mom. Our relationship isn't easy right now, but I'm not going to make a hasty decision. I love him, he just doesn't like it when I'm away. Every time we exchange faxes, he accuses me of avoiding him. And then there's all his drinking. Ohhhh! I don't know what to do. If I go to Florida, that would give us a good break, to work out our future."

Äiti just listens. I'm so lucky to have her as a mom.

*

"All set, Kati?"

"Yup."

Today I fly to the Canaries for the shoot and I'm really looking forward to it. I'm packed and ready to go. On the staircase coming down from my room, I grab on to the wall. Damn these dizzy spells! I gotta remember not to move too suddenly.

"Kati, I don't think you should go. You're not well," says Isa.

"Come on! You think I'm going to miss this? They paid for me to come here. I mean, they paid for my flight. If I don't show up they won't pay for my flight back to LA, and they'll never hire me again. I can't miss this. Anyway, I'm fine. Just a little dizzy. You heard the doctor, Äiti, it's just a stupid cold."

I kiss them both, then pop a couple of Advil on the way out the door.

I'm going by bus to the airport, which is good because I think if my parents drove me to Helsinki they would turn around and bring me home. To be honest, I feel like I'm going to throw up and like my head is splitting open at the same time. I'm trying to breathe deeply, to get lots of oxygen into my system, but I'm feeling worse and worse. The Advil has had zero effect on this headache, my head is throbbing like there's no tomorrow, and that's not all.

I can't even look out of the window, because the trees are spinning and making my eyeballs feel like they're floating around inside my head. I'm breaking out into a sweat, I'm *so* dizzy, and I wonder if I throw up will I feel better? But I mustn't do that. I can't get to the back of the bus, because if I try I'm sure I'll pass out completely, then who knows what'd happen to me? No, I've got to hide this, get over it, and get onto that plane.

I am sick, I have to admit. A cold? Throat infection? Actually, I feel like I'd like to be put out of my misery, like what they do to horses with a broken leg, but I put a smile on my face as I hop off the bus and carry my stuff into the airport. Miss Self-Sufficiency better not show how rotten she feels in front of everyone. I gotta get on that plane.

I smile through security, and head straight for my gate.

I'd still like to throw up, but somehow I manage to keep myself going forward to the flight. As soon as I get to the gate I make a beeline for some empty chairs, and lie across them. Whooo. I'll just relax here until they call the flight. Then I'll be fine. It'd be nice to have an ice pack for my forehead.

I guess it's pretty obvious I'm not feeling great, because some of the personnel start hovering over me, telling me not to take the flight.

"Are you all right, Miss?"

"Yeah, yeah I'm fine. Just tired."

"You're on this flight, Miss ..."

"Lepistö."

"Miss Lepistö, really you shouldn't fly in this condition."

"What condition? I'm fine. Just a little tired. And I haven't eaten. Models don't get to eat as much as other people." I'm not going to let some dizziness stop me from making this shoot. "I promise as soon as I get on the plane, you can serve me something and I'll eat it. I'll be fine. Honestly."

And it's true! As soon as we take off, I feel absolutely fine. Air pressure equilibrium, I guess. I nibble on something to keep the stewards happy, but the nausea, headache, dizziness are all gone, finally. Presto!

I phone my parents as soon as I get to my hotel room, and tell them I'm fine, so they won't worry.

"Ah, Canary magic," I whisper as I gaze out of my hotel room window. It's gorgeous. I suppose I shouldn't push myself with a workout, but I will go for a gentle swim. Gentle? Me? Well, this time I'm in no mood to work out too hard, in case it makes me feel sick again. Maybe when I get back to Mikkeli I should see the doctor and tell him about the headaches. I don't think I've told a doctor they've been going on for a few months now.

"Helena, this is a wonderful place isn't it?" Helena Karihtala and I will be doing the shoot together, and the client has us sharing a room.

"Yes, it's great," she says.

When I wake up in the morning, I realise something's missing. What is it? Then I realise – oh man, let me live in the Canary Islands. There are no headaches here. I've been living with a headache since September, but here, finally, I'm over it.

I think this shoot is one of the best I've ever done. Up at 7.00 a.m. every day is invigorating, and it feels so easy. Being with Helena is inspiring. Helena is one of the most famous models in Finland. In 1988 she was one of the contestants in the Miss Finland pageant where she was the favourite of the press, a really nice, down-to-earth lady. Elegant looking, the shorthaired brunette is petite next to long-and-lanky me, and there's one male model too, a nice guy. The photographer is a dream to work with. In fact, we all work really well together. I'm sure the client will ask me again. I love working with this team.

The last night of the shoot we stay up late, doing a bit of bar hopping together, and hanging out over some wine. This has really been a rewarding gig.

"Yes, we'll keep in touch," Helena and I promise each other. It's special when you find someone you work really well with. You don't want to lose the connection.

The return flight is fine, but with a three-hour ride from the airport to home too, it's no wonder I feel exhausted when I walk through the door. And it's a dull, grey January. Well, now I've got time on my hands to rest. Time to think seriously about where I go from here as a model.

The next day my mom is on my case.

"Kati, you're not eating again."

The headache is back. "I know, Äiti. I feel like I'm going to throw up. It's definitely being back here, because I felt totally fine on the shoot. Ever since I got back here, I've been feeling sick again. I hate this blackness in Finland in the winter."

"I don't think it is just blackness. I'm taking you to the doctor."

She's already made the appointment and I can tell she won't take no for an answer. Deep down, I have to admit, I never in my life felt faint before this dizziness started. I don't know what good going to a doctor will do, but I guess it can't hurt. I'd better tell him about the headaches.

The health centre is quiet, and the appointment is brief.

"Are you on any medication?"

"Nope, I'm totally healthy. Normally, except for occasional throat infections and headaches."

They do some tests and we wait for the results.

"The laboratory tests don't show us anything to be worried about," the doctor says. "Get some rest, eat more, get your strength up. It's just a bit of flu."

That's exactly what I figured he'd say. And I have been resting.

"I've decided when I go back to LA, I'm going to move to Florida, Mom, at least for a while."

"What about Warren?"

"Ah, I guess we need a break for a while. He gets upset every day I'm here. If I send ten faxes a day he still thinks I've left him for good. It's driving us both crazy."

But I can't seem to shake this nauseous feeling.

"They didn't do a pregnancy test. Maybe they should," Äiti says. I know she's just trying to find a reason for me feeling so nauseous.

"But I'm not pregnant, Mom, I'm on the pill."

She just looks at me.

"Whaaaat?"

"Did you just hear yourself?" she asks. "Ba I no prenan," she repeats.

Yeah, I guess my speech did slur a bit.

Back at the clinic, they look at me again.

"Sometimes her speech is slurred, like she's drunk," Äiti tells the doctor. "But she's not drunk," she insists.

"And sometimes I feel like I'm being pulled to the right when I'm walking," I tell them. "I'm like a car that won't drive straight unless you grip the wheel really tight."

"Well, the flu can make you quite weak and uncoordinated. You'll mend. You need to drink fluids," the doctor instructs. "And you need to eat better. More. You models..." He mutters something I don't quite pick up.

"It's worse than the last time I was here," I confess.

"This will pass with some tender loving care," he says to my mother. It's as if I didn't speak at all.

So, I just have to wait it out, whatever *it* is, until I am better. It's hard to think clearly when I'm feeling nauseous all the time, but I'm determined to ignore it. I'm not used to being sick. I'm a perfectly healthy young woman, so I'll just have to get over it. At least I haven't felt like fainting since I've been back in Finland. That was obviously just a combination of the California heat and the hard, early morning workouts.

Thinking about going back to LA, should I stop taking the pill if I'm going to Florida anyway? I know I've got to break it to Warren gradually. I'm going to Florida. But I really don't want to hurt him. And anyway, our reunion will be wonderful. It always is. So I need the pill for a while longer at least.

It's my mom's birthday in a few days and I haven't even gone shopping for a present yet. I nearly forgot – except I *never* forget. I can't seem to think straight. I'll go shopping for her present tomorrow. If Irina hadn't moved to Sweden she'd come with me. Maybe Anu will.

Tuesday, 9 January 1995. The evening starts out as normal; a quiet evening at home, just watching television. One of the cats sits on my lap, but I'm feeling heavy, and it takes all my energy just to move from the couch to get a glass of water. I'm so tired, I feel like I'm drunk, but I haven't had any alcohol.

I pass the kitchen on my way upstairs to my room.

"I goiii to ress fo a whyl," I tell my mom.

It seems to take me a long time to climb the stairs and my bed seems very far away. When I get to it, I practically collapse onto it.

Äiti comes in shortly after and sits next to me.

"Kati?"

After a while I answer her.

"I jus feeeel..."

"I don't like the sound of your voice," she says to me. "I heard it downstairs too. This isn't all right."

"Yeah," I have to agree, it sounds cloudy, and my tongue feels like lead in my mouth.

"And you don't look right either, sprawled out on your bed like this."

"Hmm."

"Come on. We're going. I'm taking you to the doctor."

Back to the clinic. Except when I try to stand, it's impossible. Instead I slip back onto the bed.

"KATI!"

Next thing I know, Mom has put me in her old black Mercedes. Isa has to work the next day, so he'll stay home with the cats. We're off to the health centre again. But then I'm dragged to the hospital because the doctor at the health centre just tells us to go home.

"No," says Äiti. "This has gone on long enough. Throat infection, cold, flu, whatever this is, it's getting really serious."

At the hospital for the first time, I'm questioned.

"What drugs were you on in the States?" the doctor on call asks. Does she think I'm high?

My mom and I look at each other and glare at the doctor, but neither of us has the energy to get angry. Nice diagnosis. If I felt stronger, I would tell her off. I've never taken a drug in my life. I barely drink. The only drugs I take are Advil and the pill.

"My daughter does not take drugs!" my mom says emphatically.

Tests are ordered. We wait some more. Finally, I throw up, which gives me some relief.

Sitting, waiting to be tested, there's nothing to do. I'm conscious but drowsy, incapable of doing anything, so drained of energy. It was bad at home, but it's even worse now. Totally lethargic. Staff take some samples. More waiting. I feel like I'm getting weaker and weaker, heavier and heavier. But nobody asks me how I am. More time passes, waiting. Shouldn't they have some test results by now? I'm sitting, doing nothing, sinking, while I'm waiting for the doctor to come back. Äiti's bouncing up and down, on the phone to Isa, then pacing. She can see I'm fading. She asks a nurse for water for me. Then she asks for help, but we're ignored. This is a hospital? They don't seem to realise I'm getting weaker and weaker. Suddenly, I start to slide out of the chair, and I can't stop myself.

"Nurse!" Äiti shouts. Some staff member notices and calls for help.

"Here, climb up here," says someone else. But I can't climb, so they lift me onto a bed in the outpatient clinic.

Äiti is pacing. More hours pass. I don't want to worry her even more, but now my legs feel like lead. Good thing I'm lying down.

Mom's got enough energy for both of us. I wish she didn't look so worried though. "Excuse me," I hear her calling to a nurse. I reach out my left hand to her, and Mom comes near my face.

I whisper, "Mom, I'm not paralysed, I just have no energy to move." My speech is slurred. I lie back in silence. Even talking takes too much effort. I feel myself drowning. I know I should swim, but I can't save myself. I've given up trying. Instead, I'll just wait for morning, and whatever they do, in their own time, will make me all right. Occasionally during the night, the doctor on call comes and tests my reflexes. She takes the blunt side of a cold knife blade and scrapes it from my heel to my toes on each foot. It's not very gentle! Maybe she's finally realised I can't move? But doesn't she know I can certainly feel what she's doing?

"You don't take any medication for anything?" she asks.

I have enough energy to shake my head a little.

Äiti explains, "She has been taking something for headaches, and that's it. Oh, and the pill, she's on the pill."

Advil and the pill are hardly medication.

"That isn't on the chart," the doctor says. "What pill?"

Mom roots around in my purse.

"Femoden," she says. The doctor looks at the package. "And it looks like Advil for the headaches, right, Kati?"

My hand begins to twitch. I'm not trying, but they notice. The doctor writes something in the chart. Äiti is staring.

"She's been getting headaches for a few months. Nothing that stops her from her routines, and she's been taking a mild painkiller for them."

"How long has she been on the pill?"

"Since the summer. She got the prescription when she was here in the summer."

"And the headaches started...?"

"A few months ago, Kati?" Mom asks. I nod.

They started just after I got back to LA from Finland. That's four months ago. September. The doctor glares at me. Then she walks off.

More time passes. Now my eyes begin to twitch, really weird. The doctors have us waiting for the test results. We'll talk to them about this new eye-twitch when they come back.

After what seems like hours, the doctor returns. The test results have finally come back. The eye-twitch has stopped.

"The results are showing something called nystagmus. There is indication of some inflammation of the equilibrium nerve. It may be cerebral haemorrhaging or cerebral meningitis. We don't know the cause of your slurred speech or nausea. We've ordered a CAT scan. We'll keep you here overnight if necessary."

It's definitely necessary. I can't even move! I don't want to make a fuss though, because it'll worry Äiti.

She asks me some questions, but I don't answer her. I haven't got the energy to move my mouth or my body. Actually, I'm finding it impossible to get my sentences out. It must be the exhaustion. There's the CAT scan and more waiting.

The CAT scan shows nothing. There is nothing unusual, no swelling, no haemorrhaging, no clotting.

"We'll keep you in overnight," the doctor says. She seems a little more focused. I bet she's changed her tune. My condition has gone from drug-induced self-destruction to some real health matter.

Äiti is pacing. She's looking at me, trying to smile, but I see she's desperately worried. It's 3.00 a.m. I have no energy even to move my head. Äiti is going back and forth to the nurses and looking for help. They are chatting away, going about their duties, as if everything is perfectly normal. But this isn't normal for me. I feel numb, and have zero energy even to scratch my nose.

"We think it's some sort of virus." The doctor looks puzzled. "We're going to move you to the intensive care unit, Kati."

"Sleep, Kati," my mom whispers as they wheel me away. They've offered her an unused bed in a storeroom to sleep. We're both exhausted.

I don't sleep. I am fully conscious, although I don't feel totally clear-headed. Energy is leaving my body, like a trail of water seeping out of a pail, and I can't even try to block the seepage. I'm helpless, unable to move or speak, helpless like a baby, too exhausted to cry. When they figure out what's wrong and fix it, then I'll relax.

The morning comes and the doctor returns.

"I've called the neurologist. He wasn't on duty last night but he's looked at your EEG. We think you have some inflammation of the brain. We're going to take the swelling down, with some antibiotics."

"Look at this, Kati. Here's what they've written," says my mom, and she shows me the chart. "The patient stares, doesn't answer questions, and is drowsy. Hands are rigged and twitch 'oddly'," she reads. She looks at my hands. They've stopped twitching. There's no mention of the eye-twitch. Of course not. They weren't around to see it and they didn't ask.

It will be good when they can get the swelling down and I can be well again. Right now, my eyes don't move, my hands don't move, my legs don't move. And I can't get my words out. I admit, it's scary, feeling totally helpless. Äiti looks scared too.

"The symptoms seem to describe a stroke," we hear someone say. "Of course that's virtually impossible, in such a young person."

CHAPTER 9

Marjatta and Risto

Marjatta Appelqvist Lepistö is energetic, determined and very protective. She has the heart of a lioness. If anyone crosses her family, she protects and helps us to pull through in every situation. She embodies all that is best about Finnish people: she is hardworking, loyal and devoted, and always willing to help. She's a great mom; she offers sound wisdom when necessary, but she doesn't interfere. She has always let me live as I know I need to live. She taught me responsibility when I was little, and then trusted me to be responsible.

When she took me to the hospital it was because she knew there was no other option. I only wish the doctors would have been smarter and more engaged with me, to stop the progress of what was happening. Mom did everything she could to get their attention, and mine, in the first place.

When I was growing up, both my parents were totally devoted to making the family happy, safe and healthy. It would take too many pages to talk about all the things my dad did to make our lives good, and all the things my mom did to ensure my brother and I were safe and well-behaved children. We both grew up feeling loved and confident in ourselves.

My mom was raised Lutheran. She believes in God and likes the traditions of the church, believing we must tell the truth, be respectful, and responsible. Risto Lepistö, my dad, is the same. I learnt how to work hard, to persevere, to be loyal to others and trustworthy through the example they set for me.

You will see, as things unfold about my life, after I turned twenty, after our trip to ER in the Mikkeli hospital that at the heart of all of it, is my mom. She changed her whole life to ensure I had one. And my dad, by the way, never asked for anything different.

My dad was hit especially hard by the stroke. He said to a close friend much later, "What happened to my beautiful girl?" when his own dark days were only just behind him. Just after the stroke he was angry and might have sued the doctor, but the rest of us said, "No, let it be." The stress of pursuing a court case would have been too much on top of the paralysis. So he let it go, because that's what we asked. He is the most giving, unselfish person I know. In his quiet way, he has always been supportive of me, always ready to help me if I needed it, always rooting for me to be strong and capable, and never interfering, even though he didn't always like the choices I made. He never liked me going to America, but he let me make my choice.

I owe my life to my parents.

There will be critical moments from now on where, if it wasn't for my mom, who kept me going in the dark days after the stroke, I probably would not be here to tell this story. Everyone who is successful has someone backing them. With my mom, I could do anything. It's funny, but I was always Little Miss Independent yet if it wasn't for her, I wouldn't have been independent. And if I hadn't been independent, I don't think I would have found the will to survive after the stroke.

Feisty Marjatta has a spirit of survival. After I came home from rehab she worked from 8.00 a.m. to 4.00 p.m. every day, and then came home to take care of me every evening, through the night, and all weekend. To this day she says she never felt tired in all those months. And when I told her I wanted to give up, she kept me going. She has always been the one person I could depend on to understand me, support me, and travel with me.

A couple of years after the stroke we started to travel. Äiti has supported my insistence to see the world, because, especially in the early years after the stroke, she knew I needed it to keep me going. Travel has given me something to look forward to, a reason for happiness, and a hope for treatment that would help me, if not to cure me then at least to improve my condition. Although when the stroke first happened, Äiti was devastated, she never complained. When asked later about this time she described it this way:

"There was just a black hole, it is something difficult to explain. To tell the truth, I no longer remember this or want to remember this. We would spend the nights in the hospital and the morning we would be awakened by a terrible cry, which lasted and lasted until you just didn't hear it anymore. My husband and I forgot to eat or drink, and only our son reminding us, forcing us, ensured we did."

We are about to take you on many journeys. My mom was always with me. Usually, she was physically present, but at those times when I had to do it on my own, she was with me in spirit.

When we face adversity, the will to carry on up the mountain has to come from somewhere. In Finland, we say it is a spirit of *Sisu* – the ability to persevere, keep going no matter what the odds, and not give in. I must have got the *Sisu* I have from my mom. She has always gone along with my crazy ideas and has always believed in me. If one saying is, 'behind every successful man is a good woman,' I'd say, 'behind every strong woman is a fantastic mom.'

Marjatta has put her life on hold until recently. "Now," she says since I got married, "I can die in peace." My mom is such a lioness that even if illness or old age came after her, she would refuse to give up unless she could be sure I was taken care of. After the illness she even arranged for private custodial care with her best friend if she were to die, to ensure I would never be institutionalised.

My mom is my heroine, and I will always be grateful for everything she has ever done for me, and for our family.

Kati one year old

Kati four years old with her family

Kati six years old with her mother

Kati eight years old with her mother

Modeling in the Bahamas

With her car in California

Photoshoot in the Mojave desert

Portfolio picture

Portfolio cover

Photoshoot in
Los Angeles

Canary Islands one week before
the stroke

Part 2: Underwater

'Waking up from a lovely dream to the horror of real life, every day, sensing that vast distance, the gulf between myself and other people, a desperation only my mother seemed to be able to touch, to grasp my needs and answer them.'

Kati (Lepistö) van der Hoeven

CHAPTER 10

Sentencing

Slowly, I open my eyes. Even though it's a dark January day in Finland, my eyes hurt from the light that is coming in through the window.

I'm not at home. Where am I? I'm in a big white room; there are machines everywhere, and I have a tube coming out from my nose. I want to pull it out, but I can't lift my hand to remove it.

Then I remember the night before: feeling nauseous, almost fainting, my legs heavy as lead, my arms too, and... oh yes, I couldn't even talk last night. So tired. I don't feel as tired now. In fact, I'm quite alert. My parents have realised I'm awake, and they've stood up and come to stand over me. They look worried, as they stand over the bed, together.

I open my jaw a little, but there's no sound. I want to ask them what's going on, but the words just don't come out. It feels like neither my tongue nor my lips want to move, no matter how hard I try.

"What's happening?" But I don't say the words out loud. I try again, but as hard as I try, over and over, the words just won't come out. Then I remember the night before – the doctor checking my reflexes every hour, running a blunt blade across my feet. I wiggle my toes now, as I think of the blade, but my toes don't move. I remember my hands twitching. I try to make them twitch now, but they don't move. I can't even make my fingers move. No matter how I command my hands and feet, they won't move. And I can barely swallow. I can feel my face, but I can't move it, and I can't touch it.

I can't move.

I can't speak.

I can't do anything.

I begin to cry. Yes, I can do that.

I stare at my mother. She looks so lost.

Who is lost? Her, or is it me?

Oh my god. I'm frozen.

How long is this going to last?

I look at my dad. "Isa." But I can't speak his name. I can't call to him for help. I can only stare.

They understand. I'm sure they do. I see it in their faces.

"Doctor, doctor," my mother calls. My dad looks as frozen as I feel.

Oh my god.

I remember everything now. Everything that happened last night. Only it wasn't last night. I hear them talking. I'm finally awake after three days.

It was three nights ago. I've been in and out of consciousness for three days, but I don't remember. No wonder I can't move. Now I understand – I'm stiff as a board from being in bed.

"When will I get out of here?" I look at my äiti. But she can't hear me. "Why can't I speak? Do you know I can't speak?" Again, I'm looking at her.

"What is it, Kati?" she asks.

But my mouth is frozen. I feel. I feel the sheets on me, I feel the air around me, I feel when someone leans on the bed and I tip. But I can't touch; I can't stop myself from falling over. And I can't say a word.

Tears start to trickle down my cheeks. It tickles. But I can't wipe them away.

At first, when I woke up, I thought that the night in the hospital, waiting, was a horrible dream. But it wasn't, was it? This frozen, incapable baby isn't dreaming. This is a nightmare and I'm wide awake. This is reality.

What can I do? Blink! That's about all I can do. How long is this reality going to last? I stare at Isa. He's crying too. Who is going to tell me what is going on?

I look at my mother. She's trying to smile, but she can't any more than I can. She sees me crying. I can't hide. She sees me crying and she just watches. Why is she watching? Now we're just staring at each other.

"Kati?" she says.

I can't respond. I'm thinking, Äiti, *Mom, I can hear you. I can see you. But I can't tell you.*

I hear the doctor speaking, but I can't see him. Where is he?

"She's awake now. We can take her to the Kuopio University Hospital and find out what exactly is going on. We'll take an MRI. Then we'll know what caused her to collapse."

But I didn't collapse. I had a slow fade, like a final photo on a reel being gradually faded to black.

What the hell is going on? But no one can hear me no matter how loud I shout. Because I'm not making any noise whatsoever.

My muscles are so tense. I try to move, but at first I can't, and then my leg moves. Oh good! I can move! But when I try to relax, when I try to put my leg down, I can't.

Everybody's staring at me. I can feel it. Äiti and Isa are staring at my leg, which is straight up in the air.

The doctor finally appears in my line of sight. He doesn't look at me, but puts his hand on my leg and pushes down hard. But my leg doesn't move. I'm not holding it up. Believe me, if I could stop it from sticking up in the air I would. But I can't let it drop any more than I could have willingly lifted it up in the first place.

I'm hardly breathing now. Not because I can't breathe but because I'm so scared. It's embarrassing having your leg stuck up in the air, but I don't care what people think. It's just stupid and I can't do anything about it. I'm helpless, stuck – literally – unable to do anything. My mind is full of words, but I say nothing. I'm totally alert and completely incapable of saying a thing.

What's happened? What happened last night, or whatever night it was? So slowly, so gradually, something terrible happened, like falling down in slow motion. Moment by moment all my energy just slipped away, and I didn't even know what was happening. Fatigue was creeping in, stealing my life, and I didn't even know it. I remember I just wanted to sleep.

Now I'm awake, but I seem to have lost every bit of freedom I ever had, all while I was sitting in the hospital, waiting for a cure for feeling so sick and so tired. Now they've got a much bigger problem to solve. How are they going to fix frozen me? I suppose I'm in the right place. Now that we all know I'm frozen, they'll have to unfreeze me. But how long is that going to take? I'm supposed to fly back to LA. Supposed to move to Florida, and then to Milan for good. How long does it take to unfreeze a whole animal carcass? Because that's what I feel like right now. Just a hunk of dead flesh that needs to be woken up.

"Kati?" says Dad.

I just look. I'm thinking, *Hi, Isa,* but I can't say it. How can I think it but not say it?

"They're going to take you to the hospital at the university now. They're going to do some more tests and figure out everything, okay?" Mom looks at me. I think she knows I'm saying, "Okay," even though I can't say, "Okay," because she looks at the doctor.

"Let's go. Let's go now, as soon as you can," she says to the doctor.

What a relief. Something is going to happen now to fix this horrible mess. Except when it's time for us to go, I have to be lifted, and put onto a mobile bed, and wheeled into an ambulance. Embarrassing, unattractive, moving through the hospital in my pjs with tubes running in and out of me. At least my headache has gone. I don't feel like I'm going to throw up anymore, and I'm not tired either. But can you really call that an improvement? No, under the circumstances, I suppose not.

It's really hard for me to let the nurses lift me and move me onto the gurney. To let someone roll me to the ambulance and take me anywhere is so hard for me. But what choice do I have? None.

Mom comes with me in the ambulance. They aren't ringing that horrible siren. There's no rush? I guess not. Well, I'm not dying.

It's really hard to breathe. It has been since I've been awake, and it just gets harder and harder. I feel like every inhale is a chore. I've got this stupid tube and it's full of gunk, from mucus I guess, from me.

While I'm waiting at the second hospital, someone tries to clean out the gunk from my tube. It's gross, but it means

I can breathe a little better. My mom holds my hand. I try to smile, but there is a tube in the way, so I can't really move my mouth.

Some medical staff person leads me away to get the MRI scan and I can't even say, "See you later." So much is happening, and yet I'm doing nothing. Time is just passing. Oh, it must be 13 January – Mom's birthday. This was no way to spend her birthday. I didn't even get her present yet. I watch the distance between us grow as I'm wheeled away from her. I can't even shout, "Happy birthday, Äiti."

I'm taken to a big, empty room except for a large, tubular machine. The nurse there explains to me that I'll go inside it and tests will be taken with this huge machine. It will look at my brain and will tell me what's wrong. Then I guess they'll finally know what's wrong with me and how to fix it after that.

I'm going into this cavity head first; it's like a tubular metal cave. How long am I going to be stuck in here? It's so noisy, making a big, steady whirring sound. At least it doesn't hurt. I'm crying again. I'm trying not to panic. *Breathe*, I tell myself, but that's hard to do too.

Everything takes so long in these stupid hospitals. How could my parents bear it while I was sleeping for three days? I'll be glad when this is all over and we can put it in our memory banks of forgettable experiences. I guess there's a lesson here though. If you've got a headache, get it checked out. It's not worth letting it get worse.

The MRI is finished and there's more waiting. I suppose I should be used to that by now. At least they take me back to my parents, and we can wait all together. Eventually, the doctor approaches from down the hall. I'm still lying on a bed but they've turned it, so I can see along the corridor. The doctor has a dark expression on his face; he reminds me of that doctor who checked my eyes when I was twelve, only this one actually looks at me more than at his paperwork. That's something.

"Hi, Kati," he says. I look at him. It's my way of showing him I'm paying attention.

He looks at my parents. He sighs. He looks like he's going to say something horrible. What's he going to say that can be any worse than lying here being unable to move? I'm not going to die. My brain is fine, my mind is fine, my heart is fine, so just hurry up and tell me what's wrong and start to make it better. That's why we came to the hospital in the first place!

"Kati."

Oh good. Here it comes, the problem and the solution.

"You've had a brain infarction. It happened very slowly. Usually it happens over about six minutes; yours seemed to have been very gradual. That, and because you're so young, we didn't pick it up. You are a very special case – twenty years old with a brain infarction? Very, very unusual. It means that certain areas of your brain stem, the bottom part of your brain, have been affected. Some of it has been destroyed and we cannot repair it. We can help you to rehabilitate, so you can learn to cope with the situation now."

"*What?*" I want to scream it, but of course nothing comes out.

"What do you mean, doctor?" Isa asks. I've never heard his voice so *distant* before, as if he's not speaking from his whole body but somehow he's somewhere else.

"What the hell is a brain infarction? What do you mean 'cope with the situation now'? What situation? I can't move. I can't speak. You've got to help me so I *can* move and so I *can* speak." But of course, no one hears me.

"When did this happen?" Äiti asks.

"It must have been the night she went to the hospital. It must have started some time that evening. It brought you in, and the situation progressed."

"Progressed how?" Isa asks.

"Well, it seems Kati was able to speak and move normally for a while when she was here, but gradually, she was no longer able to do so."

"You mean you could have stopped it?" asks my mother.

"When someone has a stroke, survival is a matter of several factors."

"Stroke. Is that what happened?"

"Yes, Mrs Lepistö. Kati has had a stroke."

Oh my god. I'm twenty. How could I have had a stroke? Never mind that. People recover from strokes. I've heard it all the time.

"People recover from strokes though," says my dad, still sounding soft and far away. "It can take a lot of hard work, recovering speech and flexibility, but Kati's a hard worker. No one is as stubborn and persistent as she is. She'll put everything she has..." Isa stops speaking.

The doctor is looking grim. "I'm afraid the possibility of Kati recovering is pretty much non-existent, Mr Lepistö."

Silence.

I'm holding my breath, as if I could even breathe now.

"You see, the brainstem that receives commands for movement, is completely gone. The stroke destroyed it. Her mind knows what she wants to do, but there is no way for her muscles to receive the messages from her brain."

"But her eyes are moving."

"Yes, she appears to be able to move her eyes, and to see. Sometimes that is lost too."

To be blind as well? Is that going to happen next? I start

to shake all over. I start to cry. And there is someone nearby that's wailing. Who is it? My mom? My dad? No, it's me!

The doctor keeps talking. "Judging from the tests, and the fact that the incident is over, we don't expect there to be any further damage. However, there won't be much progress either. Kati is paralysed. It takes muscles to move her tongue and jaw, to speak. We don't think she'll regain that either."

"No!" my mom shouts. Then she puts her hand over her mouth. "That can't be true," she whispers.

"Look, I've seen the MRI. She's paralysed. She won't recover. Kati, we want to help you as much as we can. You'll go back to Mikkeli, and we'll put you on the neurology ward. And when you're ready, we'll send you to a rehabilitation clinic in Helsinki. Maybe you'll make a little progress, but there isn't much hope for improvement. I must tell you this, because if you expect much change, you will be disappointed. Mr and Mrs Lepistö, there are programmes, and compensation from the government, for people with disabilities. I suggest you look into those, familiarise yourself with what is available. Once we feel Kati is ready, we'll give her the best rehabilitation available in the country. Kati, I am sorry. We'll do what we can here to prepare you for the next steps."

Then he turns and walks away from us, down the hall and turns the corner.

You're sorry? Yeah, sure you are. Steps? What steps? I can't take any steps. What the ... You've just told me I won't ever walk again!

People say the stupidest things sometimes, if they only realised.

Even if I could talk, I'd still be speechless.

CHAPTER 11

The New Reality

Dancing, dancing – I love the beat! Suddenly, I grip myself. I'm frightened. I feel as if I'm falling and can't stop myself. I brace myself, to make sure I don't trip. Just in time – I'm safe and I relax.

There's a moment for anybody, as we wake up from a night's sleep, when we experience internal stillness. It's like living in another world, a world of quiet solitude between dreams finishing and full consciousness, before reality sets in. This is true for me, as I move from dreamy sleep and settle into wakefulness. I'm enjoying this moment, until I stretch. But nothing moves. I open my eyes and see the hospital room, and then I remember everything.

Some god-awful howling comes from nowhere. I'd cover my ears if I could to block out the noise, before I realise the sound is coming from me. I don't even know how to stop it. I'm trapped, and my own body is the prison. How did this happen? Why would the doctor say I am paralysed? He thinks it will last... forever. But how can that be? I'm young and healthy, and that's a death sentence. If it's true, I'm better off dead.

What about my family? The howl turns into wailing, and my tears are making my pillow wet. My nose starts to run uncontrollably. I can't stop any of it, and I can't even wipe the snot away.

I've got to move. I've got to. To prove that doctor wrong. I'm willing my hand to move.

Move! But it doesn't. I can't make my muscles move. I try so hard, but I can't move no matter how hard I concentrate. I can't make my emotions stop. I'm thinking, trying, working so hard, but I'm helpless, like a new-born baby. Oh God, I can't bear this.

Suddenly someone is above me. A nurse. She leans over me, staring; eyeball to eyeball, she tells me to hush. "Be grateful you're alive," she says coldly.

Really?

Everything is coming back to me. I'm remembering the night before. The long night. The slow fade. As I was sleeping, I turned. I remember. She must have turned me. If not this nurse, another.

How many times do we move in the night? It's involuntary, while we sleep, but I can't do that? Our brain must tell us to move, otherwise I could do it on my own. But I can't do it myself. I can't even rock, never mind roll over.

What happened to me? What did the doctor say? A stroke has destroyed my brainstem. That's the part of my brain that relays my brain's instructions to move. All night long my brain must be telling my body to move. But I can't move. Poor brain. How many times did I used to turn in the night, effortlessly, all by myself, without even waking up? Why can't I do that now, in my sleep, without even thinking about it, unconsciously? Poor tired, useless brain.

It's quiet. I've stopped making wailing noises. Thinking has been a good distraction.

The nurse comes back with another one. They are going to move me, one says to the other. Where am I going? The two don't look at me. They just roll my little body back and forth, changing the sheets and moving my position at the same time. The bed is a rollercoaster, and I'm going for a ride. I'm rocked side to side and back again, until my sheets are changed. They leave me flat on my back, staring at the ceiling. Nothing is happening on the ceiling. Nothing is happening in my life.

I hear footsteps.

"Kati, you are awake. This is good, this is good," Äiti says. I can see my mom and she's trying to smile. She brings her face to my eyes. I don't want to disappoint her, but I have no desire to be awake or to smile.

She calls for a nurse and asks if I can be propped up. No one comes.

"I'll be right back," she says, and leaves.

My dad was standing right behind her. He takes my hand. He's crying. I start to cry.

The nurse comes in with my mother. She sighs, and forces her way between my dad and me. She rolls me away to stuff some pillows behind my shoulders. Then she puts her arms under my armpits and heaves me towards the head of the bed. Now I'm looking at the corner of the wall, and my back is arched. The pillows are lumpy. She shows my mother a button and tells her how to make the bed rise, and then the nurse leaves. My mom stares at the buttons, and then at me.

"Comfortable?" she asks. How do I answer her? How do I tell her, "No, there's a lump in my back from the pillow"?

"Blink once for 'yes' and twice for 'no'," she says.

I blink twice.

"Okay," she says. Gently, Äiti leans me forward,

supporting me with one arm, and with the other she adjusts the pillows. It takes two tries but finally, I can blink once. She nods. "It's a start," she says.

Funny. I feel triumphant because I can blink my eyes. I was dreaming before I woke up. In my dream, I was normal. I was dancing to Prince. I was free. I turn my face away from my parents, tears rolling down again.

"Kati! Your head moved. Don't worry, you will work hard and get much better. You'll see." Äiti wipes my face. She's so good. If I died it would break her heart. I do not want to break Äiti's heart. But I do not want to be trapped either. So I will work hard and I will get better. I'll work until I can move again. What do stupid doctors know? I remember when I was twelve and the doctor couldn't even figure out that I needed glasses. What did that one say yesterday? I will not walk again. Well, it might take some time, but I will show him. I can do this. I can make my brain work again.

Very soon I learn that the neurology ward is full of people who can move, even though they are seriously ill. The nurses have to attend to some life-and-death emergencies, which I am not. There aren't enough nurses on the ward. None of them are used to caring for a total invalid. There is no high-dependency ward in the Mikkeli hospital, and since I have a brain injury, they think this is the best care they have to offer. If it weren't for my mom coming every day, and running after nurses to get their help, or helping me herself, I'd sit and I'd sit, staring at the blank walls and ceiling. How would a nurse know when to come to help me when I have to pee?

The longer I lie in this bed, the more I feel my body stiffen and stiffen, and there's nothing I can do about it. My fingers are in a permanent spasm. They've curled to look half their length, and it hides my nice nail polish. It doesn't hurt but it is ugly. My new normal.

Every day my mom and dad come into the hospital. When my dad sees me, he cries. It makes me cry too. Jukka comes with Anu. He brings food for my parents, otherwise I don't think they'd eat. Dad is so sad; I think he feels helpless. Mom is so busy. It's been about two weeks since the stroke, and she's been telling my friends what's happened. One by one she's getting in touch with them. This is very difficult for her, because many of them only speak English and she is not very confident with her English. She makes the best out of this hospital room, decorating the walls with all the cards I've received. She's brought Prince posters too, and sticks them up. Maybe that's why I dream about dancing? It feels like I'm a teenager again, and it's fun.

Another morning comes and I wake up howling. I cannot stop myself. I wake up from a dream of normal life to the horror of reality. This morning, before they come in, I hear my parents whispering at the door of my room. Perhaps they think I'm asleep.

"I want to make her see what she's done," Isa is saying.

"It won't make any difference to Kati. Let it be, leave it alone. She won't care anyway."

Who are they talking about?

"If that so-called doctor had cared instead of making stupid assumptions when you came into emergency, Kati would have been protected."

"We don't know that. We don't know they could have stopped this."

"We don't know they couldn't have either."

Ah, they are talking about the doctor who thought I was on drugs when I was having a stroke. She is a stupid doctor. But she will not learn, or at least not from us. Eventually,

Isa and Äiti come into the room. They see I'm awake and try to think of things to say.

They have taken sick leave from their jobs, but they will have to return to work soon. For a few weeks they make the impossible possible, helping me to exist. The nurses can't take care of me exclusively, or offer the attention any completely immobile person needs. They haven't the time to communicate with me, or the interest. I can see it in their eyes, and in their impatient looks, in their huffing when they have to lift me. It is difficult enough for my parents, but at least they want to do it. It requires more than time to learn compassion.

We've worked out a system. If something is very wrong, I let my eyelids flutter. But for the system to work, people have to look at me. My mother looks at me all the time. The nurses don't notice, even when they are dealing with the tubes and I'm in pain, or the bedding when I'm being rolled like a piece of carpet rather than a human being. My mom had an emergency-call alarm system placed right by my head. Since I have a little movement in my head and neck, I can trigger it. But sometimes it slips out of my reach. The nurses don't pay attention when they move me, or notice if the button shifts out of reach. There are no guarantees I can reach it. When you are immobile, you are totally helpless.

When I sit up in bed, saliva runs down my chin, and I can feel it on my skin. It's embarrassing that I cannot even control my spit. I have tubes going in and out of me. The tubes going into my nose deliver food. Since my jaw and tongue don't work, the doctors ordered a tube through my nose and down my throat that goes straight into my stomach. My taste buds aren't in my stomach, so I can't taste the food that keeps me alive. I'm getting nutrition, I guess. But what is the point of eating if you can't even enjoy it?

I've got another tube, which has been cut into my throat to help me breathe. When I was taken to the other hospital for the MRI it was practically impossible to breathe. It got worse and worse. They had to do it, I guess, to keep me alive. I remember in the ambulance driving back to Mikkeli Hospital after the MRI scan, all the way the nurse had to suck slime from my throat. When we got back to the hospital, they decided to cut a hole in my throat and put in another tube to make it easier for me to breathe. But they gave me no warning, and it will leave a scar, I'm sure, right in the centre of my neck. Not good for a model. Anyway, why bother? Why try to keep a person alive who'd rather be dead than live like a vegetable? Worse than a vegetable; I'm fully capable of thinking and feeling, I just can't move a muscle, and they tell me I never will. What sort of a future is that?

They've discovered I can move my jaw a little, so they decide to test to see if I can swallow. Will I be able to eat without the tubes? Yes, they will try! This is exciting. I'll get to taste something nice. It's something to look forward to in this otherwise prison existence.

The hospital staff are unfeeling and uncaring. They don't communicate with me. Yoo-hoo! Hello, I'm not a zombie! But they treat me as if I am. They don't ask or even think about what I want to eat, or even what I *can* eat. The first food they offer me is fish and a boiled potato. How could I eat a boiled potato, or raw fish, without being able to chew? It's been days without being able to eat, and I'm not even asked what I like. I don't mean to sound ungrateful, but I'm brought the most horrible fish on earth – raw herring. It's as if no one reads on the chart that I cannot chew. And even if I could, the food is tasteless, or worse. Isn't this supposed to motivate me, and lift my spirits? The whole experience is totally impossible and painfully disappointing.

There is an irony to this horrible existence. The only way I can deal with the frustration of being immobile is to grind my teeth. Ironic, since I can't even chew. Can no one imagine what it's like to be twenty and paralysed? I'm still a normal person with likes and dislikes, needs and hopes, but if it wasn't for my parents' help and love, and Jukka's taking care of them, I'd be treated like an inhuman blob.

The next day there is a tiny improvement – they bring me puree. I'm being fed like a baby and eating baby food. It's humiliating, but actually it doesn't taste too bad. It's a lot better than herring and boiled potato. I have to stay hopeful, no matter what they say or do. Little by little, I'm making progress, and I have to think of it that way.

*

"Dance, dance, dance."

The steps are really complicated, but I'm mastering them perfectly. The cameras are picking up every footstep, every swivel, and the crew is having fun.

Then I wake up. Crash down as reality sets in again. The involuntarily howling starts; the day's routine has begun.

My dreams keep me going. In my dreams I am a normal person. I can express myself and move the way I used to. It's a wonderful feeling. Too bad it's just a dream. In dreamland, I have 100 per cent clarity, I live a high quality of life – even higher than my old reality. I'm a better dancer and I'm totally healthy.

I'm getting used to waking up and remembering that I'm trapped. It's a very sad moment when I do, but I'm glad I dream. It lets me feel fully alive. It's honestly worth the emotional crash when I wake up.

Though the sedentary days are long, the nights are even longer. Insomnia haunts me. Days I stare at the ceiling;

nights I cannot even see the ceiling and can only stare into the blackness.

My life when I'm awake is like living in sleep paralysis permanently: that moment before being fully awake, when we can't move or speak, we're in limbo between sleepiness and wakefulness. But that is my permanent state. Every morning when I become fully conscious, I howl. I can't help it. When I realise the horror all over again, that today I'm paralysed and nothing has changed from yesterday, I can't help but to howl and cry, howl and cry, howl and cry, day after day. Thank God I remember my dreams, where I'm still free and healthy, and living my dream.

My reality is nothing but needing help from people constantly. My life has gone from being super independent to having the dependency of an infant, just like that. It's hard. Sometimes I just want to give up, but although my life is hopeless, deep down I know it has to get better. It has to.

It's this I think about at night, during the insomnia. Sometimes though, I allow my mind to go on interesting journeys, even lingering over memories of various modelling trips. International modelling seems so far away from me right now, but for a little while, my fantasies lift my spirits and I can lead the life of independence and excitement that I love. There is no frustration and no physical pain in my memories, or in the fantasies I create.

When I'm awake, the greatest pain is not from my aching muscles, but from my frustration. I can't share my thoughts or feelings. It isn't just whether I'm comfortable or in pain that matters, but what I'm thinking about, or want to know about someone else. I can't ask my mom if she's feeling all right today. I can't ask the nurse if she has a family. I can't share my dreams – well not that I have any left.

I have been learning to spell with my eyes using an alphabet system. I look at the letters on the alphabet board they've provided, and spell out what I want to say. It is slow communication, but nurses know it and my parents learn very quickly. It makes life better to be able to express what I'm thinking or feeling. I have a lot of time to think. I'm trying to look at the good side of things. Not all the nurses are horrible; some are very nice. They stay and talk with me because they actually want to. I see the pity in their eyes, and I don't like that, but they can't help it. Then there are the nurses that pretend I don't exist. They don't realise I feel everything. Sometimes they are really rough with me. But I suppose I'm an oddity to them, and they don't think about how I might be feeling. They're scared or uncomfortable or freaked out by this young invalid, and they don't want to give me time or attention. I guess I creep them out.

The longer I lie in this hospital, with nothing to do but think and stare, the more I'm aware of time slipping away. What about Milan and the agency there? What about Florida and the boost I got from Rico, the photographer who said I was beautiful, a great model, and to go where the models are? What about Korea, and LA? LA, and Warren. What about Warren?

Äiti has told him about my situation. Every time he calls we both cry over the phone. It's crazy. What are we going to do? I really don't know. I didn't know when I was healthy, and I'm supposed to know now?

I have always been independent. But like any person, I have friends and need to share experiences with people my age. Now I am learning that I have some very dear friends. My mother has put so many cards on the walls of my room; I can barely see the paint. But not everybody comes to see me. I don't blame them. It is pretty depressing. Äiti has told all my friends about the stroke and almost everyone has been sending cards and letters, including Irina.

She moved to Sweden to follow her own dreams a long time ago. I don't expect to see her, but she phones me to tell me she misses me. I can only listen as Isa holds the phone to my ear.

"Kati, I miss you," Irina says. "Hey, you must keep busy. Read. Think about what you can do to make this work for you."

No one has told her my eyes aren't working properly. I can't even have a television in the room because I can't see what's on it. I definitely can't read, and even if I could, who would hold the magazine up for me?

"Kati, I'm coming."

Oh no, Irina must not come here. I start to wail.

"Kati?"

"It's Marjatta, Irina. Kati needs to ... to rest now. Thank you for calling. I know Kati is so happy to hear from you."

Äiti looks at me. I blink once.

"Yes, she is so happy to hear from you."

I don't want Irina to leave Sweden to visit me. She is working hard and needs to stay there with her crazy boyfriend. I don't want her dreams destroyed too, all because of me. No, I want her to do just as she's wanted to for years, to study and live in Sweden. *Please, Irina, do not come to see my pathetic self. Do not risk your own future.* But Irina cannot hear my silent wishes, or my wailing prayers.

Another day. Today is passing by, like yesterday, and the day before, and the day before that. I'm thinking about home. Where is home? I guess it's here in Finland again. I don't want to live here, but my other choices are not possible now. I'm remembering school of all things, and the way

I used to help the teachers to prepare the classroom. It's kind of funny. With the trips and moving away from home, I never once felt homesick. Now, I wish I could go back to my little bedroom and see it as it is. But I won't even be able to get up the stairs.

Suddenly, standing in the doorway is Irina. Is she real? Are my eyes in focus? Or am I just imagining her? "Kati. Oh Kati." She puts her arms around me gently. She always has been a very tactile person. She is real. And we cry and cry together.

"My, my Kati." She sits next to me and looks at me, saying nothing. She is probably waiting for me to speak, but of course I don't. She takes my hand very carefully, so as not to disturb any tubes, I guess. "I ... you'll be mad at me for coming, I know. But I had to. I couldn't imagine you here and me there. I had to come."

I just cry. Somehow, the howling doesn't come out, which is good. I don't want her to ruin her life. But she won't change her mind when it's made up. Well, she's here now. I might as well enjoy her company. I smile with my eyes, the best I can, even though they are full of tears.

I think she understands because she smiles too, wipes my eyes and nose, and hugs me again. I must look scary and ugly: my legs are dangling over the bed rails, tubes are coming in and out of me, I haven't had a bath in I don't know how many days (the nurses do their best to sponge-bathe me), and my hair must be a sight! But my best friend is beside me. It's good to see her.

Irina and I are such good friends that, when I look in her face, I think I see my face. She looks tense and nervous, frustrated and in pain, just like how I feel. She holds my hand, and tries to chat, but eventually she stops and just sits looking at me. It's what happens with everybody: Mom,

Dad, Jukka, and his girlfriend, Anu. Well, I can't contribute so I guess conversations just die eventually.

I look at her and remember so many times when we laughed together. She tells me stories of stupid things we did together, where we went shopping, great outfits we bought.

"Remember the first thing you said to me?" she asks. "You said, 'Do you want to buy something?' That was when we first met, while you were working at the shop and I used to come in just to touch the fabrics."

I start to cry again. I guess I'm wondering if I'll ever go shopping again.

"I'm so sorry, Kati." She cries too.

The next day she comes in smiling and brings me a magazine; we look over it. I cry because I can't be in it anymore, and I laugh because some of the ads are so silly.

Irina knows me so well. There is no elephant in the room. How can there be? She shows me the pictures, and makes up stories about the models and what they have gone through to get these jobs. Torture, it's all torture, and we laugh and cry because I can't do it. Some people would look at us and think we're insane, but it's good to laugh, and it passes the time. Otherwise, I lie here alone, counting the seconds, minutes, hours, days, weeks... you get the idea.

I realise I have a lot of work to do if I'm ever going to model again. Seriously, I have to try. What's the alternative?

Irina is looking at me. Can she read my mind?

"Kati, you can do this if you want to. There will be a way. There has to be. You'll be on the cover of *Vogue* one day. You'll see."

We both laugh a little, because she knows I like *Bazaar* better! Then there is the silence again. The deafening silence that says, "We can't have a conversation."

My laugh is as strange as my crying. It's like I hold my breath, not on purpose, and bits of sound manage to escape out of me. When I cry it's howling; when I laugh it's a bit like a pig's grunt. Not pretty.

"I have a confession to make, Kati." She lowers her voice. "I almost couldn't come in. The first time, it was really hard. I'm so sorry. I..."

I look pretty awful. What's happened is pretty bad. And she's come all the way from Sweden. How can I blame her for finding it hard to walk into this horrible room? How can I tell her not to feel bad? I can only hope she gets the message.

"No," I blink.

"Yeah, I get it. You think I shouldn't be here. And now that I am, you think I shouldn't be hard on myself. Yeah, I get that. But still, I shouldn't have been scared. Anyway, I'm here now and I won't leave until you get well." I think – *she can't live here in the hospital!*

"Oh, not *here*, not in the hospital of course, but in Mikkeli. I'm moving back."

I feel my eyes going big. She can't make herself stay in Mikkeli. My eyes fill with water.

"Anyway, that's what I'm thinking."

"*No!*" I blink. Oh, I don't want her to ruin her life. But it is so good to have her here. I have to confess, it's good she's here with me. More silence. Maybe it's a sign of true friendship when you don't have to say any words.

A nurse comes in. Remember the breathing tube they installed directly into my throat after I got *The Sentence*? It's been there for days and I guess they think I can manage on my own now.

"This won't hurt," the nurse promises. She's going to pull it out. But she pulls and it *does* hurt – a lot. Even worse, the gunk inside splatters all over the room, all over the Prince posters Äiti put up to make the room my own. The nurse grimaces. She's grossed out, obviously.

"Sorry to be an inconvenience," I'd say to her, if I could. I glare at her, but she doesn't dare look at me. I'm a non-person, a lump of flesh that's a bother to her. That's obvious. But she doesn't look at my mom who's nearby, or Irina. She just makes a quick exit. The posters are ruined and will have to be thrown away.

Each time my dad sees me I cry, and then he cries too. It's hard to see your isa, the strongest person in your whole world, cry, and doubly hard when you know you are the cause.

"Look here," he says smiling one day. He's brought Eetu, our cat. "To keep your hands warm," he says.

Yes, it's hard to stay warm when you cannot move. And Eetu is my favourite feline. Eetu is completely gentle. He does not pad his paws into my lap, like cats usually do when they want to settle themselves to make themselves comfortable. Instead, he remains where he's put down, as though he understands he is helping me. I love his purr and I can feel the vibration through my skin. It makes the day better.

"Tomorrow," he says, "you're going to be given a wheelchair."

"You'll see the sights," my mom adds. They are trying so hard to be positive.

Apparently I am improving. I am ready for a wheelchair, I guess it's because I can sit upright.

The next day arrives, as they all do: I dream, I wake, I howl. But there's something else. It's early, even before my parents have arrived like clockwork. The nurses have come in and brought a huge contraption.

"This is a hoist. It will lift you from the bed to the chair."
It's terrifying. What if I fall out of the hoist? I wish
my parents were here. They would make sure I didn't
fall. My limbs are stiff because I haven't moved in weeks.
They become stiffer than usual now, and my legs jump
involuntarily. I never used to be afraid of anything. Now
I'm afraid I'll fall from my bed to the floor, even though
there are bars to protect me, and staff, however cold and
unfeeling, to make sure I don't. What does this terrified
person do when she can't run away or plead for help? I just
howl.

I'm alone with these nurses, who I know are impatient
and cold. They strap me in, looking everywhere but at my
face. I'm blinking and blinking rapidly, my code to get their
attention. But they don't see me. I can feel everything, I
just can't move. Don't they know this? They are rough and
my muscles go into spasm. I'm like a corpse being dragged
from the dead, and howling. Can't they realise I wouldn't
howl if I weren't scared or in pain? Don't they care? I'm
skinny and every bump hurts. I don't have a lot of padding
to protect me from bruises. They just ignore me. They stuff
me into the chair and prop me up like a dummy, pushing
my feet onto the footrest. I keep slipping to the right. I lean,
they prop me up; I lean, they prop me up again. Eventually,
one of them gets a flash of genius and props my elbows on
the chair arms for balance. She grips my elbows so hard I'm
wondering, will there be a bruise later? I'm still leaning,
and the whole world is lopsided, but at least I'm not falling
over. And then, my parents walk in. If the nurses had
waited fifteen minutes until my parents arrived, they could
have helped and it would have been easier on everyone. My
parents have been doing so much lifting and helping. My
mother practically lives at the hospital because there just

aren't enough nurses to give me the round-the-clock care I need. I'm in the wrong place, and of course it's at the wrong time of my life. I'm twenty years old, in the prime of life.

I'm in a chair. I look around the room. I'm mobile, not that I can do anything about it. And it isn't very comfortable to have pressure on my small, bony model's bum. But there's no point telling them. I've never seen the point of complaining about discomfort. Get pity points? Better to just deal with it. I can't *really* do anything about it, even if I want to. And the wheelchair will offer a change of scenery, so I'll try to be grateful for it. Maybe we can go for walks on sunny days.

A phone call comes in, this time from LA.

"I'm coming over, Kati," Warren cries into the phone. "I'll see you soon."

I look at my mom, who's holding the phone. I don't want him to come. I blink twice.

"Warren, I think you should give it some time. Allow yourself time to get over the shock." I know she's saying the right thing.

He's crying. He's got me crying. In my fragile emotional state, it takes very little to trigger me. The thought of Warren coming here and seeing me like this, like a helpless – and unattractive – baby, distresses me. His phone call is a reminder of what was and is no more. Gradually, very gradually, I'm getting used to this existence. I can't go back and I don't want to see my LA past brought to me.

To help me adjust to life now, I keep reminding myself of my condition: I suffer from locked-in syndrome, which means my brain cannot send signals to my muscles to make them move. I am fully functioning in my thoughts, but I cannot move or speak. It happened because I had a stroke. But what makes it even worse is that it was a very slow process. When most people suffer a stroke it's all over in six minutes, mine lasted almost twenty-four hours, during which I was awake the whole time, realising moment by moment that I was slipping away, or my functions were slipping away. I just never realised at the time that it would be permanent. Slowly, gradually, I was losing my ability to use my muscles. Stupid really. My body didn't understand what was happening and so, to protect itself (ha!), it began to destroy healthy cells making the situation 100 per cent worse. It destroyed the cells that make up my brainstem, or the part of my brainstem that receives messages so I can move. Whoever made this human body was actually really stupid. Would a computer, for example, not have a good back-up system? How could it be possible to destroy a complicated human body so easily? And if the hospital staff had responded differently, could they have stopped the destruction? I think if it had been realised sooner, that process could have been stopped and I would have had less damage. But we can't know that for sure. And what good does it do to focus on what's already happened? None. Instead, I have to look forward and work hard to improve. There are such things as miracles, and I will fully cooperate to make sure I get mine.

How long have I been in this hospital? Only two weeks? It seems like an eternity. If Warren comes, the emotions will all come flooding back: the shock, the pain, the shame. No, I don't think emotional Warren would add anything good to this situation.

It isn't just Warren. Some days people come and I send them away. Sometimes I just have to be on my own. Once Äiti walked into the room.

"No, no, *no!*" I blinked to her. *Just go away!* My own mother! It must have made her cry, and I'm sorry.

So no, I don't want Warren to come.

She hangs up the phone, and I can see Mom is exhausted. Jukka arrives soon after with some food for her. He has done the same every day since the stroke. I think if my brother didn't remind them, Isa and Äiti wouldn't eat at all. My dad looks skin and bone now. Ha – like a model.

Sometimes my thoughts make me laugh. But the long days tick by, one by one, so slowly.

I never see Jukka cry, but I know he cares. He's making sure our parents get rest. Anu comes with him almost every time he visits. They can't come too often; he has work, she has training. Before Jukka, Anu was going to take part in the Olympics in horse dressage. She's made do with staying in Finland, but I think she likes being near Jukka. They have something special.

"Hey, Kalle. I brought you something. Actually, Anu picked it out."

He opens a small parcel of royal blue tissue paper. Anu is standing next to him, trying to smile. I can tell she's been crying though.

"See?" He holds it up.

It's a beautiful scarf. Anu's eyes light up. Maybe she can tell I'm happy.

"Do you like it?"

"Yes," I blink. "Yes, yes, yes."

"Yes – no – yes?" they say, then they realise I'm being enthusiastic and we all laugh.

Anu holds up the scarf. It's many shades of blue. It's one we saw when we were shopping together. I didn't buy it because I wanted to save my money for photographs. She puts it on top of my hands so I can feel it. It's cool and light. It must be silk.

"Yes," I blink once more.

It's amazing how much you can say with a vocabulary of only two words.

At night a nurse, Linda, visits me.

"Tomorrow, we are going to try a bath," Linda says. She's the kindest of all the nurses.

"Yes," I blink. At last, I'll get a real wash! But I'm learning, usually things that sound good end up being too good to be true.

Another nurse, Janna, says, "It'll be good to feel the water wash over you. It'll be good for your tight muscles. You'll see."

Of all the nurses, and there are quite a number, there are those who are kind, those who are not, and those who are just neutral. To be honest, some of them I do not understand. Why are they nurses at all if they can't be patient and gentle? They're meant to help others in need, and they only seem resentful. I feel like a blob of meat, who is an inconvenience to some of them.

Janna is very nice, but always works nights. I wish she worked days because then maybe she'd be the one doing the bathing. The day nurses are not usually talkative, and they don't smile. I guess they're too busy. Two of them never look at me at all. They just roll me over to change my bed, and roll me back again. I always see these two together. They work in pairs.

Bath day comes, and with it the bathing nurses. I haven't moved my muscles in days, except to be put in that wheelchair, and I'm stiff as a board. There's been no massage; that would help to loosen up my body. The nurses don't understand how painful it is to be moved. I'm moved from my bed again and put onto this gizmo, which hauls me onto a cart and takes me to a bath.

OMG. I just remembered: the tube that they yanked out of my throat, that made all the gunk spray over the Prince posters, has been out of my throat for only a few days. "Don't let water get in it or she'll drown," they told my parents. Do the people giving me a bath know this?

"Rita," one says to the other, "just watch what I do and follow me."

Is Rita a trainee? Oh! Can we stop this?

"We're going to put you on a rubber float so you'll be buoyant," the experienced nurse says to me. "That way we don't have to hold you and you can feel the water all around you. We let the rubber float fill a little bit."

Fill? With water? How am I going to keep my throat from getting water down it? And is the bath stable? Do they realise I could drown?

It hurts like hell just being put into the water. The rubber float does fill up and I think my misery is about to end because I'm sure I'm going to drown today. I'm so scared; I'm sweating more than any bath can wash off. If this is meant to relax me, it isn't working. But miracle of miracles, I survive, somehow. At the end of it I can clock up another terrifying adventure. I'm not sure which is worse: feeling filthy dirty, or having a bath surrounded by nurses who watch as the rubber float they've put me in, sinks.

Time just seems to roll on, day after day, night after night. The highlights are what puree I eat, and the occasional change in routine, such as having a terrifying and painful bath. Will that be the sum total of my life? Well, I know one thing – I won't be staying in this hospital forever.

*

"You are being released, Kati," says the head nurse.

I've never seen a doctor since one told me I would be paralysed for life. With news like that, who needs them? It's been one month since the stroke, one month of horror, of being totally dependent. There is nothing more the hospital can offer me.

"You're going to the Käpylä Physical Rehabilitation Centre in Helsinki." It's what the doctor promised, the best centre for stroke patients in the country. Although moving to the clinic in Helsinki frightens me, it means I will get the help I need to get better. I will have physiotherapy every day and a special diet, and they even have a gym. (What am I going to do in a gym?)

Physio sounds promising, but I'm terrified. Helsinki is hours away; I'll be all alone. My parents and friends have to work. I don't know people in Helsinki. And I have to leave Janna, and the other nice nurses. I don't mind leaving some of them, like the rolling pair. I have to believe this is a good step. I'm scared, but it's going to be okay. They are sending me to a place that offers rehabilitation. They won't tell me there's hope, but they are showing me there is. I can – and I must – improve.

CHAPTER 12

Warren

While I am still in hospital, Warren comes from LA to Finland, just like he said he would.

"Kati, my darling Kati. What has happened to you? This is awful. Oh Kati, I miss you so much. I need you, Kati. You don't know how everyone misses you. You have to get better. I need you. Oh my precious Kati."

We hold on to each other for what seems like hours. Well, he holds on to me. I just lie here, holding my breath so I don't wail, but I'm crying on his shirt. And he's crying too.

Every day he comes to see me. Every night he stays at my parents'. It is a very traumatic time. Love doesn't die just because we're miles apart. It doesn't die because I'm paralysed. It doesn't even die because we argue, although obviously we don't now.

This morning, my mother comes early to the hospital. Warren will come later. She tells me what it was like at home the night before when Warren returned from the hospital.

"Last night he wandered through the house after we went to bed. I'm sure he was drinking. He fell over something and made such a noise that it woke me up. Risto was already awake."

Yes, Risto isn't sleeping much. She has told me this before. But maybe it's worse with Warren walking around the house, drunk, all night.

"I got up, Kati, and he was in the bathroom, with a cloth on his head and pills in his hands. 'Sleeping pills,' he said. But pills and alcohol don't mix, Kati. It's very disturbing." I'm glad I never told her about him cutting his chest.

I see the look in my mother's eyes. "Was he like this before?" she asks. She looks very worried for me. She does not need me to answer. She knows. "It's the same every night, Kati. Drinking, stumbling. It was just noisier last night." She shakes her head. Warren's habits make her very sad.

There is no point staying together now. What's the point? I was nearly going to end it before I got sick. I know what I have to do.

Warren! He barges in, half dressed.

"I walked," he says, and laughs like a maniac. He's walked to the hospital in shorts and bare feet. It's January in Finland. He's crazy. Is this love? Is this really love?

"Kati, I'm going crazy without you. What happened to you? Oh, my beautiful Kati," and he throws himself onto my chest and weeps again.

I cry. My mother must be watching. What are we going to do? He's worse than when we were in LA. What's wrong with him that he can't stay off booze and pills? I'm a quadriplegic who can't talk and he's drinking because he's upset? It's crazy behaviour.

More days pass, each one the same as the one before. Warren tells me he's going to have to go back to LA, back to work. I knew this day was going to come. I have mixed feelings.

"Car sales aren't too bad. A bit better than this time last year," he says.

He's calm today. He's talking about some of the good times we've had. I like him sitting on the bed, holding my hand, smiling.

"Remember when..." and we're doing a lot of that. Remembering good times.

The next day he comes dressed for winter, with a coat. He's borrowed one from Isa. My whole family is trying to help through this whole mess. They never complain.

"Here, Kati, I want you to have this."

Warren takes off his heavy gold link necklace and unclips it. In order to put it on me, he has to put it under the tubes to clip it around my neck.

"Here," he says, and puts his face to my ear. "When I come back, it will be an engagement ring, my beautiful princess."

Ah!

He kisses me, for a long time. I start to cry, but I manage to hold back some tears. If he sees me crying, I'm certain it will make him cry all over again.

"I'll call you when I land," he says. And he does. He does for days and weeks.

Warren!

After he leaves, I'm alone for the rest of the day. No one comes to visit tonight, not even my parents. I'm sure they know there's no point in coming. I can't stop crying.

Sadly, my mother and I were proven right. He should not have come. It's good that Warren left. His being here made it so obvious how bad my condition is. He wants to be with me, to support me, I know, but his presence just reminds me of how it used to be, how I used to be, how I used to live in LA and work and dance and have fun. Now I can't do any of that. What kind of future is there for Warren and me? There isn't even a future for me. He has promised to come back with an engagement ring, but do I want him to come back?

*

Today, it's sunny outside. I allow my parents to wheel me out, but it's hard to enjoy it. I used to like it when the sun shone. Looking out of the window now just makes me angry. At least I'm going to the rehabilitation centre soon. But what will that mean? It's in Helsinki, which is hours away and I won't know anybody. What if they are horrible there? What if there are no nice nurses? I'll be so far away from my parents. I'm scared, but I don't want to tell anyone. I can't bear it, but I know I must go. If there is any hope for me to get better, I have to go and do everything I can to be able to move again, to be able to live again.

CHAPTER 13

A Night of Reflection

It's night time, the most peaceful time. I'm thinking, consolidating the facts of my condition, to figure out where I go from here. I go through it in my mind again and again: I'm locked-in, so my perfectly functioning brain cannot send the signals from my brain to my muscles to make them move. My own brain cells self-destructed to try to protect me. My brain didn't know what was happening to me the long night I had the stroke, so they did a suicide attack on my brainstem. Stupid brain. Stupid system. I can't keep thinking about this. Instead, I have to think: now what? How do I get back on track?

It's February, icy cold, bleak. There hasn't been much progress in the last month, but I am going to be sent to a new place, where I can get physiotherapy designed for people who have had a stroke and are locked-in. That will be good. I will meet other people just like me. I'll learn how they're coping. Somehow, we'll help each other.

After a month in this room, I know every fleck on the ceiling and get well greeting card that's been stuck on the wall by my amazing mother. I don't have any plans, except to recover. That will take all my focus for a while. Nights pass very slowly when I can't sleep. When I'm lying in bed at night, perfectly still, and it's calm and quiet around me, I have to mentally pinch myself to believe I am in hospital at all, and that my life has completely changed. I remind myself of what that night was like. It happened so slowly, so gradually, and I was so totally unaware of what was really happening. It was like a slow motion movie that I was in. It was half real, all nightmare, like being tied up in a straitjacket, locked inside a glass box and thrown into a pool. I could see everybody standing around, looking at me sinking. No one, except my mom, was aware I was drowning. I was in the pool, going down, trying to yell out loud, but the words just wouldn't come out. I'm not Harry Houdini. I couldn't escape.

I had no concept of time or space that night. I didn't have any idea what was happening to me, I couldn't move at all, and even worse, I couldn't explain. I could not say how or what I was feeling. All I could do was to look around me and see the desperation in my mother's eyes. I could see that even though she was moving, she felt as paralysed as I was. Not so funny; I didn't even realise I was paralysed. I just felt weak, tired and I wanted to sleep. I think about that night, the most horrific night anyone could live through, and I realise it taught me something: When the worst thing in life happens, don't give up and don't self-pity. Instead, I must face this horror and find the energy I need to cope. It has destroyed enough of me. It won't destroy any more of me. Sometimes I have the strength to keep going. Sometimes. But I don't know where it comes from.

The doctor has given his comments and they will be sent to the rehab centre in Helsinki. We don't really agree, but he is the doctor, so I'll give his medical explanation of my situation:

"Stroke is an injury to the brain due to blockage or rupture of a blood vessel. The brain requires a constant flow of blood to carry oxygen and nutrients to nerve cells. Four main arteries carry blood to the brain: the right and left carotid arteries and the right and left vertebral arteries. In Kati's case – damage to nerve tracks passing through the brainstem disconnected the upper parts of the brain, the cerebral hemispheres, from the spinal cord and the body. Kati became locked-in – her intact cerebral hemispheres enabling her to be awake and aware, but unable to move her limbs or facial muscles because the connections between the cerebral hemispheres and the spinal cord were injured by the stroke. Stroke is the third leading cause of death and the leading cause of disability in the developed world. Stroke is often thought of as a disease of the elderly. However, strokes do commonly affect middle-aged adults, young adults, and even children. Up to one-third of all strokes occur in individuals under the age of sixty-five."

It's a very clinical report. Cold, detached, unfeeling, just like the hospital. Imagine that. I'm not surprised.

Originally, I was told to recognise that I really wouldn't improve, that I should just accept that I'll be a vegetable for the rest of my life. But I won't. Why should I? There isn't anything a person can't do if they put their mind to it. I'm determined; I have a plan for my life. I'll get through this.

The report that the doctors have given to my parents isn't detailed; it doesn't describe what my life is like every day, or how my family and friends are suffering because they see that I'm helpless and totally dependent for everything.

I'm not the independent Kati they remember. It doesn't say anything about that. Totally inhumane. What they need to realise is the person I am, the people my family are, and how we are going to get through this. What I really want is for a medical person to say I'm going to be okay. But they don't offer anything like that. No encouragement, no hope, only negative remarks. Why can't they tell me I can improve? I know I can!

So, here's a mental record of what I'm experiencing now, in detail, because I can't tell anyone. I just have to remember so that I will recognise my improvements as I make them.

» I'm paralysed, but there is nothing wrong with my muscles or nerves. I can move and I can feel. I just can't *make* my muscles move. Many people think paralysis means the muscles are dead and you cannot move or feel your limbs. This is not my situation. I can feel everything, so if a fly lands on my nose it tickles and I want to brush it off. But I can't, and I can't ask anybody else to either. It is very frustrating.

» I'm mute. I cannot speak because my brain can't tell my tongue, which is a muscle, to move. I still have a voice box though, and I can make very loud noises. For example, if someone startles me I scream. That requires no thinking and no speech.

» My eye muscles are beginning to work. At first I couldn't see very well. I couldn't even watch TV. But I have always been able to blink. Now I'm also working on making the muscles of my eyes work, so that I will be able to focus better.

» My skin is super-sensitive to touch. Sometimes the bed sheets feel rough and what I wear needs to be soft and light, or I become very uncomfortable. People need to be gentle with me too, because I can feel everything much more than before I was paralysed. Sometimes my muscles are so tense that moving me is very difficult, and when pressure is applied to my muscles it hurts my skin.

» Muscle spasms happen automatically sometimes and there is nothing I can do about them. My muscles are very strong and so it's hard for anyone else to handle me when my muscle becomes automatically contracted.

» One month since the stroke, I can tell my hearing is much better than it used to be. I'm discovering that I focus on sounds and can recognise where they are coming from, even when they are far away. People whispering around me are not able to keep their secrets!

» I have been using my memory so that I can remember things I've been told or conversations I've had. For example, I practically memorised the doctor's long report.

» My brain is funky! The more I'm interacting with people the more alert I am becoming. I'm going to stimulate my brain to make sure I keep improving. If I have to do crossword puzzles (boring!) I'll do them. If I can't exercise physically then I'll exercise mentally. One way or another, I will keep fit and I'll keep improving.

So there it is, the sum total of my abilities. Not very exciting news for some people, but for me it's what I have, and it's written down so I can compare when I improve, to know how far I've come.

Tomorrow I go to rehab. This is very scary, but it is very necessary too, so I have to make myself say goodbye to this time in my life. Good riddance, you might say, but some of the hospital staff have been really nice and I will miss those people. And I leave my family behind.

Helsinki, here I come.

CHAPTER 14

Starting Rehab

It's nearly a three-hour taxi ride from the hospital in Mikkeli to the Käpylä Rehabilitation Centre in Helsinki. I spend these hours staring at the dirty spots on the taxi's ceiling along the way. Well, it's a change from the hospital room ceiling, I guess.

My mom travels with me. She doesn't say much, but I'm glad to have her here. My father has to work. My mother's workplace is extremely generous throughout this time, and allows her the time she needs, whenever she needs it, to care for me. I'm so glad she's with me, especially when we arrive at the rehabilitation centre.

The doorway is narrow. Inside the lobby it's dark. *Is this the fine place where I'm supposed to be rehabilitated?* I'm thinking. It's gloomy and stark.

It suddenly hits me that no one knows my routine and I'm going to have to start all over again with different nurses. They won't know me, or how to communicate with me. I think of the carpet rollers and the hoist and the crane at the hospital. Panic starts to come over me and a howl fills the hallway where we are; I hate the fact that the sound is coming from me. I look at my mom and she looks like she's about to break down too. Oh God, what am I doing here? Not only is this hospital dingy and dark, but it's really small too. This cutting-edge hospital for the whole country is tiny. Is this where I've put all my hopes? Really? All of a sudden I feel sick to my stomach. I expected so much. I don't mean to sound ungrateful. It's thanks to one professor's recommendation that I'm allowed to come here at all, and much sooner after the stroke than it might have been. Yes, I should be grateful.

Äiti grips my hand to encourage me, but I sense she needs the contact as much as I do. She looks as anxious as I feel inside. Looking around the centre, I'm definitely the youngest patient here. There are other people in the reception area who are in wheelchairs, but most of them are navigating themselves. They can't walk, but they can move their arms. No one else I see has a condition as bad as mine.

"Hello, Kati, we've been looking forward to your coming. Hello, Mrs Lepistö. I'm the administrator. Kati, have you brought a lot with you? We encourage our patients to make themselves as comfortable as possible. And your mother can visit as frequently as she is able. I understand you live in Mikkeli. It is quite far away, so you can stay overnight, next door in our guest house, whenever you come to visit."

She's very friendly, calm and welcoming.

"Yes, thank you." My mom's voice sounds very quiet.

"Nurse Leena will show you the way to your room, Kati, and she will help you unpack. If you don't need to start your journey right away," she says to my mom, "you're welcome to help Kati adjust." She is very nice. She looks straight at me and I can tell I'm a person to her, not a blob. My panic has gone. I blink once, to let her know I'm okay.

"Good. Kati, you'll have a speech therapist as well as regular physio. We're going to work you very hard," she says with a smile. "You have had some physio at the hospital?"

"Yes." I pause. "No," I blink twice. The truth is there wasn't much and if she thinks I can't move rather than I'm as stiff as a board from a month of doing almost nothing, then maybe she won't work me as hard. I have let her know I can always do more. Always.

"My daughter is a very hard worker. She will not give you any rest," says my mom.

"Excellent," says the administrator. "We want our team to work hard for our patients. Nurse Leena," she calls.

The nurse leads us to what will be my new room. I'd better get used to it because I might be here for a while.

"Hi, Kati, the room is just down here. It isn't very special, but you will have privacy, even though it's a double room. You can make it your own. I'm Leena. I'm sure I'll see you a lot, and if you need anything tonight, I'll be here."

"Do you know the spell chart?" my mother asks her.

"A little. I'll learn." She smiles. And I believe her.

Saying goodbye to my mom is something I got used to when I started to travel, but now? How am I going to manage here alone? Äiti practically lived at the hospital. I can see she looks a bit sick. I guess she's worried about leaving me here. I manage not to howl and hope she doesn't notice how scared I am. She looks around the room they've brought us to. It's nothing special, just like any hospital room. She squeezes my shoulder. Our family is tough, but since the stroke my parents have become very gentle. We all feel a bit fragile, I guess. But I must never give in; I have to beat this situation, and if I'm strong, my family will be strong too.

At least I can spell out words. Ever since the hospital taught me to use an alphabet board, we use it all the time.

I use my eyes to spell out what I want to say, but it seems like I'm the only one who has one here at Käpylä. That must mean everyone else can speak. So am I the most disabled? Will all the staff here know the alphabet board? I've been waiting to get here, to get better, but now that I am, I'm worried. I haven't even tried any rehab yet, but all of a sudden I feel like there's no point, because it isn't going to work.

Nurse Leena looks straight at me. "It's going to be all right, Kati."

"We'll take good care of her," she says to Äiti. "I'll be back in a few minutes."

She's left us to let us say goodbye in private. That's really thoughtful.

"Kati, are you going to be all right?" Äiti asks me. "The staff here seem really nice."

"Yes," I blink. I know I should have a lot to say but right now I can't think.

Goodbyes are really hard, but my äiti says she and Isa will be back in a couple of weeks. Maybe I'll be much better by then. Maybe we'll have something to celebrate.

It's a big room – big enough for two patients. But I'm the only one here. The other bed is empty and unmade. I'm glad Nurse Leena said I'll have my own room.

I'm not left sitting, waiting for even a second. Someone new walks in. That's a good start, I think.

"Hello, Kati. I am Sinikka Soderholm, and I will be your speech therapist."

I spell.

"You are spelling 'Hello' but you are using letter placements that are a little bit different. We'll teach you another pattern that's easier on your eyes. It is not too different, and it is more popular." Her smile makes me like her right away.

Leena has returned before Sinikka has to leave. It's time to eat and soon after, time to go to bed. Once I'm in bed I feel nervous. What if I fall out? I'm trying to speak so a bit of grunting comes out to get Leena's attention.

"What's upsetting you?" she asks me. I spell using the only alphabet pattern I know. She's really patient and eventually she says, "Ah. Try not to worry. The sides of the bed are very sturdy." She demonstrates. "We have never let anyone fall out of bed yet." Her warm smile doesn't take all my fear away, but it helps.

*

When I was at the university hospital in Kuopio for the MRI scan, a psychiatrist there wanted to put me on medication for my head, including sleeping pills so that I could sleep. I guess he thought I needed to blur my thinking so I wouldn't have to face the horrible truth of the disability. But I said, "no way," to any of it. I was sad and miserable most of the time (who wouldn't be in this situation?) but I made myself live out each day. That's the only way to get stronger and better.

I won't take anything for my head here either. I have to be alert, not mushy-brained, which is what the medication would do to me. It's bad enough I can't move. At least I can still think. And that's what I do most of tonight at the rehab centre. The staff come in to check on me throughout the night, and every single one looks to see if I'm asleep. When I'm not, they stay with me for a while and talk. It's nice.

When I'm alone, I listen to passing traffic, of cars slowing down for the stop light, and then starting up again. Suddenly, there's a siren outside, an ambulance passing. I can see the glow of lights as it passes. Will the person inside survive? Will she be a vegetable or free to live life as she used to? Who is it? What's happened to her – or him?

I hear voices from down the hallway, of staff murmuring. I can't make out what they are saying. Someone has a television on, a patient in his room, I guess, even though it's the middle of the night.

I suppose eventually I do fall asleep, because all of a sudden, there is a glimmer of daylight. Finland in winter. I don't know where I am, and for a second I'm terrified. The howling starts and then I realise where I am. The rehab centre. The howling won't stop and it's embarrassing. It doesn't give a great first impression, but I can't help it. Every morning when I wake up I remember all over again that I can't walk, I can't talk. The shock is still overwhelming. But I'm not alone for long. A nurse comes in and introduces himself. He surprises me, and that's enough to stop me from howling. It's amazing how quickly he came after I woke up.

*

Day one – eating. I can swallow more easily than I could right after the stroke. They give me pureed food here like they started to do at the hospital, which I hate, but at least I'm tasting food, rather than getting nutrients through a tube. Focus on the best, try to ignore the worst. That should be my motto. I will get through this.

Sinikka, the speech therapist, is back this morning.

"We have a lot of work to do, Kati, but I understand you are a hard worker. So first, a facial massage. This is both for eating and general muscle flexibility.

"First, the sweep." Holding up two fingers so I can see, she starts from my forehead, then moves around eyes, cheeks, nose to my chin. Then she does the same thing, swiping with a frozen Q-tip. It feels awful. But whatever will work to help me so I can eat real food is worth it.

She has brought a new alphabet chart, with a new configuration, on Plexiglass.

"Spelling will bring your expression back. Your facial muscles need exercise, Kati, and as well as daily massage you'll practise your spelling. Anyone who learns the placement of the letters will be able to communicate with you. Anyone who doesn't know it can learn, or you can have them hold this up while you spell out words. Sound good to you?"

I blink once.

"This instrument has been available for years, so the system has been proven to work really well. Do you see, each letter has a place? When you focus, one letter at a time, you can spell out what you want to communicate. And whoever you are speaking with repeats the letter to make sure it's correct, and you continue. Letter by letter, you spell out words, and word by word you create sentences, communicating what you want the other person to understand."

We try it. At first, I'm speechless; I mean, don't know what to say, believe it or not. But eventually, we are sharing back and forth. I feel like I can actually have a conversation with her, even though she's a stranger. It's slow, really slow, but it's working. It's better than not being able to communicate. And it's better than the system at the hospital, which was similar but there was no board and the letter order was more difficult to learn. Only my mother got really good at it, and half the time it was because she was able to guess a lot of what I was trying to say.

"There are computers too," Sinikka explains. "You'll be able to use it hands-free, to write to anyone you want. There is email. These are possibilities for communication that didn't used to exist." She smiles.

I blink.

"We'll look at that program soon too, but for now we'll get you used to this spell chart." She pauses. She looks as if she's going to speak, but she doesn't for a while. We're just sitting opposite each other. I like her, and I think she can help me a lot.

"It is going to be a very long process, Kati. It will take a long time for you to improve, but I've observed that you can move your jaw even a miniscule amount. This is good. The basis for rehabilitation is, we take what you can already do and work to improve it. Do you understand?"

"Yes," I blink.

"So, I think – and I hope you'll find this good news – I think you'll be able to eat eventually, and not just pureed foods. I think you'll be able to eat solid foods. As soon as you're ready, let's start the process."

Yes! Wow! I'll be able to eat again. How soon? I notice she hasn't said anything about speaking yet.

Physio begins on the same day. They don't waste any time here. They are going to keep me busy, and this approach suits me. The gym. It's so exciting to think I'll be going to the gym. But when I get there reality hits me in the eyes. Is it possible to be any more embarrassed than going to a gym, which I *love*, and being unable to do *anything*? My joints are *so* stiff that it feels like I need oil for their hinges. There are other people there, but they have voices and working arms. I seem to be so much worse. Ohhh... I don't want to get upset again.

"Hello, I am Riitta," says the physiotherapist.

Am I the only one here with locked-in syndrome? It seems that the majority of the clients are paralysed just from the waist down and still able to talk. I'm staring around the gym.

"The others here are not locked-in as you are, but I know the alphabet and I have had clients in the past. You don't have to feel ashamed or embarrassed. Are you ready to begin?"

She begins working with me, to see what I can do, which is nothing. It hurts and she's not very gentle, but she does persist and gets my knees to move a little.

"Kati, we will try new things every day until you find what you can do. We'll progress at your rate."

Well, I'm young, and I can build my strength. Mobility is possible. If I work hard and am strong in my mind, I will improve. I can't deny that progress is going to be slow, but there's only one way to go and that's up.

The next day I meet another physiotherapist named Virpi. What I like about being here is that, even though the medical doctor in Mikkeli said the situation is hopeless, here they move my joints so I don't get stiff and I am loosening up. In the hospital they wanted to give me drugs for my head, which I refused. Here it's very different.

Virpi says, "Kati, your muscles are very stiff. You haven't moved your joints in a month and so we want to give you a medicine to release the stiffness. Is that all right?"

"W-h-a-t-w-i-l-l-i-t-d-o-t-o-m-y-b-r-a-i-n"? I spell.

I've been given the new spell chart, and I've practically memorised it already.

"Do you mean will it blur your thinking?"

"Yes," I blink.

"No, it won't affect your mind at all."

"Yes," I blink.

"You'll take it?"

"Yes," I blink.

And it doesn't take long before I notice a difference in my frozen bones.

The physiotherapists visit my room or take me to the gym every day. Sometimes the nurses also massage and stretch my muscles. They all know this spelling alphabet. They don't have a lot of time to talk, but they try when they are working with me.

"Kati, you have strength in your arm!" one nurse says and smiles.

I smile and laugh. Oh yes, my laugh still sounds like a donkey honking, but so what? It's good to laugh. I know the process will be long, but here in this centre they won't give up on me. I know I can improve. I know I can surprise everybody. I just need the time to do it.

"We think Kati might have a tiny nerve still functioning, still connected to her brainstem," they tell us on my parents' first visit. I'm exhausted and the time since they left has been, to be honest, a total blur. It's almost as if I've had a stroke all over again. Oh, not really, not physically, but in my memory and in my focus. How long am I going to have to be here? At the rate I'm going, I'll be here for... I don't imagine how long. It's too awful to think about.

"It will take a very long time for you to improve," I remember being told. Yeah, I guess it will. But they don't give up on me, I'll do it!

One morning, out of the blue, I get a phone call. One of the nurses comes in. She has the phone and says a man named Luigi is on the phone. She holds it to my ear.

"Please let me come see you, Kati. I love you. I want see you. I want take care of you. Let me come." Oh, that beautiful Italian accent, that tender voice is Luigi's. But I can't let him come. Tears roll down my face. It is just too shameful. My condition is so unattractive and I do not want him to see me this way. When I get better, I can see him. I can go to him. And anyway, even if I never see him again, this is no place for him to visit. He is so beautiful and perfect. This is not the time nor place for him.

I blink twice.

"Kati says no, Luigi. It is not a place for you." She sees I'm crying. "She is sad but she does not want you to see her like this." She expresses my feelings perfectly. Then she hangs up, and leaves the room.

Luigi was so beautiful. I will never forget him.

I don't socialise at the centre. Other patients don't really want to *talk* to me. They don't know the alphabet and they seem afraid of me. Even though they are in their wheelchairs, and it's only that they can't walk, some don't seem to have much power in their arms either, so even if they wanted to, they couldn't hold my alphabet board to talk with me. Anyway, I don't think they want to.

It is lonely, but the nurses are nice, the physios are good, and Sinikka is a good friend. I have so much work to put my energy to; I don't really have time to make friends anyway.

After a few weeks, I'm able to relax a little. I have my routine, new posters my mom has brought, and I'm used to the staff. Best of all, I can communicate with the outside world, the world outside of my head that is, using the spell chart and the computer.

Luigi and other people have sent me cards and letters, and my mother displays the cards in my room. But there is an improvement in rehab that has nothing to do with my physical condition or the decorations in my room. They have given me a computer and told me I can use it to write to other people. Since I can be strapped into a wheelchair, they set me up to use the Internet with a gizmo that lets me spell, letter by letter, using a mouse and a program that doesn't need fingers or hands. "Hello, World, I'm still here!" I'm getting used to this program and it's making the days a little shorter and life a little better.

Luigi tells me in his first letter that he uses email, so he becomes my first email friend. I write to him and he sends a message that is cheerful and warm. I write back. Then he writes again. In fact Luigi writes, over and over again. My Italian love. He wants to come to see me, but I've said no, so he keeps writing about other things. I couldn't bear him to see me like this. I like his messages though. Email allows me to share with him without him having to see me. We can still be friends.

The special computer program works really well. Writing an email is slow but steady, and I'm so grateful for it. I can communicate just as well as anybody else when it's computer to computer. Over time, I will write to more of my friends. When my mother writes and sends my letters, which I dictate, I give out my email address.

Physically, has my condition improved? Well, I haven't progressed very much. I'm better than when I came in here, but that's not saying much. That isn't to blame Sinikka, or Riitta and Virpi my physiotherapists, or even myself. I'm working so hard but I don't seem to be getting any better. I know they told me progress would be painfully slow, but at this point it doesn't seem to be happening at all. I can't give up. But it doesn't seem like I'm ever going to get better. The staff keep telling me not to get my hopes up, but how else can I keep going?

One idea I do have is to write everything down. I can record every experience on this computer. I don't know why I should, except that it will give me something to do besides staring at the ceiling. And maybe it will be useful, somehow, to know what I experience to help me find out how I can get better. I have an idea that one day I'll write a book, so that everyone who has this problem can know things can get better. For now, I'm keeping a record of every step of change and improvement. Some days there isn't much to write.

Every week Warren calls me. We cry, he tells me he still loves me. Sometimes we send faxes to each other. It's crazy. How much longer can we go on like this? Not long, I think.

CHAPTER 15

My Progress: Aches, Pains and Standing Upright

Physiotherapy is never boring.

The therapist moves my legs and arms, bending my elbows, bending my knees. One day I'm able to bend my knee all on my own. It's a triumph. Another day, my left arm. Another triumph. When I manage to sit on the edge of the bed unsupported for five minutes, I'm truly on the road to recovery.

Today I'm introduced to the exercise ball. I used to roll on one of these every time I went to the gym in LA – we're old friends. Here, I'm set onto the ball, but the physios go too fast and suddenly I'm rolling away from them, rolling until I fall off. I land with a thud and they come running after me, but I'm laughing hard so they won't be worried. They lift up my head and shoulders. We're all laughing. Sometimes you just gotta laugh. There's just nothing better to do.

I remember the first day I entered the gym, I felt *so* hopeless. I'm advancing a little every day now. They tell me my muscles and mobility are improving, although I don't feel it. Some people have degenerative diseases and are fading away, while I'm getting stronger. It definitely makes me appreciate my condition, no matter how bad it may seem. When I can just make my body do what my brain tells it to, then I'll be fine. It may seem weird to someone who is not paralysed, but I do feel my limbs, I just can't move them. And of course I can't move so I can't touch them either.

The physios work to keep my muscles fit and supple, otherwise they hurt. Imagine waking up in the middle of the night with a muscle spasm or a cramp. My muscles are very tense even without a cramp. Sometimes if I'm startled or excited, one leg will involuntarily kick out at the knee. It's a bit embarrassing. You know how stiff you can get sitting on a plane? For me, being in a wheelchair is like that. I get stiff and sore very easily. So the therapist takes my knees and ankles, one at a time, and gently moves one leg at the knee back and forth. It's how I get exercise. My ankles get spasms too. One ankle got hurt during the stroke – of course I don't know how – so that has to be massaged, stretched and worked out even more often than the rest of me. My fingers are permanently cramped too. But here at Käpylä they are already stretching out my fingers. The therapists are firm but gentle, so it doesn't hurt too much. Gradually, my hands have opened up. I feel so much better without the tension. I had stopped letting my fingernails grow because my fingers were digging into my palms. That's stopped now, and so I do have my nails manicured again, like I used to. Little changes in the right direction, and patience, show I'm getting better. The main thing about my arms and legs is to get them moving, so the physios work on all my joints and hinges to get me loosened up. They are very patient and it is helping me to stay relaxed for longer periods.

Something that is quite scary is that I have shaking attacks every day. Its technical name is clonus. Sometimes, my leg from the knee to my foot just starts to shake and I can't do anything about it. Once someone applies firm pressure to the part of me that's shaking, it gradually stops. It used to freak me out when it first happened. It felt like an internal earthquake, and that is one LA experience I don't ever want to repeat. These spasms have been happening every day for weeks now, so I have sort of gotten used to them. No choice anyway. It might be my body trying to receive messages from my brain and it can't understand yet.

I also burst out with emotion. It's involuntary, but sometimes the expression doesn't even match what I'm feeling. I can be quite happy and cry, or I can be quite sad and laugh. The most embarrassing moment was while we were all watching *Schindler's List*. I burst out laughing. Everybody else looked at me like I was heartless. I've been told this strange behaviour happens because the emotion parts of my brain are near to one another, and I can get expression confused. Well, at least I can express emotion. I feel like a robot doll sitting in a chair all the time. At least I can feel and express it, even if sometimes what I show doesn't match what I'm feeling. I'll have to watch that movie again sometime though, and cry. It really is very sad.

The hardest thing for me to put up with is standing. The first time I was put on a tilt-table, which is the name for an electronic platform on wheels, I felt like I was on some kind of rollercoaster ride. The dizziness reminded me of the warning spells I had before the stroke. I started out lying down and was gradually brought to a vertical position. It made my head swim, and it hurt my weak ankle. I tried not to moan because I want to improve, but this standing thing just made me physically ill, like coming off a fairground ride, and feeling like I was going to pass out. One of the worst experiences as a paralysed person is standing. I mean, apparently lots of other quadriplegics hate it too, so I'm in good company. It sounds crazy. You'd think it's something I'd want to do, but I hate it. I look forward to standing one day, when my head doesn't swim and I don't keel over either.

CHAPTER 16

Progress at the Gym

"Today we're going to try something new, Kati."
Every day there's something new, and I'm always ready for it.

I'm wheeled to the gym and I can see a harness hanging from the ceiling.

"We're going to try to get you walking today."

Oh wow! *I can do this, I can do this,* I tell myself. This is a great chance to test myself.

They put me inside the harness, and I'm dangling like a baby. (How humiliating.) On each side of me is a physiotherapist.

"We're going to get your legs moving."

I'm looking down on them as though I'm the instructor about to teach them something. It makes me laugh – donkey honk, again!

"Okay, Kati. Let's see you walk."

My saggy body hangs limp in the harness and it's really painful on my crotch. My hips feel as if they're being plunged up into my ribs. It hurts, but I won't give up. I am getting the hang of the movement, but they are moving my legs a little too fast and I can't quite keep up. I'm trying, but it's so difficult. It's painful. I'm breathing hard. I can hear myself. I want to tell them to slow down.

"Does it hurt, Kati?"

"No," I blink.

I want to keep going. But they don't look up at me to watch me spell. They stop moving my legs. I groan some more, to signal I want them to keep going, but they don't understand. They start to undo the harness.

"No!" I blink and blink and blink, but they must think I want to stop.

Of course I don't want them to stop. It might be days before I get this chance again. I'm frustrated. I could have kept going. But they put me back in my wheelchair.

"Kati, don't worry about it. You did your best."

But I didn't. I could have done so much more.

"When will I be able to do it again?" I spell out.

They look at each other.

"We'll see," one of them says.

I hate that. I hate not knowing. I hate having to be taken everywhere, on everyone else's timetable. I start to howl. I can't control it. Oh, I hate this!

Eventually, I calm down.

Although the centre is small and unattractive, the people who work here are really good at their jobs. The physios don't really get personal at all, but they treat me so well, and give me *the works* – every programme imaginable. They spare no expense, and I feel like nothing is too inconvenient. Apparently I'm a very strange case – everything works but I can't make anything work! So they keep coming up with new ideas. I sure can't complain about their treatment of me.

CHAPTER 17

Eating and Speech Therapy

Sinikka has taken me under her wing. She's amazing. I know it's her job, but I have to remind myself, because she doesn't treat me like a patient. When I'm with her she's like a big sister. She has incredible compassion and patience. She's like... my rock. Every day I look forward to seeing her and she seems to look forward to seeing me too. In a way, I hate the weekends, because she has her own life and she doesn't come into the centre. It's like she's become my best friend, and I'm so glad I have her. She's the best part of being here, my salvation in this place.

Sinikka thinks she can make my facial muscles work. She says I can practise and fine-tune the vocal sounds that I can already make. She says everything is worth a try. She knows me and understands my work ethic and attitude. I'm especially able to connect with her and I think this is very helpful. She understands me and develops a treatment structure specifically for me. She uses the Plexiglass letter chart a lot to get me to respond. She's going to get my facial muscles moving, so I can express myself in ways other than blinking and spelling.

"Great!" I tell myself.

Maybe I can be a close-up face model. My dream isn't totally dead. Well, it's a very small chance, but it's a little goal. I can keep going when I have a goal. It's crucial to set goals in rehab and work my butt off to reach them. Working hard comes easily to me. I've always been a workaholic.

Sinikka likes the fact that I have jaw movement. 'Microscopic' is how she described it the first day I worked with her, and she wants to build on that.

"I want you to learn a new way to eat. First, for two months you have to be fed on the tube again."

I start to cry. She touches my hands, "I know it's not nice, but it's just for two months, while you learn a new way of eating. How about if you make it a goal? You can break it into stages over the first month? Then in the second month, until you can eat, chew and swallow the new foods, you'll mimic it. I promise we'll try new foods, things you like. You can tell me the foods you want to try when you're ready, okay?"

I nod. I can nod, just a little, already. The tubes will go in, but it'll be worth it because when they come back out, Sinikka is going to teach me how to eat *real food*.

She's clever too. One day she told me something and I actually don't quite know how she managed to get me to accept it – I guess it isn't very likely I'm going to talk again.

"Kati, darling, your tongue doesn't really want to move on its own. You make clear sounds, but..."

She's looking at me and we start to laugh. Sounds, yes, like a donkey when I laugh and a coyote when I cry. Sounds are loud and clear, but no words. She's made an understatement, and manages to make me laugh about myself. After the laughter dies down, she continues.

"I want you to think, 'It doesn't matter that I can't talk'. Sure, you want to, and you'll try, but don't let the frustration overwhelm you and get you down. Just keep working. I've never seen anyone ever work as hard as you do. You're amazing. Just keep at it and we'll make the most of it. And don't worry; I won't give up on you. If anything can happen, we'll make it happen."

Wow, she's so helpful. She speaks my language – the language of trying no matter what, trying in spite of all the odds, trying because it makes life worth living. If I don't try, I'll die. Or want to. Maybe somehow she knows this.

Some days aren't so great. Sinikka takes me into a forest area behind the rehab centre. It's a place where I can make my clumsy sounds without having to feel self-conscious and where I can be loud without shocking or disturbing anyone else. I hate going to the woods. I don't like making weird sounds but she has convinced me it makes a difference to my progress, so I let it rip! When it's over, I'm always relieved to get back inside.

I haven't wanted to have visitors here in rehab. I don't want them to see this place, or to see me this way. I can focus better too, if I'm on my own. My parents come, but I don't want anybody else. However, one day, while I'm sitting in the wheelchair alone in my room, a visitor comes unexpectedly.

Jari! I can't help myself: I laugh my horrible-sounding laugh. He looks surprised, but he laughs too and there is no awkward moment. He's as beautiful as ever, and it is so wonderful to see him, even though I don't want him here. It's so horrible for someone to have to come here.

He has flowers for me. "My beautiful Kati, this is tragic, but you are still beautiful," he says. The flowers are really nice, but I blink twice because I don't feel beautiful. I feel wretched. Some days are better than others for me, but they are all horrible really.

He kisses me on my forehead. I stare at him.

There are too many tubes to kiss me on the mouth. He tries, but ends up kissing my tube. We laugh a little.

Jari! I cannot say his name of course. He sees in my eyes he is welcome here.

He sits on the bed and describes his sailboat. He's going to go around the world. We talk – he talks – as though we've never been apart. We will be best friends, he says. He will stay in contact, always.

"I have missed you, Kati. All that time you were living away. Milan, yes? And LA?" He tells me he loves me and misses me. I just stare at him.

Jari lives in Helsinki.

"I'll come back again soon."

Some days I don't want visitors, but I admit, seeing Jari always makes me smile. He's so gorgeous and interesting. It doesn't take him long to learn how to spell and we can talk back and forth. I know he will sail away soon, over the horizon. He's another world traveller, like me, who is destined for life beyond Finland. Except I will be in Finland now. In little Mikkeli, forever. I feel a lump in my throat, and I'm remembering my dreams of modelling, and the reality of modelling, and how far away I am from all of that now.

"Kati?" Jari touches my hand.

I look up at him. I'm sure he can tell I'm about to cry. I don't want him to miss his dream because of me. He has to live his desires, but I am sad because I can't live mine. I shouldn't think like that. I should think of all the wonderful things that he can see and do.

*

The two months with the tubes pass slowly.

"Kati, we'll take the tube out tomorrow and start you on puree."

Finally! Finally I will be able to leave boiled potato and pickled herring memories behind forever. Finally, I'll be able to eat food that looks and tastes like adult food. Finally, I'll get to eat a burger.

Eating is a time-filling activity, and when you're immobile, you need to keep busy somehow. When you don't have mealtimes, it's a hole in the day that needs filling. I've been doing all the exercises to get ready for real food. I have been receiving my facial massages every day. All the nurses know how to do it – and they do.

Sinikka massages my face with her two fingers on either side.

"We'll start tomorrow with drinking and puree, to get you used to digesting again. Soon we'll test your eating skills. I'm sure you'll pass with flying colours. Ready?"

The special thing about Sinikka compared to the other people who try to help me is that she knows that I need to know what's going on. She always tells me what's coming before it comes so I can prepare myself. I wish everyone was like that. It seems like she can put herself in my shoes, and knows what it feels like not to be able to control my own life.

"Sinikka, you understand me so well," I spell one day.

"I know what it's like to feel helpless," she says. I look at her canes. Sinikka has her own disability, obviously not as bad as mine, but she can't walk unaided.

"How?"

"When I was younger I had a real problem with my ankles. That's why I walk with canes. I had a year of treatment in London, England. It hurt like hell, but I'm glad I went through it, because now I know how difficult it is to overcome any disability."

That's getting a positive from a negative experience. It's nice that she talks to me about herself too. I feel like there's a real bond between us, and tomorrow is the first day I get to eat real food. That's something to look forward to.

Tomorrow comes, and before any food there's another face massage. A nurse will massage my face every time I'm going to eat, even if it's only a little bit. First, she uses two fingers from each hand, one on either side of my face. When I'm a bit relaxed, she does the same circular movements with the icy Q-tip (Brrr!). It's chilling, but I put up with it because it's worth it to think I'll be able to do facial modelling and I'll be able to eat. Sometimes I get massaged with an electric toothbrush (tickle, tickle). I'm trying to be light-hearted about it, but it's *so* irritating.

Now I get to eat. The puree is better than the tube. It tastes okay, although it's like slime going down my throat, which isn't very nice. Drinking proves very difficult at first, taking just a spoonful of liquid at a time, and initially, it goes down the wrong pipe. It takes a lot of mixing of the liquid to make it thick enough to only want to go down the right tube. Sparkling drinks like cola, which aren't so easy to go down the wrong tube, are good, so I don't end up in coughing fits.

Another day comes, and another. Practice makes perfect. "Kati, you're ready for solid foods!" She's as happy as I am.

The food has to be cut into tiny, tiny pieces, but as soon as I get used to it we'll be moving on to bigger pieces. Burger, here I come!

One day, I'm given candy to chew on that is held by a cloth. Only part of it goes into my mouth. That way, it won't accidentally slip down my throat and choke me. The next day, I'm given pieces of fruit to suck. I'm eating and it tastes fantastic.

At night when I'm lying in bed, I think of what I can eat the next day. Little by little, I'm able to eat more complicated foods. I'm so happy. I fall asleep thinking about Äiti's cooking. Of course, when I dream I can do anything as though I never had a stroke; it's a time when I can feel really free. When I go to sleep, my brain doesn't remember I'm locked-in. Maybe it does that so I can experience a normal life when I'm asleep. It's still a horrible feeling when I wake up, but not as big a shock as it used to be. Maybe I'll never get over this horrible situation, but little by little I'm accepting my limitations at the same time as I'm working to get rid of them totally.

"Kati, I know you're a model, and you aren't used to eating much, but really you need to eat more to keep strong. Even breathing uses calories because it's a bit hard for you. As you eat, you are practising, so your jaw gets stronger. We know you can use your jaw, so let's practise with eating," Sinikka tells me one day.

"What about the calories?" I ask, spelling out the words.

"Breathing burns calories," she says.

So I learn to eat. And I eat. They offer me whatever I want. I'm like a princess with a whim for this or a craving for that. Sure, there are foods I can't eat: apples, nuts, boiled potatoes (as if I'd miss those!), but I learn to cooperate with eating because I'm using my jaw muscles, building up flexibility and strength, and enjoying my food. Life may feel like a prison right now, but at least I get to enjoy eating. And to a model, that is a huge change. I learn to enjoy my food. It's a tiny piece of freedom: chocolate puddings, fresh avocado, pieces of hamburger, anything I want.

Occasionally I choke on a piece of food, which gets the nurses moving. Sometimes I have to have the Heimlich manoeuvre so I can spit out a piece of trapped food. Not pretty. Fortunately, it doesn't happen too often. I would be very upset if they stopped feeding me solid foods.

The weeks pass, and as I enjoy my food, I begin to realise breathing doesn't actually burn that many calories, certainly not as many as I'm taking in. For the first time in my life, my helpless body is not only useless but it also feels disgusting. It must look disgusting too (although I don't dare look in a mirror). What should I do?

Jari has not seen me in a few weeks, and when he surprises me with a visit I feel totally aware of how fat I am. He doesn't say anything about it, but I'm not sure my clothes are hiding it.

"I'm going to sail soon, Kati." I knew this day was coming. Even though he has so much to do to get his boat ready, he has still come to visit me, and this time it's going to be to say goodbye for a while. I can feel it. I can see it in his eyes. He's leaving. He has to. He has to live his dream.

"I'll come back to see you. By the time I'm back you'll be home again, in our little home town. And while I'm sailing, I'll send you messages. We'll talk on the computer the whole time I'm away."

"W-e-h-a-v-e-a-n-e-l-e-c-t-r-i-c-r-e-l-a-t-i-o-n-s-h-i-p," I spell. It makes him laugh a little bit.

"Like no other," he says. "Ah, I'd like to marry you, Kati, one day, and take care of you."

"O-k-a-y," I spell.

"Well, here is our secret promise then. One day we will get married. One day we'll go down the aisle together as husband and wife."

"You didn't say walk down the aisle. We'll roll down the aisle."

"Well, let's get some crazy music and we'll rock *and* roll. Sound good?"

We laugh. We always laugh. Jari is so wonderful. And he didn't say I got fat. Thanks for that! He kisses me before he leaves. It's a wonderful kiss. It stays on my lips all day. After Jari leaves, the silence creeps in. It's quiet because it's night time, but I don't mean that kind of silence. There is still dull noise in the hallway, because people are talking and some patients have televisions in their rooms. But surrounding me is a big bubble of silence. I'm scared.

Jari said I'll be in Mikkeli. That's true, I guess. I'm not improving enough, am I, to think I could travel on my own again, and work? What is going to happen to me? The reality is I'm never alone, because I can't be; I'm totally dependent. For the first time in my life, I feel so lonely, and I'm fat too. I'm full of food for the first time in my life, but I feel so empty.

I used to like being alone. I had friends but I also travelled a lot on my own to get to shoots or castings. I don't remember ever feeling lonely. A model doesn't have a set job, but goes to many different places and is always meeting new people. I used to like meeting new people. Now I don't want to because they stare, because I can't talk to them, and because they think I'm mentally handicapped. They either totally ignore me or patronise me.

I need somebody to help me with everything. In fact, it isn't even help I need, because to say I need help implies I can do some things with help from others. The truth is, I cannot do anything. I can only hum to get someone's attention so I can ask them for what I need. The forecast for me is like a bad winter's day: grey, dark and wet. I try not to think about it, but sometimes I can't help it. When I do, I start to find it hard to breathe, as though I'm suffocating from my thoughts and fears. I thought I would get better, but it isn't happening, is it? I thought I would get better and prove to the doctors that they were wrong. But maybe they weren't. Maybe they were right. Maybe I am going to be a vegetable. Not in how I think, but in how I live, like sitting on a shelf and waiting to be noticed and taken off the shelf. If nobody notices me, I just keep sitting. Nothing else to do, nothing else to offer.

Jari will be on his boat, sailing around the world soon. I'm glad. It's his dream to sail around the world. I of all people know how important it is to live your dream.

Warren calls me every week. He doesn't have a dream. He needs one. I'm not his dream anymore, but he doesn't know it. He needs to figure it out, like I have. At first, I like that he calls, but it only makes my condition seem more hopeless, and emphasises how far away he is from me, and how much life has changed from when I lived in LA. It hasn't even been six months since I lived there, and life has changed so much. Every time Warren calls, I have such a deep loneliness, even worse than I was feeling before he called. Sometimes I'm busy being stretched and I stop to listen to him. Sometimes I'm just sitting looking out of a window. But always, I feel worse after he's called than I did before. So, it is finally time to make the change. I don't want to be heartless, but being a couple just doesn't make sense anymore.

What did I do to deserve this paralysis? How did this happen? It doesn't do any good to look back. It kills me. So no, I have to look forward only. Forward into this abyss. Forward into loneliness. Forward into a life alone, with no family of my own. Alone with my very wonderful parents until they die. And then what? I am needy and have nothing to offer, I have nothing to do, and now I've become fat too.

CHAPTER 18

Facing Reality

*D*ear Isa,
All the exercising I do doesn't help, I hate it here. I do not want any guests, because I do not want them to see me like this and pity me, it hurts too much. Nobody understands me when I blink my eyes, or they just do not look, you do not either.

The blonde nurse has too little experience; she does not know how to feed people. If I could just speak, I'd tell them all I am so fed up with all of this.

This is a letter I wrote four months ago to my dad, when I was feeling pretty hopeless. Now I look at it again and see all the optimism and hard work, and loneliness hasn't changed anything. Oh, except one thing: the blonde nurse is used to feeding me now. That's the only improvement.

The computer has made a difference; it's a window looking out on the world. But I can't enter that world, not anymore, I'm stuck on the other side for the rest of my life.

Maybe it's time I looked in the mirror to face the horror in front of me. I haven't looked at myself in months.

I'm in the shower and my hair is being washed. I tilt my neck back and suddenly, it's like I'm on a free acid trip or something. I have a weird out-of-body feeling, which lasts only for couple seconds, but even in that time I already hope it will pass quickly. I've never tried drugs, but I imagine it can be like that, with some sort of very strange clarity in my thoughts and a feeling of watching myself, not in a dream but in another world entirely. There are thoughts that for an instant make me think that I'm enlightened, making me question how utterly stupid and useless this life is, that there is something more I should be experiencing. Maybe for some people this *enlightenment* feels great, and like there is some superior understanding available that elevates us. But not me. It's only horrible and I want it to end so that I can go back to my stupid mundane life.

I have a faint memory of this happening before, way before I had the stroke. When I was a little girl, I was once standing on the back porch and looking into the backyard. I felt like I was watching myself playing *in* the yard. Another time, when I was a teenager, I felt like I was watching myself. Could there be something weird with my brain that was there all along, something that was made worse by the stroke that ended up destroying me? How could I just fall apart the night of the stroke? I can't understand how I could get so sick and it end like this, like a vegetable in body, but not in mind.

As for superior insight? Of course I don't have superior insight, but I can't go back to my ordinary life either because I am paralysed for life. Yeah, I have to admit it, finally – I'm stuck like this forever. Frozen silence, that's what my present is, and what my future will be. I've been in this rehab clinic for four months. How much has changed? Not very much. I can communicate only by spelling with my eyes, or typing on a computer. I can sit up, but only because I've relearnt how to balance. I can lift my chin, and eat food as long as someone feeds me. I can wash, and poo, as long as someone takes me. I have to admit it, I'm locked-in for life and this stroke was a death sentence. Not death in my brain but death in my body. A healthy body that can't move might as well be a dead body.

I remember when we were still in the hospital. First, the doctors told my parents about institutions where I could be sent to live.

"That's not going to happen!" my mother said.

Another time, both Äiti and Isa were visiting, and the hospital staff had us into the office.

"I think it would be wise to start planning to make changes to the home, so it will fit a wheelchair patient. These things take time. Perhaps you can do that while she's at the rehabilitation clinic."

Later that day in my room, Äiti said, "Change the house? Sure we could. But hey, who's going to need a wheelchair? They don't know our Kati! Or maybe they think we'll be expecting guests." She made me laugh.

Another day during a physiotherapy session at the hospital, Äiti said she'd buy me a red sports car as soon as I could drive it.

"They're looking at us, Kati. Do you think they think we're crazy?" Äiti whispers.

"I wouldn't buy that sports car just yet, Mrs Lepistö," said the physio.

I remember thinking of the song lyric: "Baby you can drive my car."

The staff thought we were crazy, and we were. Crazy hopeful. What's wrong with that? Nothing. Except now, I have to admit it *was* just a dream. I'm never going to drive a red sports car. I'm never going to drive any car. Not ever again. My mom has fought hard for me. But we both knew, didn't we, deep down, it was never going to happen? I was never going to get well. She knew. She said she'd get me a car to make me laugh, to keep me going, to keep me hoping. Maybe that shower did bring me insight. I see the reality now, and it makes me so mad I want to throw something. But of course I can't move to pick up anything. I can't even lurch and throw myself because I'm strapped into my chair so I won't fall over. Funny. I'm protected against what? Hurting myself? That's funny. Who cares if I hurt myself? I'm dead anyway.

My mind is in a daily struggle. Constantly, I'm torn between hope and defeat. I'm not depressed, but I'm sure not optimistic either. I'm looking through glass at my future: I'm going to have to live my life, if you can call it that, at a slow pace and in a different way than I ever expected. I am supposed to accept this, but how? How do I, Kati Lepistö, who has always been the most fiercely independent woman in the world, cope with total dependency? Maybe some people use drugs to cope with disappointment. Well, here is disappointment smacking me right in the face. It hurts. But I can feel it. I'm alive. I just don't know how to live it yet.

CHAPTER 19

Learning to Adapt

The computer has come in very handy. I can't even bear to think what existence would be like if I didn't have the possibility to communicate with friends and family, far and near, through the computer. I guess I should say it has been a life saver.

The computer has a software program called *Dragger*, which moves the cursor. Another software program called *Grid* has an on-screen keyboard so that I can write. To use *Dragger* an infrared camera is placed above the monitor and a metallic reflecting sticker is put on my forehead. The camera sends out the infrared light and picks up the reflection and thus the cursor moves. It's a brilliant invention and opens up the whole world to someone who is otherwise locked-in.

Moving to Helsinki and the rehab clinic has been good for me physically, but not socially. I didn't want visitors, to be stared at or to see the pity in their eyes. Most of all, I just wanted to work hard to get better, and start to live a normal life again. But that decision makes for lonely weekends. That's when physio pauses. Staff need a break from work and supposedly patients need rest. I'd rather just keep doing the physio even on weekends, because I don't want my progress to slow down. Also, I admit, when routine stops I start thinking about my situation: my Rolls Royce wheelchair, my strange and unusual dead-end life. That's too miserable to think about, no matter how I try to perk it up with smart-ass comments.

I remember the first time the doctor came to see me when I first had access to a computer, to see if I could manage to use it, but even more to see if I was coherent – able to think straight. I wrote to him, "Shit happens." Do you think he recognised I was coherent? I think I made it pretty clear.

Sometimes my parents come and take me for family drives at the weekend, or for wheelchair strolls. At first it was horrible to go to public places and have people staring at me in this chair. It hurt to think they thought I was stupid as well as immobile, but then I remembered how I coped with people staring during photo shoots. I'm looking through people now when they stare, and it doesn't bother me so much anymore. It's always good to see my mom and dad. They cheer me up. They state the obvious and make light of my paralysis. People call it black humour, black because it's based in sadness and disappointment, humour because it allows us to laugh at ourselves. I know I'm really lucky to have parents like them. Yeah, I feel like I'm a boxer and I've got two excellent trainers in my corner, Isa and Äiti, Dad and Mom. I couldn't have better parents.

Humour gets me through a bad day. Äiti and I have a very similar sense of humour. When we're out and people stare at me I ignore it. I'm so used to it from modelling that I can just blank it out. When people notice me and acknowledge me, that's a different thing. For example, recently we were at a restaurant.

"Would the other lady like something?"

"Ask her," says my mom.

The waitress bends down to my eye level and in a nursery nurse's high pitched, very slow voice says, "Hello, would you like something?"

I spell for my mom.

"Oh wow," the waitress says, "she can spell. That's neat."

"Oh yes," says my mom, "and she can read too."

Ouch. I'm not sure the waitress caught the joke, but we did and laughed.

Then my mom said, "And she can laugh too." But that got lost in our hysteria.

As for the waitress, she brought our order, and was very pleasant. She just didn't understand us at all, but she meant to be kind. Yeah, sometimes you've just gotta laugh.

Another thing I'm learning to laugh about is itches. I used to love summer, but in Finland, with sunshine comes mosquitos – and itching. It's amazing how many insects come at us and we don't even know it – far more than we realise. Until this paralysed summer, I never really noticed.

Well, I notice every single one, because I can't just brush them aside unconsciously.

"C-a-n-y-o-u-s-e-e-t-h-a-t-m-o-s-q-u-i-t-o?"

Well, by the time I've spelled it the damn thing has drawn its blood and is long gone.

To have an itch scratched, I have to spell it out, and by the time I get attention, describe where it is, and have it scratched (which is never quite in the right place, by the way), I could explode. I do have a sharp tongue, but I am realising that the sharp tongue – which of course is silent but deadly – has to be saved for important matters. If every itch mattered, I'd have exploded a long time ago. So, instead, I make a joke of it. The best secret on how to cope with embarrassment is to make it a feature.

One time my seat belt wasn't done up and I had an itch and wanted to squirm to try to make it better. Instead, my legs spasmed and went straight out in front, and I slid off the chair and onto the floor. Fortunately, I didn't hurt myself. When a nurse came running to rescue me, I spelled, "C-a-n-y-o-u-s-w-e-e-p-m-y-n-o-s-e? I-s-e-e-m-t-o-h-a-v-e-a-h-a-i-r-o-u-t-o-f-p-l-a-c-e."

I was never left unbuckled again. The lesson: it's very important to drive with your seat belt buckled up.

Everybody has to have a hobby to keep them busy at stressful times, or to entertain themselves, to build up skills, or to learn. My hobby is a bit surreal. I stare at the ceiling. It's a bit of a weird pastime, but it isn't stressful, which is what a hobby is meant to be, right? Sometimes when I'm staring I'm thinking. One thing has not been resolved yet, which is really bugging my dad especially – how did I get to the point of absolute helplessness at the age of twenty-one?

Like always, I'm still able to tell my mom anything. We talk plenty, but for serious stuff I'm learning to use the computer. We realised very soon after leaning the spelling that emotional stuff is just too hard to discuss. Crying and using my eyes, slowly, slowly, trying to express my emotions, is too difficult and too frustrating. Instead I write to her, and she writes back. The computer is very handy. With the computer I can be myself, and express myself, through my own words. I keep in contact with everybody. Without it, I'd be trapped without any way to communicate with the world the way 'normal' people can. I don't even want to think about what life would be like without email.

I've found some things out on the Internet too. The doctors say I'm stuck living like this forever, but I know there are other treatments. Alternative medicines can help me. If things don't improve significantly in rehab – which they aren't very much – I can go to other places to get help. When I leave this place, which will happen one day, I may not be perfectly back to normal, but I have other options.

CHAPTER 20

Home Again, Naturally

I'm looking out a window. No one sees me from outside.
I'm calling. No one hears me.

I'm throwing my fists against the glass.

No one notices.

I wake up.

This is the only dream I've had since the stroke that
isn't nice. But it is how I feel, trapped inside myself. It's
a life where only the computer hears me, only the screen
sees me. If I thought I'd live like this forever – dramatic,
emotional and self-conscious – I think I'd die of despair. It
isn't an option for me.

I didn't literally dream this; I imagine it while I am fully
awake, not every day, but some days. My dreams are actually
about modelling days, and walking along the California
beaches. Some of my dreams are real memories, some
are just nice situations of what could be. None are about
entrapment. Thanks for that! I guess my subconscious has
a way of dealing with this situation by letting me remember
and relive movement and sound. At least in real life I can

see, I can hear, I can feel. Just because I can't talk, or move, or touch doesn't mean I'm not alive. I just have to learn to live differently. At least this is what I tell myself. This is how I go forward. This is how I return to Mikkeli, to my childhood home, to the cold darkness of Finnish winter. Well, at least it's summer, and it won't be cold for another couple of months. Always, I look for the positive side of things.

This morning I've been left alone for a few minutes. It won't be for long because a nurse will come in soon – totally alone is rare in the daytime, but she just left me in the bathroom for a moment. I look up and there I am. For the first time since the stroke, I look into a mirror and see myself.

I remember when I could not even lift my chin. Äiti offered to hold her compact for me, so I could look in a mirror. But I closed my eyes. She brought a hand mirror. I blinked, "No". She gave up after a few more tries. But today it is time.

When I look at this face, I see a girl I don't recognise. I look older. My hair is brushed – the nurses here are very careful to do that for me. My face looks clean and there is a bit of make-up, done well, around my eyes. It's not the make-up I would wear though. She hasn't put on any lipstick yet. The worst thing is, my face is round, fat! It's awful, staring at a fat face, a fat woman, who used to be super skinny, sleek and beautiful.

Who is Kati Lepistö now? A fat cripple. But no! That's not all of me. I'm still a woman with a heart and a soul. I still long to be held, long for sex. I still love clothes (naturally), and food (more than any self-respecting model ever should).

The people here have tried really hard and have helped my medical situation a little. But my heart is broken and my soul is empty. How do you fix an empty soul? No one else can. I have to fix it myself. Today I'm going home. It will be safe, but I'm so scared. While I'm staring at my face, like all the other people have been staring at me for the last five months, I tell myself what I see: I see a person sitting in a wheelchair. She's fat, but she wouldn't be if she could walk. What else? Oh God, I don't know. Oh, I don't know. I have a name and a face and a useless body, but I don't know who I am!

Then the howling starts. Damn! I won't be alone now. I liked this, and I've ruined it because I can't control myself or stop myself from howling.

Leena comes in. I'm glad it's Leena.

"Kati, are you okay?"

"Yes," I blink. I don't know who I am, but I know I'm okay.

Residential rehab is over and it's time for goodbyes. The hardest one will be saying goodbye to Sinikki. While I've been at Käpylä, Sinikki has been the best speech therapist and friend I could ever ask for.

"Kati, as we finish here, I think you can reward yourself with a little trip. Maybe you'd like to take a short cruise to Norway or Sweden. It isn't too far, and shouldn't be too tiring. What do you think? A change of scenery would be good for you, and the air will be very healthy."

"We're going to Florida," Mom tells them.

I'm packing to return home, to Mikkeli. I'm the best I'll be, they think. I can't talk, I can't walk, I can't even move, and – this is it. But I can travel. Well, baby, this girl is gonna travel!

Hot sun, palm trees and happy faces. That's where we're going. The staff stare at us as if we're insane. Well, if we are, so what? Life is to be lived, made the most of.

I've been cooped up here with a death sentence, so it's time to roll and go. And so we will, very soon. Sure, there are some practical things to organise at my parents' house: assistance, accommodation changes, but a holiday is in order and yes, we are going to go for it.

All the physiotherapists, led by Riitta and Virpi, come to my room to say goodbye.

"She was our most challenging case ever," says Riitta to my parents. "No one has ever worked harder, and it was so rewarding for us to work with her. We all think so." There are nods and applause. I start to cry, laughing like a donkey at the same time. Finnish people do not normally show their gratitude or congratulate each other. It is a nice American way of expression, but it's rare in Finland. I guess I've made an impression here, and the people are genuinely sad to see me go. Other nursing staff flow into the room. It's getting crowded. It isn't the first time I'm going home, but this time I won't be coming back. I've had home visits to get used to things and to spend time with family. But now it's permanent.

I've written something on the computer for them, to say thank you: "I have met many interesting and wonderful people here. I have experienced so much kindness and genuine caring and warmth. I will never forget this. Thank you." My mom reads it out and tries, unsuccessfully, not to cry.

There are many, many hugs. Even my dad hugs some of the nurses that he knows. He's changed so much since the stroke. He's always been caring, but he shows it in a tender way now.

I cannot even say I look out the back window as we drive from that place, since obviously I cannot even turn around.

As we leave Helsinki, all of the nurses on the ward where I lived for six months of my life come into my mind. Every day I looked forward to seeing them and they always went out of their way for me. All the nurses were wonderful, male and female. When a person is in hospital for months, she needs to see familiar, friendly faces. I got used to everything and everyone. I appreciate every single thing the nurses did for me – and there were many. Each day, they'd spend time with me, no matter how busy they were. They never ignored me or lost patience with me. I will always remember them with the greatest respect and appreciation – even though some of them think we're crazy! I will miss them all.

I dread moving home. At least the option of a nursing home is out of the question. My parents would not abandon me to that sort of life, and I'm grateful for that. But I have to accept my fate, focus on each day as it comes, and look for other ways to improve. I will live in Finland for the foreseeable future. That is my reality and I have to be strong now. I'm scared, not knowing what the future holds, and so a bit of involuntary howling comes out of me as we drive. Funny thing about my condition – I can't hold it in even if I try. I guess we'd all better prepare for random outbursts. There's nothing I can do about them, if they come. And I suppose they will come.

One of the great things about going home is my mom's cooking. At Käpylä they let me eat whatever I wanted, and let me order my food, but at home it will be very different; it isn't cafeteria food. She makes the most delicious dishes imaginable, and since I haven't got much to look forward to, at least I can look forward to my meals. However, my äiti will help me so that I don't eat too much. I will have to lose this weight I gained at Käpylä.

Every one of my family and close friends can spell so I can talk to anyone, and they will take time to be with me and to have a conversation. There isn't a computer for me at home, but we'll manage.

I think I'm pretty ready to move back home, but when we get to the driveway, I start to shake. Terror sweeps over me, and panic and despair, and helplessness. I'm going home to what? I've lost everything: my modelling life, my possessions – my pearl green Cadillac, my independence. As I'm wheeled to the door, I feel worse than I ever imagined possible. I'm moving back home, like a little girl who can't make it in the world on her own. Jeez, can't even walk in the door of the house where I grew up.

Every memory of the stroke comes flooding back to me. I feel dizzy all over again as I see the staircase to my room and remember that night – the last night I was in my room. I can't go there now.

My feet stick out and get in the way of the doorway. Another spasm. My fingers clench. The howling starts. I feel like a dying animal about to be put down, but doesn't want to – wait! On the other hand, I think I would celebrate it.

I have no plans. What am I doing here? What will I do with my life? Nothing. I'm only going to waste my time and my parents' time. Just sitting. That's my future. Just sitting silently, unless I get to howling like I am now.

Oh!!!!!!!!!!!! OWE!!!!!!!! HOWL!!!!!!!!!!

"Florida," my mom shouts over the noise, my noise. "Florida, Kati. We're going to Florida, remember?"

"Florida, Florida," my dad chips in.

My noise stops. Silence. They look at me.

"Ah," I say. And then we all laugh. Yes, we are a crazy bunch.

Returning home brings cherished memories, painful reminders of who I used to be. I'm totally aware that I will never be that person again. I'm mourning my own death, but I'm living in a horrible hell amidst the surroundings and people I grew up with, people who love me, and want the best for me. What torture can be worse than this? It hurts so much. I want to throw myself into a bottomless lake. Yet there's something else too: I feel sorry for them, all of them. Not just for me, because I just have to put up with this, but I can see they feel so bad, and I feel bad for them. Yeah, they feel helpless, and there's nothing I can do to make them feel better. It's horrible. I'm ruining their happiness, and it isn't even my fault. How can I make this better, when I'm the cause of their sadness? Something is changing in me. I'm not sure what it is, but something. I want to die, and yet I see the pity in their eyes, and mourn for them. What is this difference, and is it worth living for?

CHAPTER 21

Learning to Cope

I feel like I'm stuck on a rollercoaster. You know, they are fun for a ride, but not as a lifestyle. One day up, one day down. Sometimes I think I'll get better, other days I don't. But there has to be a way off this ride, so I'm going to find it. If there IS a way to regain my health, I'll try everything I can.

Irina lights up the room when she walks in.

"Kati! It's so good to see you." Although there is a tinge of sadness in her eyes, I know she means it.

"Oh, it's not as cosy as upstairs, but it's still nice! And at least this way, you don't have to have everything in your room from the time you were five years old." She rolls her eyes.

Yeah, all moms like to keep us as little girls, don't they? But mine has let me choose to leave most things up in my bedroom. I have some nice things here: some mementos and some new things, to make the space my own.

"So," she says, "shopping is going to be different. But so what? We can still shop."

You bet. And it is going to be different. I'm going to buy things I like and not wait. Wait for what? Life is too short. I'm going to dress up for today. There is no reason to save something for a special day or a special occasion. Today is the special day. Today's the special day because I'm alive and with my best friend. Today is special because I can breathe. Today is special and I'll dress for it.

I won't save and save anymore either. I used to do that, but from now on I'll enjoy the money I have to spend. One thing I've learnt is to buy what I want (as long as I can afford it, of course) and not always wait for the sales or think too long about it, wondering, "Should I? Shouldn't I?" Instead, I'll just get what I like and enjoy it. That's my motto.

The great thing about being with Irina is, because we know each other so well, we don't always have to use words. That's good, because I don't have any to say. Also, she doesn't avoid the 'elephant in the room'. She doesn't pretend like there's nothing wrong or changed, but she doesn't let that bother her or interrupt life.

"Let's eat," she says at the shopping mall. And we do. Sure, she has to feed me, and yes, people are staring. Sometimes a waitress will ask her if I need an extra napkin or she'll bend down and talk to me as though I'm four years old, but we just laugh about it after the waitress goes. We both know she means well and just doesn't know what to do.

Days out with Irina are fun, and the moments of silence between us just show how close we are. Other days are bad, for no particular reason. My state of mind seems to match the state of the house; a bit of adjustment is being undertaken so the house is adapted for me. The inside has to be changed to fit a wheelchair throughout the downstairs. Since the stairway going upstairs to my tiny haven is narrow, there is no doubt that I will ever go up to see my room again, not unless I can walk. The living room is my bedroom, temporarily, but an extension is being built to create a permanent bedroom for me. I'm trying to keep positive.

The builders are outside working and each morning they hear howling, but they can't find a dog, so today they asked Isa, "Where's the dog?"

Oh, how embarrassing. I wonder what my dad said? I know this whole situation is hurting him so much. My whole family is doing everything for me. They love me so much, they are sparing no time or expense to care for me. I see how it is changing – distorting – their lives. I am the cause. If the doctors are right, and I will be as I am today forever, then nothing is ever going to change for my parents. It's too much for them, or for me, to live with. But I can change this, and I will. I've thought of a simple solution that will help everybody.

My mom is home for the day. I'm ready to tell her something. Today I will need her help, but if she agrees, it will be the last time.

"A-i-t-i."

"Yes, Kati."

"H-e-l-p-m-e."

"What do you need, Kati?"

Äiti, *it's time. You have to let me go. I just want... to die. You know that. Now it's time.* I have to tell her all this, get her to listen, get her to help me.

"Äiti." I stare for a long time, to get her to watch me closely. "It's time to give up."

She turns and grabs the handlebars so fast, and wheels me outside. There's a blast of sunshine into my eyes. Today I hate the sunshine. At least if it rained it would be easier to be miserable.

"Kati, you are tired and you are scared," she says. Her voice is quiet but very stern.

"No," I blink. "J-u-s-t-h-e-l-p-m-e-d-i-e. L-e-t-m-e-d-i-e. P-l-e-a-s-e!"

She looks me in the eye, and doesn't even pause to think. "Give it a year," she says. "If nothing changes for the better in that time, we'll talk about it then."

I can tell she won't budge. Stubbornness runs in the family. Mostly she has always let me do what I wanted. Rarely did she ever insist on her way. But occasionally she called the shots. I can see she won't budge on this one. All right then, one year. The clock starts now.

She starts to stroke my hair. She doesn't say anything, but I can hear her breathing. Actually, her presence and her voice are so calming. I'm her little girl again, afraid of a thunderstorm and the lightning in the dark. Except this is not a freak of nature. This is a nightmare monster that's as real as any can ever be. So, that's the deal – one more year. Okay, I have to get through this. What choice have I got?

Some days I get letters or phone calls from friends overseas. That's exciting. It's hard on Äiti when there is an international phone call. When my American friends call she finds it really hard because her English isn't very good. It is getting better.

"Who is that?" she'll say loudly, as if speaking louder will help them get past her accent.

Then she points the phone at me so I can hear. We get by, that's all I can say, because my mom is an amazing woman.

Mom's routine is crazy. She works all day, and then she comes home at night and takes over from the assistant. Obviously, I have to have assistance around the clock, but the government will only supply one during the day. So when Äiti comes home from work she looks after me, evenings and weekends, and in the middle of the night when I need turning in bed, she gets up and does it for me. No more carpet rolling. She's a gentle, real-deal lady, and she says she doesn't mind, that she's able to go right back to sleep. When we go for outings, she has to lift me in and out of the car. She does all this (my dad's heart is a bit weak) and never complains. I could have been put in an institution, but she wouldn't allow that. I'm glad. But still, it has made her life very hard.

I have to tell the truth – some days are very dark. When I write letters on those days, I spell everything to my mom, and she writes every word I dictate. These letters are very hard, but with close friends I have to be honest.

Dear Jamie,

Well, you know about the stroke. I'm home at my parents' now. And I just want to die. My mother has said I must wait a year before discussing it again. I wait, and I hope somehow, I'll just die.

That's the sort of letter my mother writes for me. It can't be easy for her, but she does it, and she sends it; I know I can trust her to do that.

I get letters back from these friends too, letters that tell me they're sorry for what has happened to me, and to hang on, that something good will happen for me, to keep going and not to give up.

I'm not able to do anything for myself and because I'm not even supposed to be left alone very much, it means my mother and I have to hire assistants to take care of me. Eventually, we are able to have a second assistant. That's good news in that my mom won't have to do as much as she did when I first came home. But it isn't easy to hire someone, and having assistants in your life is difficult for lots of reasons. It means I have no privacy. It's one thing to have your mother look after you; it's another to have total strangers. I can't even go to the toilet by myself. How do I cope? I just blank out whoever is with me. Not in a rude way, but I sort of pretend I'm by myself. Fortunately, it's a skill I perfected when I was modelling and people stared at me in the street. It's come in handy so that now I don't live my entire life feeling embarrassed.

I've had to learn to trust complete strangers. An assistant is a stranger at first. Sure, they have an interview with Äiti and me, but an hour's introduction is hardly a basis on which to form an immediate, intense sort of bond. Trust is not a little part of my life – it's huge. I have to trust that my assistant won't burn my mouth with hot food, or drop me while she's lifting me from my bed to a chair, or let me drown when I'm bathing. In a way, I have to trust this person with my whole life, sometimes being with them for hours at home, with no one else around.

One time, my assistant was wheeling me around downtown, and she got lost in her own thoughts. A car was driving straight at me! Obviously I wasn't struck, but it was a close call.

I have to trust that I won't be forgotten in the shower, or on the toilet.

I have to believe someone will wake up and turn me at night. This is very inconvenient for her, but very important to me. I have to be put in the foetal position, otherwise I can't fall asleep. I need the cooperation of another person to have patience and get my body position just right, with a cushion against my back to keep my body from rolling. My neck, arms, hands, legs and ankles all have to be in a relaxed position. Then, in the middle of the night, someone needs to be available to hear me wake them so that I can be turned, otherwise the pain and stiffness become impossible to bear.

I do let myself see the funny side of life. Once the assistant took me in the car, and had to pop in somewhere for something.

"I'll be right back."

Sure, no problem.

For security, she decides to lock the door at the last minute, just so no one would hassle me. So, just as she's closing the door, she pushes the lock down, and then slams the door.

Yup, I'm safe inside – only so are the car keys. She's left the keys in the ignition. Yeah, I'm locked in the car with the keys. And I'm locked-in and can't retrieve them. The assistant realises what she's done pretty quickly.

"Oh my! I can't believe it! Kati, I'm so sorry," she shouts through the closed window.

I laugh. What else can we do? We laugh. She calls my dad. We eventually get the car opened.

My whole life is in the hands of other people, and I have to trust them to take care of me. It really is like being a helpless baby, who can only grunt, howl or cry to get attention.

They say that when you're dying you don't regret missed days at work, but you do regret missed days with family. Well, I'd say that must be true. The people who keep me going are my family and friends. Another saying is that stroke victims like me don't usually live more than a year or two after the stroke, and that it's usually even less than that. That's because they wither away and die. I think that would happen to me, except my family and friends have made darn sure it doesn't. Of course, some of my friends have found my situation too difficult to handle, and others live very far away and can only send notes or phone occasionally. But everyone who has contributed, and even those who had to leave my life after the stroke, I'm grateful to, because time with them has given me a full life.

Only sometimes do I think like this. Other times are more bitter than sweet. I'm really lonely. There's a big black hole in my life, I guess where modelling used to be. Friends try to help, family is doing everything possible, but there is nothing they can do really to change anything. I'm fat. Life is finished as I know it. I don't know how anything can change.

Mikkeli doesn't have a lot to offer, but it does have one thing – swimming. It's an activity that keeps me fighting. When I'm in the water my body is lighter, like there's less gravity, and I can move. I need help to stay afloat, but my legs do kick and I get exercise. Believe it or not, when I swim I am a moving being. My muscles are alive. It's fantastic and life feels good.

I have a physiotherapist who helps me to swim. She walks behind me, with her arms around my waist, as we walk the length of the pool. I push myself hard, even harder than the physio does. And she's willing to try new, forbidden (i.e. risky) exercises with me. I repeat and repeat exercises until my muscles start to tremble. I did it in ballet, I did it in the gym, so why wouldn't I push myself that hard now?

Swimming takes a lot of concentration. Triggering any muscle of mine takes serious work, willpower, and strength. As long as I stay patient, which I admit is a big handicap for me, I will do my best to get this stubborn body moving. The so-called experts aren't always right. I'm like a different woman in the pool. I know I look like a precious doll when I'm sitting totally still in my black Rolls Royce chair. But in the pool, I *can* walk when the therapist holds me just a little for balance. It isn't easy – yelling helps – but I *can* do it. In the water, I do push-ups, sit-ups, kicking, and I even run on my tiptoes. I keep exercising, because it feels wonderful and because I'm not waiting for some miracle to cure me. Of course, it'd be awesome if it does happen, but in the meantime, I work hard at getting my body moving. Usually after forty-five minutes in pool therapy, people get cold, but not me. I'm told I'm an unusual case. I'm out of breath and burning when I leave the pool, because I absolutely make the most of the exercise. It feels wonderful to make my muscles work. I leave the pool hot, exhausted, and happy with myself. Ta da!

To get in and out of the pool there's a hydraulic lift. It is *not* a romantic contraption, but it's secure and effective. As humiliating as this part of the procedure is, it's worth it, because with sweat pouring down my face and breath heaving, it gives me as good a feeling as I had on that last shoot in the hot Canary Island sun.

Oh! It's as if I'm on the rollercoaster again, with good days and good thoughts, bad days and bad thoughts. I just triggered my own sadness. How do I stop it? I have memories from my life before the stroke that take me down into a funk that's so hard to get back out of. Like just now. What just happened? I was happy a second ago, but then I remember being well and with friends or colleagues, and I collapse inside my head. I just want to explode. I guess sometimes loneliness tries to get out of a corner I've managed to put it in, and it stares at me. Like right now. I stare back at it, and stare and stare, until it backs down and goes back in its corner. But sometimes it doesn't back down, and it wears me out instead. Today it isn't going away. It's robbing me of this nice moment of triumph, when I've worked hard, moved my legs and feel great, but instead of joy, I feel like I'm suffocating. Like I can't breathe at all.

Get me out of here!

But where can I go? I'm stuck inside this useless body and no matter how much swimming I do, I still have to get out of the water eventually, and be like a seal flapping helplessly on land. Actually, a seal does better than I do on dry ground, because at least a seal can bounce and waddle its way back into the water.

Back at home, I listen to some funky music. It helps to lift my mood. Listening to Prince is dynamite. When I listen, I feel a perfect union between my thoughts and my emotions. I may have limitations, but what am I made of? Flesh, blood, thoughts and emotions. Only my flesh doesn't work too well. The rest of me is A1 – perfect! The music takes me off this wheel of fortune and helps me think towards making something out of my life; no matter how hard the fight must be to achieve it. It's been almost a year since the stroke and I'm fat and angry. Fat, because one pleasure I have is to eat what I want, and angry because I can't make my body do what I want it to. So, I can either stay fat and angry or do something about it. The music is loosening up my thinking. I'm beginning to see some things that I didn't see before. Maybe it's just because I'm getting older, but mostly I think it is because of this new life I'm living as a disabled person. I'm learning.

Even though this thing has happened to me, I have to make this life work. No one else can do it for me. Hey, it's the one thing I can do on my own. I do still have some independence; I have the independence to think for myself. Whee! It's a good thought, and I'm on the fun part of the rollercoaster again, feeling excited.

When I'm feeling bright, I can think straight. Now, in fact, I know there's a thing I've gotta do. I'm gonna cut someone free. Little do I realise it's going to turn out to be me.

The phone calls from Warren have continued all through my rehab and since I've been home. When he calls, I listen, he cries, and then I cry. While love can withstand anything, I realise that this is stupid. I'm ashamed to say it, but I just can't see the point of this long-distance tragedy continuing. I have nothing to offer him, and he can't offer me anything either. That's not his fault, of course, but it's just the way it is. I sent him faxes during rehab and my mom writes letters for me since I got home, but the stroke happened a year ago and really, I don't have anything left to say to him. My messages tell him about my progress, which is pathetically limited, and now that I realise nothing major is going to change, at least not for a very long time, I have to think – what is the point of continuing this relationship? We're thousands of miles apart anyway, which is another reason to end it. Of course I still love him, but there's no future. Zilch. Nothing. Honestly, we had a rocky relationship when I was healthy. He's got this huge mid-life crisis thing going on, in spite of the fact he's only thirty-one, and his bad way of handling it, with booze and pills, and cutting himself, is crazy. I remember crying to make him stop, but it never seemed to do any good. I was twenty, too young to know how to help him. Now I'm also too disabled.

Although he came here to visit after the accident, which was really romantic, it was a disaster when he was here. Sure, it was good to see him when he came from LA. I'd missed him desperately, but when he visited me in the hospital he was really a mess, and making life harder for my parents than it already was, drinking vodka in the morning and walking around the city in shorts in below-freezing weather. Didn't they have enough to cope with about me, without adding worry about him too? Even if he came here again, I doubt it would be any different. It's obvious he can't cope with this situation, and I can't help him to cope, or try to make anything better for him. Nope, there's just no future. I knew it before I had the stroke, now it's so obvious. There is really no point in continuing letters and weekly phone calls. Something has to be done to stop it. I guess it's going to be me that breaks it up, since I don't see him doing it.

This is the last letter:

Warren, you have to go on with your life and forget about me. We don't both have to suffer. I'm sick, on the other side of the world. It's okay. It's time we both moved on.

For the first time in a year, he doesn't call me at his usual time. I'm relieved. Oh, I do notice, and I cry a little when he doesn't call, but that's more because it makes it abundantly obvious that that part of my life is definitely dead. I'm relieved more than I'm sad. In a way, I had the excuse of the stroke. I didn't have to make up a reason, or argue about my career plans, or explain anything. There's a very good reason for breaking up, and I'm relieved it's done. I wish him well, but honestly, I just don't love him anymore. I hope that doesn't sound mean, but it's just the way it is. Now, I will get on with my life, such as it is. At least that part of it, the crazy Warren part, is over.

So, now what? I do have one idea, and with a bit of strategic planning it might work. There's a big day coming up that most people on earth celebrate – Christmas. I'm going to make it the time to thank other people in my life for everything they've done for me this past year.

What a year! Do I really want to celebrate this year? No way. So instead, I am going to celebrate the people that have made this impossible year possible. Christmas 1995 is going to be the most memorable Christmas, and the most generous, because I'm going to thank people for their goodness to me.

"Isa, I need your help." My dad is all eyes, as I spell out to him what I want him to do. "Take me shopping, Isa." I hope he can take me today.

"Irina, let's go shopping," I say on another day.

"Äiti, will you take me shopping?" I ask my mom. Of course she will.

I get my two assistants to help me too, and each of all these people thinks they're the only one helping me. I've asked them to keep our secret, so no one knows everything that I've bought, or where I went. Each person who took me shopping doesn't know I shopped for them with somebody else. This is going to be my big thank you Christmas surprise. I'm so excited.

Christmas 1995 arrives. I watch as each person gets a present from me although they never in a million years expected it. I'm so happy to say thank you and to surprise absolutely everyone. It's fun and it's the best day I've had since that horrible night at Mikkeli Hospital.

"Kati, this is amazing. How did you find it?"

"Kati, you've always been the best shopper. Thank you so much."

"Kati, you're the best. This is such a thoughtful gift."

Et cetera.

I'm broke now. Do I care?

Life is not about saving money. It's about using it for its purpose – to spend it to bring happiness, whether it's for me, or someone else. To be honest, it's more fun when it *is* for someone else.

Way back when I was planning this, I knew I'd have to give a message. I'd known I'd want to say to everyone how I'm feeling and what I'm thinking. I've already learnt that, for delivering serious stuff, it's much better to write it down.

In that way I can explain myself better, and there are no misunderstandings that happen with spelling (sometimes people guess and get on the wrong track). I can take time considering and creating the message, instead of delivering it, and the person receiving the message can concentrate on the message instead of reading the spelling.

A little before Christmas, we got a computer that I can use to send messages.

"Whap! Zip! Send!" The computer is great. This morning I've written a message to have Äiti read out loud to everyone.

Dear Everyone,

This has been a year to forget, except that I have to tell you, life is really good. Today life has a new meaning. You have all been so patient with me, and I am so grateful. If it hadn't been for the stroke, I would not have learnt what I've learnt, which is how much we love each other. And that no matter what life throws at us, it's a chance to learn. Challenge isn't to break us, it's to make us. So now, I'm going forward, all because of you. Merry Christmas!

Love, Kati.

As my mom finishes reading the message, everyone that's sharing Christmas at our house today is crying, including me. But they are happy tears.

I surprised them all with presents, but I got a surprise too. You know what I'm learning? Life is not about winning or losing. It's about doing our best to turn a negative into a positive. Life is full of surprises, some good ones and some terrible ones. That's just the way it is. Life is about balance and living life means balancing ups and downs. Finally, and most important of all, it's about getting on with life. It's been almost a year since I woke up in the hospital. I wanted to die, but my mom said, "Wait a year."

Now what? I'm moving on.

CHAPTER 22

How Could this Happen?

I suppose the number one question that loomed in our minds immediately after we got over the shock was: could this paralysis have been avoided if the doctors had acted quickly at the hospital?

The second question was, of course, could I have avoided this?

It's inevitable, I guess, that we should start to wonder how this crisis might have been avoided, and even to look for someone to blame. My dad especially was really angry and wanted answers. I don't think he would mind too much if the doctor on call the night of the stroke just dropped dead one day. The doctor at the clinic diagnosed a bad cold. Then, the one on night call at the hospital assumed I was on drugs, rather than in urgent need of medical attention. She was the one who could have tested for a stroke right then and there, as it was happening. I think if one day she woke up dead some people would think that was fair. Maybe. I mean that night, you'd have thought by the way the medical professionals behaved, that I had all the time in the world to be rescued. The story could have ended very differently if someone had understood what was going on and took immediate action. Maybe. But it doesn't do any good to brood over the past.

Worse is to wish for revenge. If I get even, will I be able to walk? No. So, what's the point? I've lived in LA. Lots of people sue doctors – I've never seen it make anybody happy.

I'm no detective, so maybe I'll never know how this happened, but I think the cause was stress. Sometimes our bodies warn us and we have to listen to the warning signs. I didn't. Didn't I keep being warned by headaches, fainting spells and nausea? But I just didn't get it. By the time I realised I needed help it was basically too late. That's how I look at it. In life, we get hints; we receive an intuition, or a sense of what we should do. Every time we miss that hint, that issue comes back with more intensity. After several ignored hints, I found myself in a situation where I was forced to face the fact that I was not invincible. With my health, I ignored stress, months of prolonged headaches, dizzy spells and horrible sickness, like the time on the bus on my way to Helsinki Airport. Even before I got on that bus I wasn't feeling well. I ate fruit, thinking that after eating, I would be fine. But immediately after the bus pulled out, I felt worse and worse; the bus's motion made me feel terrible. Looking out of the window, watching the trees pass by so fast – as though they were jumping – made me feel so dizzy, and sick. How did I manage to keep my lunch inside? I couldn't sleep to make the time go faster. I just sat in a crash position, with my head down on my knees, until the bus finally got to the airport. That was a big warning, but I ignored it. I just wanted to work.

Within myself, I'm an extremely competitive person. A workaholic. I never understood that I should slow down, and that's the main reason why I got this stroke, I think. I worked my body too hard. The stroke was my body's way of saying 'enough is enough'. It's been a whole year since the stroke and now is the first time I could even think about how? Or why? I think it was my own stupid fault. Now I get it. Experiencing this stroke has been a major wake-up call – I have to accept responsibility for my health.

My mother doesn't blame me. She thinks the stroke had something to do with health issues right from the start of my life.

"Kati, you were born at least ten days late. After I went to the hospital, more than once, and was sent back home, I finally insisted on staying at the hospital. Eventually, it was a caesarean birth, and everything was fine. Growing up though, you were prone to throat infections and had a tonsillectomy when you were still a little girl. After that, you still got infections. LA was particularly bad for your throat, and you had a throat infection when you came home for Christmas last year, just before the stroke. I wonder if somehow, the infection attacked your brainstem and made things much worse during the stroke. Do you remember you went to the bathroom the morning after that horrible night, the morning of the tenth? You moved then. But after another day, you didn't move anymore. Maybe the infection made things worse."

She asked the doctors once, would the stroke have been prevented if we'd gone to the hospital before I went to the Canaries? Their answer: "Probably not. Because in someone so young, it's unlikely we would have considered stroke as a possible threat, or looked for any signs."

Risto, my father, blames the doctors' incompetence. 'If only' is his way of thinking about it. If only the clinic had taken our complaint seriously. If only the doctor on call at the hospital had asked more questions at the beginning. If only the nurse's assistant had spoken up more loudly, or had been listened to. Yes, there was a nurse's assistant who told us after the stroke that she had suspected a stroke early in the evening; all the signs were there. If only the doctor had asked for a CAT scan right away. If only the nurses had watched more closely. If only the doctor had realised Kati was fading slowly, slowly – slowly becoming paralysed. If only. But my dad is gloomy, and 'if only' doesn't help him. It doesn't help anyone. He's right about one thing though, they all could have been a lot more positive in the hospitals, especially the one giving me *The Sentence* – telling me I'd never move again, and the ones getting me ready so I could go to rehab. Over and over we were told, "there's no hope." That's the worst thing they could have done.

There is one other little thing that is a part of this 'how could this happen?' that we'll never really know about for sure. That is the pill. Femoden has certain side effects and warnings that I wasn't informed about. No one said, "You might get headaches at first, or dizziness, and then these symptoms should ease off." No one told me, "The pill can cause stroke in extremely rare cases." No one explained, "If you feel unwell when you take this pill and if it gets worse, it means it doesn't suit you and you need to stop taking it." No one communicated anything. Not even that it can cause you to gain weight. If I'd known that, I might not even have taken it. I do remember having to diet extra hard after I started taking the pill, and it was harder to keep slim, but I never thought there might be a connection with taking the pill. And finally, I remember that horrible night of the stroke, and the look that on-call doctor gave me when she learnt I was on the pill. It was right after that when she started to take my deterioration seriously. I mean, shouldn't the doctor who prescribed the pill have communicated the possible dangers to me?

I suppose even the pharmaceutical companies are sensitive about this. There is actually pharmaceutical insurance for people with injuries that might be due to their use of prescription medication. I wonder how many people claim coverage for being on Femoden when they get sick? I know I'm not the only one.

My brilliant äiti found out, quite at random, that there is a pay-out for people who get a life-changing sickness while they're on prescription medication. We didn't have to sue anybody. That would have been hell to live through and even if we won it wouldn't be worth the pain and trauma caused by a court case. But there is prescription insurance and thanks to Äiti's resourcefulness, we claimed. I have received a significant settlement because I'll never be able to work. Never? Well, I have to keep trying. One day, there is going to be a place for me, where I can do something meaningful with my life. I have to believe that. All of this has happened for a reason. I didn't die; I'm totally a mess, but there is a purpose to it all, and when I find it, I'm going to tell the world.

I'm fairly philosophical about this. I mean, what's the point of answers when they won't change my condition? I've just got to get over this and move on. My mom said I had to wait a year. I'm glad she said that. I wanted to die, it's true, but dying isn't going to help anyone. There has to be a reason to live. I just have to find it.

CHAPTER 23

Riding Forward

Äiti has told me I have to go to some locked-in seminar. Why do I want to go all the way back to Helsinki for some stupid meeting with a bunch of other people who are locked-in just like me? Will we be a lot of people sitting around, staring at the ceiling together? But it's one of those rare occasions where my mom decides. I don't have a choice. It isn't as if I can refuse to go, is it? I mean, I go where I'm taken and I stay where I'm put.

The drive there is fine, and when we get there I see not everyone is able to sit up. I'm not the worst case! (I'm not the best either.) And we actually have fun. I meet some nice people and we laugh. I guess since I didn't expect anything, I wasn't disappointed. And it wasn't as bad as I thought it would be. If there's a next time, I won't be so sour about going.

The next idea my parents have is riding therapy. Actually, Riitta from the rehab centre suggested it to them on one of their conversations after they brought me home. She owns a horse herself and loves riding, so that's how she got the idea. Humph. Remember I was scared of falling out of bed, even with the bars? Well, I've basically become totally terrified of heights since the stroke. They know this. You would think they'd be sensitive to this, wouldn't you? But no – they are determined to put me on top of a horse.

"Do you want to give me a heart attack too?" I spell. Äiti really *should* have let me die when I asked her.

How the heck am I going to ride a horse? Never mind that. How are they going to get me on top of it? And once I'm there, then what?

We drive to the stables, and I'm doomed to try. As I'm wheeled towards the paddock, panic surges and I start to howl. I honestly can't help it. Then one leg kicks straight out involuntarily. I'm in an all-around bad state.

What's the point of this?

"Balance..." the therapist tells me – she looks like a nice woman, who speaks softly and looks straight at me, not at my parents, "... is a very important part of muscle development."

I get it: since I can sit in a wheelchair, I can enhance my balance.

"Are you up for it, Kati?" asks Äiti. I stare back at her. She knows me so well. She knows, now that I'm facing that stupid horse, I won't give up.

So, after all the fussing and arguing, the big moment has arrived. They manage to get me up, and I'm sitting on top of this huge horse. He's as gentle as a lamb, by the way. I think animals have a real sensitivity about people who are vulnerable. I sense that he won't cause me any pain, at least not deliberately; that's obvious by his sweet nature. Still, when I look down, the ground seems a long way away.

The horse starts to walk. I really am going to die, and I start to sound like it too. The therapist has already been well warned, I guess, so she just ignores my howls and keeps the horse going. I have to give it to him, the horse I mean, he hasn't gotten scared of me, even though I'm wailing my head off. Gradually, I manage to calm down and I'm sitting quietly on this beast of burden. I'm exhausted at the end of the experience, more because of my terror than because it's a physical ordeal.

I go back again and again; the therapy will continue for a year. I can feel my body adapting to the horse's movements, not right away, but gradually. Every time I start, I howl, but that gets shorter and the riding gets longer. I'm able to sit up better and better, without aid, which is the whole point. Each time I get on the horse, I ride for longer and longer, and my body is getting used to sitting up without my brain telling it to. The first day there was one person walking along each side of the horse, but eventually, there's only one person walking beside my horse, and that's just for security, not because I actually need their physical support.

I have never fallen. Not once. Not even when the horse galloped. This riding therapy has done wonders for my balancing. Before the horse therapy, I couldn't sit straight for very long; now I can.

Lesson: you've got to face your fears if you want to triumph.

CHAPTER 24

Florida Bound Once More

A full two years has passed, and it's 1997 before we can finally go to Florida. It beckons, and we're on our way – my mom, Irina, and me. Dad will stay at home to feed the cats, he says. Actually, he's not a fan of visiting the USA.

My attitude towards going to Florida is that I'm returning there after an unexpected delay, and with a slightly different purpose than the original one, which was to model. In fact, I won't go to the modelling agency at all. I could contact Rico, the wonderful photographer who gave me that inspirational note to 'go where the models are' but I probably won't. I'd hate to see his face when he looks at me. It would just make us both sad. Instead, I'm going with an altered purpose to the original one, you could say, but I'll enjoy Ocean Drive and the sun, and oranges aplenty.

The flight will be so l-o-n-g. I don't eat or drink anything before we go, because it would be impossible for me to get to the toilet. If nothing goes in the spout, nothing will have to come out the butt. I'll eat when I get there. Since I've always been disciplined about food, this is just a rerun of an old behaviour. It's funny the things we don't think about when we're working that we do have to think about when our situation changes. We take so much for granted. This disability has me thinking more clearly than I used to. Thinking better can't be a bad thing.

The flight is horrible. To start, the flight attendant seats us in the wrong row, which wouldn't matter at all except for a very big, very loud, very horrible man. He wants his seat. Not a row back, not a row forward, but his allocated seat. So we have to move, and it's very difficult.

"I don't care what this moron's problem is, it's *my* seat." You get the idea.

But landing is the start of our wonderful adventure, and wheeling around Miami is quite easy. The ground is smooth, the ramps are gradual, and the spaces are wide for wheelchairs. Most people are sympathetic and courteous. We have a sensational time.

When we get to the hotel, we are greeted warmly and there's a fantastic surprise in store. We get an upgrade! The three of us are sent up in the elevator to near the top floor. The suite is like something out of a James Bond film – absolutely gorgeous.

"Look at the bathroom, girls," my mom says, and Irina wheels me over. It's massive, with a sunken tub.

"Ooooh," says Irina quietly.

"Oh, Kati, you must have a bath in this!" says Äiti. I'm thinking the same thing, and I'd "Ooooh" too, if I could.

We unpack and get settled in and then Irina runs a bath for me. The others help me in and I have a wonderful, long soak. There are bubbles, candles and dim lights. It's hot and every muscle in my body gets relaxed. I'm not left alone the whole time, but we do manage to set up a way to make sure I don't slip, so they do leave me on my own for a couple of short times. It's wonderful.

After about forty-five minutes, my toes and fingers are wrinkly and it's time to come out. The water is drained; we wait patiently so I don't make them get wet. But then, we have a huge problem: I'm slippery, the bathtub is deep and my mom and Irina aren't strong enough to get me out.

I burst out laughing. Mom looks a bit worried, but Irina starts to laugh too. Äiti giggles. We try wiping me dry while I'm still in the tub, and then one of them reaches under my armpits from behind to lift me. It's a no-go. Then the other tries. No success. Then they both try, in tandem, like a two-person bicycle, one behind the other, pulling. Then they try one on each side of me. It gets harder and harder to lift, because we are all laughing so hard. We simply cannot call room service for this because I am, of course, stark naked.

"Right, I have an idea," I spell to my mom. She understands quite quickly.

"Irina, let's spread the towel behind Kati, under her back, and across the back of the tub. Then we pull together."

How did I come up with this idea? I do not know, but they pull and we manage not to tear the towel or break my back.

They heave, I breathe, trying to make myself as light (not dead weight) as possible. And, it works! Once I'm out of the bath, we're all lying on the bathroom floor in shrieks of laughter. Oh, God, that is worth the trip, and it's only our first night.

Another evening we go to see a musical, and I have to pee before the show. I cannot emphasise too much the importance of monitoring my dietary and digestive functions so that I can time my needs and not interrupt anyone, or worse, have an accident.

Mom wheels me into the toilet.

"Kati! There's no room for the wheelchair in the stall," she says.

"What?" I try to see past her.

We look at each other, and there is a moment of silence while we each are thinking what are we going to do?

"You'll just have to stand," she says.

Standing therapy, without a therapist or a stand, in the middle of a public theatre bathroom. Hmm.

The lights flash, indicating the show's about to start. I've got to try to stand, and hurry.

"Come on," she says, and unties my belt.

My legs find a strength I didn't know I had. They just keep me up like never before.

Sometimes, you just gotta do what you gotta do, when you gotta go.

When we finally get to our theatre seats, feeling like we've run the marathon, Irina knows better than to ask why we look hot and tense. I sigh, and soon we are all relaxed, and totally enjoy the show.

The trip to Florida gives me an experience of life I didn't know I could still have. Life really can go on, in spite of any challenge. Even though I am with two companions, I have time to think during my time in Florida too. One of the main changes that being paralysed has had on me is that I notice I've become emotionally very sensitive and intense. I used to be so carefree. To cope with the tension, I have learnt to numb myself, just to blank out my surroundings. Things can happen around me, and I can sit looking like there is nothing going on. On the other hand though, if something happens that touches me inside, then suddenly the clouds burst and my tears pour out. I overreact in that moment because all the other feelings that have been pent up get released. It's what was happening when Warren visited or phoned. Over the last two years I've had my fill of drama and sadness. Now, on this trip, I almost have enough laughter to make up for it all.

On our way back to Finland, of course, we have airport security in Miami. I got used to the frisking part when I was travelling as a model. There is always a woman doing this job and they do it all day long. It can't be easy, touching people as discreetly as possible, yet having to be thorough. But they do it, and always with a stony face. Until today, when the security woman sees me. The expression in her face changes totally when she has to frisk me, somebody who cannot move at all. I can't raise my arms, for example. I see she has tears in her eyes, and I feel really sorry for her. I try to joke, to make her feel comfortable. But she really finds it hard.

"She's my best friend," Irina says gently. "I promise she's not hiding smokes or alcohol," and she smiles.

The woman just nods, trying to keep her composure. Not everybody can handle the situation easily.

The flight is long again, but I'm put in my correct seat from the start and there is no disruption on the way back to Finland. As we start to descend in Helsinki, I think every architect should sit in a wheelchair and try out their street and building designs to actually feel how the new spaces will work for someone in that situation. Maybe in Florida they have rules to cover wheelchair access, or maybe some major architect's mother was wheelchair bound in Miami. Either way, if I lived in Florida permanently I'd have a much easier time than in Mikkeli.

Of course if anyone expected going to Florida would eliminate my travel bug, they'd be dead wrong. Even before we get back from our trip, I'm planning the next one, and it's going to be really super amazing!

It isn't easy returning home. I'm glad to see Isa, but I feel more helpless and useless than I did before I left, and life looks bleak. I have to figure out how to live. In Finland there has to be something to do, something to look forward to from week to week, something that will help me to keep my condition improving. But what is it?

CHAPTER 25

Searching for a Cure

Travel. It isn't everything it used to be, but it's something to look forward to and something fun. I embrace it with everything I have. It's a time when we can be together as a family, because if we go somewhere Isa likes, he'll come too.

Bali, Indonesia, sits just south of the Equator where the Indian Ocean meets the South China Sea. It's a tropical paradise, and I love to go wherever it's hot. After the trip to Florida, I set my sights on Bali.

My body has always preferred heat, and even more after the stroke. In fact, what was a preference has become a near-necessity. A person who is paralysed feels the cold more than someone who is not. There is no movement and so the body cannot keep warm naturally. I am a perfectly healthy person, apart from being immobile; I can't remember the last time I got a cold or the flu, or any aches and pains (or throat infections). Since I cannot move, I feel cold most of the time. Wind feels freezing, even if it's 15°C. In summer, I can feel a chill when shadows fall late in the day, even if it's eighty degrees. For protection against the cold I wear throws almost all the time, because if I get chilly, it takes forever to get warm again.

When it's cold outside, my body functions slow down and my whole body naturally folds inward to keep warm – my shoulders tense and curl in to protect myself from the cold and my arm and leg muscles shorten, which interferes with my sitting position because my elbows may not reach my armrests and I can fall over. And my legs go spastic, so they stick out like logs; it's difficult to be wheeled around with my appendages sticking out. Sometimes, every muscle in my body starts to hurt so that it brings even a tough girl like me to tears. Needless to say, the thought of a warm climate is inspiring.

As I'm staring at the ceiling in my room I imagine myself sitting on a warm mat next to the sunny sea, sipping a cool drink; or floating and kicking in a swimming pool, or the sea, which is as warm as bathwater; or just lying on a towel drenched in sunlight. Travelling isn't just for psychological treatment, as Sinikka Soderholm, my speech therapist, recognised, warmth is also a physical treatment for the paralysis. Bali has been calling me, and finally the day comes when I answer.

I prepare myself for the very long journey. Arriving in Bali is everything I could ever dream of. It's breathtakingly beautiful. One thing I hadn't thought of is the nightmare of being transported in a wheelchair. If Florida pavements are much better than Mikkeli's, then Bali's are a hundred times worse. I wonder if it's harder for me, being bumped and jostled over the uneven stones and dusty potholes in the roads, or for the person who is trying to push me through them.

Before being bound to the wheelchair, I never gave a thought as to how streets are uneven and full of bumps. The simplest trip can be so difficult for people in wheelchairs, especially when we have to pee. Luckily, I always have someone – or even two people – to push me. On this trip my mom and dad are with me, and also an assistant, and quickly we discover how kind and helpful all the staff are at the hotel. The hotel manager introduces herself to me; she knew we were coming because we asked specifically for a room on the ground floor, so that I could be wheeled easily here, there and everywhere, without the need of an elevator. But she is nearly crying when she speaks to me.

"You must have three hours of massage, every day. Complimentary, you no pay. I will arrange you."

Of course I do not refuse. I meet Putu, who is the hotel masseur. He is an artist, and he gives a better massage than any I have ever had. The first massage makes my muscles so relaxed that I feel like I'm cured, as though the war is over. The tension that attacks my muscles is gone; I feel light, as though I could move, rather than as though I'm lugging my limbs like pieces of lead. He also recommends that I go to see the Grandfather, an old expert.

"Maybe he cure you," Putu says.

National Geographic did a piece about the Grandfather, and so he is a Bali celebrity. He must be very wise; maybe he can do what modern European medicine cannot do. Did I come to Bali to be cured? There is always a possibility that something can take away this life in a wheelchair forever. I have to try this.

After I'd left rehab, total strangers who would recommend alternative medicines and treatments had often approached me. Some ideas sounded absurd, some seemed incredible. My reaction was always, "If there is a way to regain my health, I should try it." That's also what I think when Putu makes his suggestion.

After another massage with Putu, he reminds me about the Grandfather.

"He very hard," Putu warns. "Everyone screams when he touches." But I am tough. I may cry, but I know I can endure the pain.

To get to the Grandfather's house is an adventure in itself, even before the treatment starts. The Grandfather lives to the north in the mountains a few kilometres south of Munduk, over very difficult roads and pathways. Come with me on a four-hour drive over a volcano (inactive for now) and down into a ravine with narrow winding roads all the way. It would have been a much shorter journey if the roads hadn't been in such a bad condition. The car is screaming, and so am I. I think I'm going to throw up, but there's one good distraction – tiny monkeys along the way. They are so close we could almost reach out and touch them as we drive past. Towards the end of the road we get stuck. The car can go no further, and if we tried to use the wheelchair over the rough terrain, it would fall to pieces along the way and in the meantime, give a heart attack to the person trying to push it. As we are looking ahead at the prospect of being stuck forever, a little man appears out of the distance. It's the Grandfather, and when he comes to us, he speaks to our driver in his language. Without warning, he scoops me up in his arms, like a sack of potatoes. Everyone else follows us on foot. The walk is smooth somehow. He doesn't jostle me at all. The Grandfather is strong and wiry, and I seem to float down the rest of the way.

When he massages, his fingers are nimble and he works on my muscles for three hours. His fingers dig into me like knife blades, but I don't scream. (I confess I do cry.) It hurts like hell, and when he's finished I feel refreshed, as if I've just come out of a tough workout of ballet, stretched, invigorated and jelly-like, all at the same time.

The interpreter tells me, "This time just for muscles. Next time for cure." Is it possible? I do dare believe it. Well, he does have magic fingers. Why not for a cure?

I'm in Bali for two wonderful weeks. I make several visits to the Grandfather, but I am not cured. Some nights I cry because I'm disappointed that I still can't move. Other nights I cry because I'm so happy to feel free. The massages are worth every minute of pain, because at the end of each visit I feel like new. It's amazing what pain I was living with. If I could stay in Bali, maybe I could not move, but I would be pain free.

"I will come back," Mom says to the hotel manager for me. We have all become friends and I am so happy.

It isn't until I'm halfway home on the plane that the darkness begins to set in again. The Finnish gloom rests on me like a blanket of cloud. I do not know how to get rid of it. Promising myself another trip keeps my hopes for happiness alive.

We do return to Bali the next year for two months, and I visit Grandfather every week. We planned the long trip so I could try different therapies. We had to write to the embassy of Indonesia to ask for permission to stay that long.

It is a wonderful trip, but I am not cured. I realise this is my mission in life: find the end of my paralysis.

Next we go to Thailand, because of the weather and the hope for a cure. Throughout history, in real life and in mythology, people have gone to great lengths to find the secret of eternal youth. Let me tell you about my two experiences in Thailand, as I search for the cure for paralysis.

Like Bali, Thailand is another South China Sea oasis. I am used to long aeroplane trips, and I know as long as I don't have to go to the bathroom, I can handle the travel. We arrive at the Thai resort, a really nice hotel that promises a perfect holiday. The warm sun and some deep massages (which are less painful and less effective than Putu or the Grandfather's) make this a perfect holiday. Everybody is happy. We make friends at the hotel and have good times, eating, drinking, lazing in the sunshine. But the holiday is not over. Harri, one Finnish man we've made friends with, tells us about a man who can cure me.

"If he cannot do it, it cannot be done," he tells us. And so begins my first story: 'The Tale of the Long-Tail Boat.'

My experience is so terrifying it is hard even to put black humour into it. The excursion to meet the man who can cure me is planned, like everything in my life has to be. He lives on an island and so it will be a challenge to get to him. Do you think I'll rise to the challenge? You bet. Whatever I have to do, I'll do it, if it will get me out of this chair for good.

The next day, Harri tells us we must go on a long-tail boat. A boat ride sounds nice, I think.

The idea to take a boat ride to see this amazing man, who is sure to cure me, is irresistible, but I should have known from the way the excursion started that this was a very bad idea.

"There's the boat," Harri tells us.

Now we see why it's got its name – a long-tail boat. It's narrow and long, and looks very unstable. It's just a giant canoe.

Oh, we're going in that? I think. It's the one time ever I remember being glad I couldn't speak, because the words coming into my mind would have talked anyone out of taking me.

The pier is as rickety as the boat is wobbly. This is my second warning, but I ignore the warning. You'd have thought I'd have learnt by now not to ignore danger signs!

I can do this, I decide, and blink, "Yes," to anyone watching. Actually, everyone is watching me except Harri, who is so keen to take me on this trip he's already in the boat and waving the rest of us on.

Of course, the wheelchair cannot be wheeled onto the narrow boat; in fact, I must be placed perfectly because the boat is so narrow that if I'm in the wrong place the whole thing will tip. Safety belt on for the journey? You bet; if the boat tips and my chair goes into the water, I'll sink like a stone in one second.

Suddenly I'm lifted, chair and all, by the guides and the boatman, even some of the other thirty tourists help out – Harri's too busy waving, remember? It's a six-foot drop from the pier to the boat, so my stomach feels like I'm in an elevator in free fall until I am finally placed in the centre of the boat – dead centre, for balance.

We're off from the pier in no time and the scenery is the most beautiful I've ever seen in my life. Rocks jut out of the water up to twenty-metres high; the water meets the blue sky, blending perfectly as I gaze into the horizon. I think to myself, *Wouldn't this be a grand place for a honeymoon?*

When we see the island where we are to stop, it is too shallow for the boat to go inland. Another smaller long-tail boat approaches. We have to be transferred onto this other boat, which is just a shrunken version of the original long-tail boat, and even less stable. It takes blood, sweat and a few screams to get me onto that over-sized canoe and into the shore.

When we get to the island where the miracle worker will be, I have to be lifted off the canoe. The crowd thins quickly and there's only Harri to lift me. Of course, he can't wheel the chair on the sandy beach, so he throws me over his shoulder.

I've done this before, I think to myself. Only Harri is not wiry and muscular like Grandfather in Bali. He's tall, firm, a bit like you might imagine a Viking to be. Somehow, he manages to carry me, although during the trip up the beach I feel like I'm on a rollercoaster with a severely drunk man as the driver. Finally, Harri sets me down in a chair in a restaurant.

"Where is the miracle worker? Do we see him after lunch?" my mom asks.

"Miracle worker?" Harri pauses for a minute. "Oh, no. He's not here. That'll be another trip, another day," he says.

OMG. How can this be? I just endured the fear of my life and for nothing! I'm not very hungry for lunch. I wonder why? It's just as well; I would have thrown it all up again on the way back along the beach. I notice Harri isn't enjoying his lunch either; I'm sure he's trying to work out a better way to transport me. We don't relax, even though we do sit on the beach for a little while before it's time to get back into our canoe. I'm too worried about the trip back to the hotel to relax.

Back to the canoe and they put me on first. I am a steadying influence, it seems. They put me sideways this time, rather than facing me forward. They're sure this will have an even steadier effect, but when some big lady decides she's in a hurry and jumps into the canoe, I really do nearly fall into the sea. If a child had done that, they would have been scolded for sure. But her? She doesn't even notice. Meanwhile, my mom is in front of me, holding on to my chair. Otherwise, for sure, I would have gone under, tipping the whole boatload in the process. I'm riding high again, like an Indian princess on an elephant, until I'm transferred onto the big boat for the return ride, which is pleasant and without trauma. We're old hands at this now.

The final shock comes when we get back to the pier – the tide has gone out and we can't actually reach it, so we have to make one more trip in the shallow canoe. Another OMG moment. Everybody seems to panic that they'll have to walk back to the pier, so they all pile into the canoe at once. This time even Harri notices I'm rockin' and rollin' and about to drown. He tells them, "Calm down. Nobody will be left behind." I might have been, under the coastal waves, deep, deep under.

I've already told you that there is no spontaneity in my life and that everything has to be planned out. But even the best-laid plans can go completely haywire when we don't have proper communication.

"Oh, you thought we were going to see the miracle man today?" Harri blasts that evening over dinner. "No, that's tomorrow. Are you ready?"

It seems no matter how hard I fight, I keep having to face obstacles thrown in my way. I think I can handle something, and then a horrible twist comes along. What? Life isn't tough enough after having a stroke, I have to be paralysed? What? Life isn't difficult enough after becoming paralysed, I have to face pain? What? Life isn't difficult enough after suffering excruciating pain that I have to face drowning like a dead weight in a bottomless sea? Well, with every experience there is a lesson. I'm always keen to learn. Do I provoke the challenges? I don't know, but Thailand has one more life-changing lesson for me, and I can't resist taking it head-on.

Harri does eventually get me to the miracle man. The trip to that island is much less eventful and not worth commenting on. I don't know that he's mute, but the miracle man says nothing to me in any language. I'm laid on a mat, and my chair and assistant leave. The man begins by tapping all over my body with a bamboo stick. Right from the start, I notice his tapping is not light. Since my muscles are rock hard, it hurts a lot, but if this will cure me, then I will not resist. He taps for over an hour, hitting harder and harder, on my back, my arms, shoulders, legs, feet. I'm a tough cookie and I bear it for a long time, but eventually, even I can't stand it any longer. The tears have been coming and coming, and finally I scream. He stops.

How much longer would he have carried on if I'd not screamed? I think the man is either a sadist or an abuser. His miracle is to beat his clients with a stick in specific places all over their bodies, so that their muscles will become tender. Tenderised is more accurate! I feel like a piece of meat, bruised and beaten beyond recognition. A piece of dead beef would fare better under his stick. Practically sobbing, the assistant comes to me and I can see in her face what I must look like. We cover me so my dad won't see. I think he'll kill this miracle man if he sees my condition.

I finally get the message, not the massage, that I needed to come to Thailand to get: there is no miracle cure. There just isn't. I should have seen it coming when I got into the canoe. I should have known this was a lost cause when I saw the stick. It's time to give up this fight for a cure, and find the next fight. Sometimes, you just have to read all the signs that point to 'give up and do it'.

On the flight back to Helsinki I'm thinking about Thailand. The weather was perfect, the people were friendly and the terrain was as bumpy as Bali, but that road in Thailand led me to the end of something – the end of my search for a cure. The next logical step is to ask, "What now?" What do I do with the rest of my life, knowing I'm going to live this way forever?

I suppose deep down I've always known I would not be healed. But I had to try. It took a silent abuser to get me to finally realise it was time to give up. I suppose it's inevitable that some of the obstacles we have to face in life will defeat us. But we don't have to live defeated. I can wallow in the fact I'll never be cured, or I can accept I've endured the worst humiliation ever in search of a cure. At least I know I've tried everything – I've never given up before. This is a new experience for me. I feel oddly relieved. I don't have to fight anymore. As I gaze at the ceiling of the aeroplane, I wonder at the life lesson I'll carry forever. I realise misery is not a reality, it is a state of mind. My mind and my spirit are as invincible as I choose them to be, and paralysed or not, I don't have to give up on life. I look at my sleeve and know there are bruises underneath. Once these external bruises heal, and they will heal like all bruises do, I'm going to live accepting there is no cure. That's the only way I'm going to find out what I'm still here for. Once that happens, it won't matter that I'm paralysed, because that reality is just a part of the puzzle that is my life. I'm rockin' and rollin' for a reason. I'm just not sure what that reason is – not yet.

CHAPTER 26

Accepting the Passage of Time

We're on another trip to Bali. It will be as wonderful as before, but this time we're going to linger there for two months. It will be good to revisit our friends.

Before I go, I organise a big party to hold an auction to fundraise, so that my assistant can come with us. The party's a huge success. Seventy wonderful people come, and I surround them with good food, a beautiful candlelit setting, singing and dancing entertainment, and my dad speaks up to thank everyone for coming to the party that I planned. Assistants, family and friends helped so much. Everything was sold in the auction and I'm sure I will plan more parties like this. Now, it feels good to be returning to Bali, home away from home.

At the flight transfer at Kuala Lumpur, Malaysia, I buy a digital camera. It's a good camera – cheap price compared to Finland, although people are staring at me so much, I should have sold tickets! Do they stare because I'm blonde, or because I'm in a wheelchair? Maybe both. But they don't hide their staring. I guess culturally it's okay to stare in

Malaysia; in Finland or America it would be considered rude.

When we land in Bali, Putu meets us at the airport, and by the time we're at the hotel, we've already planned the regime treatment. I'm going to trust him with the whole thing, like putting my life in his hands. At least I know he's trustworthy. He won't bruise me or kill me with a stick. I won't be healed, but my muscles will feel restored.

It's nice to come back where they know us. We are given such a warm welcome, and I'm happy to see them; they encourage me too. They tell me I'm so much better than I was the last time I was here. I live in my skin so I can't tell, but they assure me I've made progress. Nice. There is one drawback – we always have to take the bad with the good. Somehow, I've managed to forget one entire suitcase of clothes that I'd packed, at home. How could I do that?

It is my mother's birthday. My present to her is a four-hour beauty treatment. For once she gets pampered. That doesn't happen very often, but she really deserves it. We all celebrate together with a cabaret dinner. Fun! Some people would hate to travel with their parents. Not me; I owe them my life. My mom comes on all my trips. She's put her life on hold to raise me all over again, her invalid infant-child, and I'm so glad she gets the pleasure of our travels.

I'd love to have a child. My mom's an excellent role model on how to be a mom. I suppose, though, if I had a child I'd miss being able to hold him or her, and my mom would end up doing a lot of work for both of us. That wouldn't be fair. If she didn't organise, travel with me and make sure the assistants did their jobs, who would do it? Well, the least I can do is show her my gratitude with some pampering. Four hours isn't nearly enough, but that's as long as she'd lie still anyway, and we all have fun in the evening together.

The next day, while Putu is giving my muscles their aerobic workout, I stare up at the sky – my ceiling during the treatment. I used to feel like I was in Purgatory, a sort of living hell waiting until I die. But it's funny; now that I know I can't be cured, I also know that life is the best it can be, and I am happy. I have good friends and family, I experience fun activities and surprising adventures, which are mostly safe, and of course there is even room for romance. Two adorable men in my life right now, are trustworthy, beautiful and although long distance, are good friends. They will stay in my heart forever. Would I be as attached to them if I wasn't paralysed? Thinking about them makes me wonder why I ever went out with Warren, when both of these men are healthy, kind and sane. Wouldn't you think that an ex-model, who is a non-verbal quadriplegic, would have to say goodbye to romance? Well, not this girl. It's true that I can't go dancing out on the town, but these wonderful men, whom I've known since I was in high school, have never completely left my life.

When I was seventeen, Jari and I dated for a month, but I broke it off because keeping him in my life could ruin my career – if I stayed with him I might never become a model. So many girls give up their dreams, because they fall in love and give up. After the stroke, Jari re-entered my life. He's been a good friend and a romantic one too. He comes to visit me, then he sails around the world, and although he's moved to Monaco, he visits from time to time.

"Kati, my darling, how gorgeous you look." And, "Kati, I bought this for your wrist. Oh, it's a bit small. Never mind, we can change it."

It's a bracelet and it's beautiful. It's small because I'm fat! He can't change it. He brought it from Monaco, but he's too polite to tell me I'm fat. I'm going on a diet! I've done it before and I can do it again.

The other love is Luigi – he still writes to me. Luigi; my first experience, my Italian lover. And how he writes. He writes so romantically, it's as if the stars of heaven sit on my shoulders. He says he has found no one else. Never? I can't imagine that.

Neither of them is married, but I think Jari has met someone recently because he hasn't written in a while. The last time he was in Mikkeli he didn't visit me. At first I was angry, but why should I be? He must have someone. Well, that's okay. We are still friends.

Lately, Luigi's emails have really touched my heart. Maybe I should finally let him see me. Maybe not. The shock might hurt him. But then again, if I love him, I must let him see the way I am, to see if he can get used to it. I don't know if I could live in Italy. All this time, I never stopped studying Italian. I thought I just liked the language, but maybe it's more. I would have to go there to live if we got married, because that's where he works, and he certainly can't get a job if he came to Finland.

I don't tell these things to my mom. Not even to Irina. They are my secret loves, these two men. Well, Jari isn't really a secret, he used to visit, but no one knows about our engagement. And Luigi has never been to Finland; maybe I've been a fool to keep him away. He is so loving, I can't believe I've not realised the feelings I have for him. How could I overlook that? Sometimes we don't see things that stare us straight in the face.

My mind wanders. A long massage is so liberating. There are a thousand thoughts you can have when your mind is free to wander, and sometimes they all pile up on top of each other. Being in Bali again, and for such a long time this time, allows me to see what life here would be like. It isn't a permanent place for me – it would get boring. But I am so grateful for the time here. My hair has turned blonde too, from the sun, but I think I'll keep it this way. It will be a memento of my visits here. I love Bali.

As we fly home from Bali, I don't know what's next, but whatever it is, it will be good, because I've learnt that everything is okay when you have a good attitude. It's an old saying, but I count my blessings: wonderful people, amazing adventures, life-changing lessons.

I do not forget the details of the people in my life, or the places I've been. I'm able to hold on to all my memories; it's quite easy when you have limitations to enhance your other senses and abilities. For example, I see, I hear, I taste, I smell, I just don't touch, but I do feel, and every single sense I use is heightened, not distracted, by moving around. I think I have a super-brain. I don't think it's better than other people's brains; I just use it more. It's kind of funky, the brain, it learns by interacting and whatever mental stimulation I can get makes it function better. It's bad enough that I have to fight to keep my muscles from degenerating; I refuse to let my brain go numb.

I remember the doctors said the longer I couldn't use some part of me, the less I'd ever be able to use it, but that just isn't true. Sometimes, out of nowhere, I can bend a knee or an elbow, or make some other movement. It especially happens when I'm swimming, then my body moves as it wants to, and sometimes even when I instruct it to. It's really important not to take what a doctor says as absolute truth. Oh, we shouldn't ignore medical advice entirely, but we should take it with a pinch of salt, as the saying goes.

Another thing I like to think about is how the human body moves with the tiniest detail and the smallest impulse. A lot of the time, I don't think people realise they are moving, but when you can't move at all, boy do you miss it. It's funny how we can miss great big boulders of understanding in our lives if we only pay attention to the details. I have learnt to compensate for not being able to move. I've heard that blind people have an enhanced sense of hearing, and smell. In so many ways, my other senses have been enhanced by not being able to touch. But best of all, because I can't move, and because I had such excellent therapy on my facial muscles so that I could eat, and at least move my face, I have a super-expressive face. I'm happy when wrinkles appear because it means I've been able to move my facial muscles. Hurray! I'm pretty transparent when it comes to showing my emotions, which is a real bonus shortcut to having to s-p-e-l-l everything out.

I don't think I'll be capable of getting dementia – my memory is too well-trained. I remember TV schedules, so I don't have to ask somebody what's on. I remember where I store things, so I don't have to ask somebody to look for them. I remember people's faces, voices and names, because my assistants change and I can't rely on them to remember. And I remember all my clothes and shoes. I like to dress up every day, because every day is a special occasion. I need to know which clothes are where, so I can choose what to wear. And, of course, I need to remember my wardrobe in order to choose from it. I have built up quite a wardrobe over my adult life, even if my ups and downs in weight have made some pieces obsolete from time to time.

I like to think, to get things clear in my mind. I could write a book if anybody would read my thoughts. Would anyone else be interested in what I think about? Do other people wonder about what a paralysed person does with their time? I'd be interested. I wonder if other people who are paralysed would like to know they aren't alone in their experience. I am not sure that non-paralysed people take the time to think. I didn't much. I guess that's something good about not being able to move. It slows you down; you have time to wonder. I bet most people don't make time to just look up at the ceiling, or the sky, or think about what's going on in their lives. A paralysed person can do that. A paralysed person can do a lot more than people think they can; especially more than what the doctors expect.

I'm no longer a model, and yet I still have the starvation dieting for losing weight. I need to apply it again. Sure, I can swim, but that's about the only real calorie-burner I can do, so I have to watch what I eat. I'm just like anybody else who goes on holiday. Most people on holiday overeat, right?

Once I lost twenty-five kilos, that was when I was in the absolute pit of despair. I was so low I didn't even realise it wasn't normal to want to die. The fog I lived under was a constant drain. It was a couple of years after the stroke, before Jukka and Anu were getting married, that I was shamed into dealing with the depression and the weight issue that symbolised it. Thank God for my brother's wedding, or else I might still be in that horrible state.

After rehab, I had decided that eating was my one pleasure, and I continued on the same path of eating to get some enjoyment in life that I picked up at the Käpylä Rehabilitation Centre. I do not blame anyone for this, because I was used to having what I wanted in life, and I think anyone who was caring for me didn't want to deny me this one freedom I still had. My mother knew I wanted to die, so she let me eat what I wanted to cheer me up. I guess in a way it was a slow, tasty kind of suicide.

Eating wasn't just for pleasure, but to hide behind my despair. I mean, when a twenty-year-old's life and dreams are killed in one night, I guess it's pretty understandable that she would want to die. Well, the eating didn't cure that, and in fact, it made the situation much worse, because it made my immobile body seem ugly to me, and made it even harder for me to move. What woke me up from this eating habit, and made me super-aware of how I was really feeling inside, began at Christmas, 1996. One year had passed since the wonder-Christmas, where I had given wonderful presents to everyone who had lovingly cared for me through the stroke. That was a happy time, but by Christmas 1996 I was a year fatter, and although I was happy on the outside, inside I felt so lonely. Everyone else had a partner; my partner was a chair. Many others were having babies. I was so happy for them, but inside it felt like needles attacking my lifeless womb. Their lives were moving on, but mine never would. That, of course, was a lie, but depression is full of lies and loneliness is a smooth killer, let me tell you. I was suffocating, little by little, every day of my life. My psyche was deranged. My thoughts and emotions were totally messed up. In deep depression, loneliness whispered into my ears, as though it was my best friend, giving me pity, consoling me in my grief, and strangling me slowly.

In the summer came Jukka and Anu's wedding. I just didn't want to go. I – or my wheelchair – would be noticed and would take the limelight away from them. That's the excuse I made, but the deeper reason was that I was ashamed. I couldn't face people looking the way I did. I got a nice dress for the occasion, but I looked awful in it, because I was fat.

I went to the wedding, because my commitment to Jukka and Anu was stronger than my shame, but I made a promise to myself that I would lose that fat, and started immediately. Eventually, tetraplegic-me lost twenty-five kilos, by taking extreme notice of what I ate. It was damned hard, and I'll never let myself get that fat again, I promise. I also noticed during that diet that, as the kilos went, so gradually did the depression, until one day I didn't hate my situation anymore.

They say what doesn't kill you makes you stronger. Well, that is certainly true. Depression let me get fat, fat made me ashamed, and shame gave me a wake-up call to take care of myself. It's funny – I can't take care of myself at all physically, but life is a lot more than physical. Attitude is what makes you die or thrive. I reached that place of accepting the situation, even though it was a while before I gave up looking for a cure. I cannot pinpoint the exact moment acceptance came and anger left, but I understand something now – there are cards that we are dealt in life, and what matters is what we do with them. Now that I know my hand, there's nothing else for me to do but play it, and make the best out of what I have.

Sometimes, I'm reminded that some situations are not as difficult as others. My good friend, Jamie in LA, who took me to his high school talks to help kids stay away from drugs, got cancer. He has a little boy, and went through hell. I may be permanently disabled, but at least I have life. Jamie had this scare and the whole family had to go through it too. Thankfully he survived.

Making the best out of life includes people, parties and travel. That's my plan until I have a better one. I may not be healed on the outside, but I will have a rich life. The present is full of presents, the past is full of memories, and the future is full of promises waiting for me.

I have great friends all over the world, and some close to home too. Sometimes, people forget to keep in touch, but that's okay, I'm glad for what I've got. Sometimes, I do get disappointed, like not hearing from Jari for a while, but I can let that go. I am happy that Luigi and I are connected, and he may finally come to see me. We love each other, I just don't know, now that we've both admitted it, where we can take it. Some people never know love, and I do.

*

Before any romantic reunions with my long-distance men friends, I'm taking another trip, and this time it's to LA. I need to face those memories of my modelling years, and see my friends. I haven't been back since the stroke. I'll see Stephanie and Jamie too. It'll be weird to be back, but I'm so excited. Mom and I are packed and on our way.

The flight is long, but okay. It's kind of eerie at first, being back in LA. I remember all the places we used to hang out, all the shoots; it's as though I never left, but of course I've changed.

One thing about LA that is great is the variety of people you meet. Wherever I go, I meet amazing people. It happened before the stroke and it still happens now. I met the man who invented Gummy Bears and Hershey's chocolate today. I guess LA is that sort of place. I remember meeting celebrities just like they were ordinary people with regular professions, sometimes on shoots and sometimes in bars and restaurants. Cool!

Jamie's neighbour invites us for wine in his garden. It's an amazing spot, near a lake.

"Yes, I once cooked for the President of the United States," the man says.

"You like food?" says Jamie. "Come over to our house. Kati will make you a Finnish meal you'll never forget."

I want to hit him. Is he crazy? His friend cooked for the American President and I'm supposed to impress him? But

Jamie is such a good friend. He drives us around Santa Monica, our old neighbourhood. He takes me to Warren's mother's, and we have a wonderful time. When he gets a call from Warren, he does not automatically put him through to me without checking. "Thank you," I say, "no." The past is past, but eventually, I change my mind. Jamie's mom holds the phone for me.

"Oh, Kati, it is so nice to talk to you. You are in my dreams, I have never forgotten you. So beautiful you were. You are now. Okay, Kati, your life, our life together, was cut short. Oh, it's so tragic..."

Like every other reunion, there are tears, only with this one we don't really end up laughing. We hang up and I think, *yeah, we needed some closure, but I'm glad that's done.*

Next we go to see Stephanie who has lived in LA for a while now.

"Kati!" she shouts. She can totally ignore my wheelchair. She's still crazy, skinny and my best modelling girlfriend.

And then Jamie takes me to our favourite potato soup restaurant, the one in Santa Monica that we went to every week. I'm sure they cook other things, but I just have potato soup, as always. Jamie is a friend forever.

LA – it's good to come back. It makes me laugh to remember, and it makes me cry. Mostly, I'm just glad to have great memories and even better friends.

When it's time to say goodbye there are lots of tears. I can't help it. I'll never be able to control the tears. I could blame it on the stroke, but of course it isn't just that. It is wonderful to be in LA again. My life is so different now, but I wouldn't change all the wonderful people and memories. We are all born to experience life, and I've experienced more of life, more of the world, more of people than most. I have nothing to regret and no one to blame for how things are now. If I could do one thing I can't do now, it would be to dance. Apart from that, I get on the plane knowing I've got more travels ahead, and more people to meet.

"Jamie, it's been a blast," I type.

"Ditto. I'll come one day, you'll see, I'll surprise you in Finland."

I cry some more, but he doesn't seem to mind. He clings to me before I go through security. I think he's as bad a crier as I am. Good friends for life.

As I get on the plane, I know I have hours ahead of me to stare at the ceiling and to think. I have an idea of how to fill my time when I get home. I wonder what other people will think of it.

CHAPTER 27

In the Blink of an Eye

I've come back from California with a plan. Little do I know that 2005 will be a breakout year.

"Äiti?"

I bounce ideas off my family and friends.

"Irina, what do you think if I write a book?"

"Fantastic. You can do that, Kati."

I surround myself with people who believe in me. Some days are tougher than others, but the people around me are consistent. A lot of the blessings that I have are in the shape of good friends. There are those who have been here for me all along. Some others took time to adjust to my situation and gain the strength to be around me again. And, of course, there were some who vanished; I don't judge them because it's a very difficult situation to handle, and not everybody knows how to deal with it. Gee, I still meet people that don't know how to handle themselves around me.

You could say that life has been unfair to me, stripping me of all control of my body. Well, I don't have time to think about that. I want to live my life – I don't want just to survive, I want to enjoy life to the fullest, just like I was doing before the stroke. I was depressed for two years, but then I broke free. All the clouds in the gloomy sky have gone and life has opened up to me. I'm thinking about what possibilities there are for me. I can't model, but I do want to contribute. So, what have I got to offer?

I have a sharp sense of observation, sharper than I used to have, that's for sure. I notice little things, and read manners, gestures, and body language pretty well. I can sense when people are telling me the truth or when they are lying; who is sincere and who is fake; who is confident and who is nervous. I've spent years watching conversations, and learning to recognise signs that tell me what another person is hiding; I don't just hear what they're saying, but see what they're telling. I wonder how this sense of observation can be useful when I'm with other people. If they're trying to hide their unhappiness or their pain, I can communicate with them, to help them recognise what they might not even know themselves.

There's one activity that I do more than anything else, and that is keep in touch with my family and friends. I share my thoughts and feelings, and stay connected to them. I can't emphasise enough how my dark days have often been overcome simply because someone came to visit me, gave me a call, or sent me an email – responding to one of mine. So if they can do that for me, I guess I can turn on my sensitivity and be there for them too, or someone else, if they need me to be.

Ever since the stroke, I've been doing the occasional interview for magazines and organisations interested in my experience as a locked-in person. This reaches a peak with COGAIN-Network. Organised through the University of Tampere, Finland, they develop eye-tracking devices for the speech-impaired, who are also immobilised. I'm honoured to take part in testing the EU-funded high technology. I'm useful, I get to meet new people, and it's fun. I become their spokesperson for locked-in syndrome. I'm honoured to take part in this research, even though it's just to be their guinea pig. I work with Mick Donegan of Cambridge University in the UK, and learn how to 'whisper'. He spells by staring at the letter, I nod when the letter is correct. After a complete sentence, he spells it again to make sure it was correct. It's a silent but profound experience. I also meet Lisa and Kathryn, who spell in different languages. In German, for example, it's a completely different system, but it works. It's fascinating learning with people of different nationalities, as not only are spellings different, but how we spell varies. Finns are reserved; they stare and think. People of other nationalities engage in different ways, often being very animated and energised.

Unrelated to COGAIN, but equally interesting, I receive a request from the Information Technology and Communication Centre, Tikoteekki, part of FAIDD, the Finnish Association on Intellectual and Developmental Disabilities, to take part in a seminar about communication for people with complex communication needs. I am honoured to open the seminar with a speech about the importance of communication technology. R&D for people like me is really fascinating, and I get to be involved, experimenting with new technologies. Wow! How did that happen? All because one day, soon after I came home from hospital, my mother said, "You're going to a meeting," and I did.

I guess you could say I'm at a kind of crossroads now, you know, a time when I have a major decision to make – what am I going to do with the rest of my life? Well, I want to enjoy life, but living just for me isn't enough. I've always had a goal. When the goal of modelling ended abruptly, at first I didn't have another one; I tried to get well so that I could have my old life back. I travelled to find a cure. When I had to lose weight for my health and self-respect, it gave me a purpose. I did it; I pushed through. Now, I'm pretty sure that without a goal, I may go into a funk again, so, I need something to work towards. And I think I know what it is.

A book will do that. I'm disabled, which I can either see as something to stop me, or as an obstacle to get over. I'm disabled for a reason, which has changed my life, and that leads me on. It doesn't stop me, it just points me in a new direction. It's just a chapter in my life, not the end of my story. Yes, I've been through hell and living paralysed is not a delight, but when I make the best out of any situation, the situation just gets better. So, I'm going to grow into this new life, whatever it is. It sure isn't an ordinary life, but then I never wanted an ordinary life, did I? I'm going to make that disability a feature rather than a barrier. That's what a book can do.

My mind is a powerful tool. I may not have the physical choices most people have, but I have the same brain as anybody else. I'm going to put it to work in a new way. The computer is my biggest source of help in this department. That might sound ungrateful towards all the people who have cared for me, but they care for me because I can't care for myself. The computer helps me to be independent, and it's the one way I can be, and the one way I can help others, because with the computer, I'm on a level playing field. Because of the computer, I can write. It's the one thing I can do on my own. Using the computer isn't easy, in fact it is super tedious, but I have a program on the screen, and a gizmo that gives me a mouse on my forehead, and I can move that mouse to touch the letters on the program one by one. Yeah, it's slow, but I like work, and I can sit at the computer for twelve hours a day if I have to – I want to. I can do the same thing that other Internet users do on the computer – I can communicate to the world. "Hello, World. Who's out there?"

A few years ago I did an interview for a magazine, because the editor heard about me and thought I made a good human-interest story. That article got a really good reaction, which shows people are interested. There have been other interviews since. A book will offer more detail and more help. I'm going to start my book knowing it will make my situation, which is pretty unusual, public. People will be interested, and even more, some who go through hell like me can get a new perspective. I want to give hope to people like me, who are locked-in or in some other way are limited by their physical situation.

It's a total surprise to me that I'm in much better condition than some others with this fate. When I was in rehab, I hated the gym because everyone else had the use of their arms and their voices. My condition was so much worse than other people's, but since then, whenever I've been to group meetings, I've seen that others who are locked-in have it far worse than I do. I think I can help.

I realise I am a very strong person, and I believe God doesn't give a person a burden that is unbearable. In fact, I think only strong people are given such challenges. That's a message of hope to everyone in my situation, including their family and friends. I should share it with other people, to give them a new perspective. I don't wish anybody to go through this, but some do, so if I can at least make it easier by sharing what I've learnt, then I will be making a difference, and that is a good purpose.

I plan to write about my life being locked-in. It won't be filled with pity-party tear-jerker emotional helplessness stuff. No way; it'll be an autobiography to give the details of my life and what I think. Why? Because I think I can give hope and strength to other people and their families to keep going, no matter how tough life is.

In fact, I just remembered something... Wow! I'm surprised at myself. When I was a child I thought it would be awesome to write a book, but that it could actually happen never crossed my mind. Now I'm thinking about it again. Well, I like to dream big. Let's see what happens. Where should I start?

I've seen that most people look at a person who has a serious disability with pity. The message is: that person has a right to feel sorry for themselves, and to be cynical, or bitter, or sarcastic is totally understandable. Well, I disagree. It's okay for dark humour, but not to be taken seriously, because pity and all these traps that go with it are negative and destructive. Why, if you've already got a disability, would you add to it by being fearful, or angry, or full of hate? Those are monsters that'll kill any life in you, and let's face it; life's tough enough without adding to the task.

I'm learning that the attitude I have is just as important as the attitude others have who are around me. If I deal with challenges with a cool head, knowing I'll get through them, I do. If I think I can't, I won't. That's just the way it is. Sometimes you have to give up, like when I tried to find a cure for my paralysis. I needed to be smart to know when to give up. But mostly, if you try long enough and hard enough, you'll succeed. I know I have a stubborn temper that I'm trying to improve, but in the meantime, I know it's something that gives me the fight to get through adversity, no matter how difficult. And hey, every day is a challenge, so keeping my temper cool is a bonus to making life better for me and everybody around me. The point is to look at the positive side to everything; there always is one, and that will give you a good attitude to whatever you face.

I'm wondering how I can write about this, and then I realise, I just have.

Once you develop a good, positive attitude, you've got to keep it. How do I do that? I learn to go with the flow, which is actually very hard for me. I had to learn it when I became paralysed. Until then, I organised everything. Now, I have to practise when I go out into the Internet world and share my thoughts. I have to be ready to try but willing to fail, and in the process be willing to change. I don't know what's coming next in this life (I think it's a book), but I want all the good that's available. To get that, I have to be ready to let it come to me in whatever way it might. I realise I can't expect something to come a certain way, but need to let my eyes see, and ears hear, my destiny coming. It will show itself step by step, and I have to be willing to take them. Funny that I can't walk but I can take steps.

I am definitely going to write that book. With all the journaling and email correspondences, I have been preparing myself without even knowing it. How shall I start? I think I know someone who can help me.

I helped with a magazine article once, shortly after I left rehab. Sinikka put me onto it. My good friend and speech therapist at the Käpylä Rehab Clinic, who is so kind, so wise and so generous, connected me to *Suomen Kuvalehti* magazine, to discuss locked-in syndrome. She knew I needed something to do and the country needed to know about this condition. Sinikka asked me if I'd do an interview for a magazine. I said, "Why not? I'm not doing anything else."

Leeni Peltonen from *Suomen Kuvalehti* magazine was the journalist who interviewed me. She wrote a great article that helped a lot of people. For a while, people were contacting me by email just to find out more about how I cope with being locked-in, and Leeni and I stayed in touch. I think if I ask her to help me with a book, she will.

"Kati, this interview has been really good. It's amazing we can talk to each other without sound. I love it!" That's what she had said after the interview. I think she might like to work together again.

"Hi, Leeni, will you help me write a book about my story? Love, Kati."

"Sure."

I almost can't believe it. I'm staring at my computer screen, at Leeni's answer. All this is possible because I went with the flow a few years ago, in spite of how low I was feeling. Now I'm going to co-write a book. It just proves, when someone asks you for something, say, "Yes" because it's helpful and because you never know what can come of it.

*

Some months later.

I want other people to learn that having a disability, or being different in some way, doesn't mean being less of a person. *In the Blink of an Eye* is about to be published, copyright 2006. I'm so excited. It's a journal of my life from before the stroke, through to now.

I love the title. Today, my favourite sentence in the book is, "Kati wrote in her diary, 'I love life. Those that complain have had a life that's too easy'." This about sums it up for me. If anybody wants to read a journal of my life from California in 1993 to Finland in 2005 the book is available.

It has been such an experience working on this book with Leeni. It demonstrates how important email is. With anyone, whenever I have something serious to express, air-spelling just isn't the right way to do it. I can explain myself and there are no misunderstandings when I can write it all down. Even though I have to do letter by letter, it's still faster on computer than air-spelling. Another weakness of air-spelling is that my face shows my emotions. But sometimes how my face looks isn't connected to what I'm trying to say through the spelling, so the person I'm communicating with is confused. Leeni and I did so much emailing and it was a great way to communicate. Communication is the most important and hardest part of relationships, and I think ours has been really good.

My friends and family respond to *Blink* really enthusiastically, and so do the Finnish public. I get letters from people who read it, and they say how strong I am to still be able to move forward with my life after the circumstances of the stroke. When I was a child, or a model, I didn't think about strength, perseverance, resilience or grit; I knew I was strong, but no stronger than anybody else, no stronger than I needed to be.

The responses from readers make me wonder: how did I do this? How did I move on when I wasn't able to move? The doctors had given me a sentence – I would be a virtual vegetable for the rest of my life – but they were only looking at the physical me. Neither they, nor I, knew I had the strength to overcome the situation. No one knows the extent of their strength until it is tested.

There is a saying, 'If you stand still, you are moving backwards'. Well, I don't believe it. In physics, it isn't true; even if you stand still, you are still moving forward, because time always moves forward and the earth moves.

With every breath, we move forward. I look at my life and I recognise, I am strong. I have a choice: to wither or to carry on. I choose to live and refuse to wither. So, I guess that's a kind of strength I never knew I had, until I was tested.

In the Blink of an Eye sold out really quickly. It was a real success.

"Let's have a party to celebrate," everybody says.

"Yes."

We arrange a celebration, with dinner and a party singer, only at the last minute, he gets sick and we need a substitute.

Mario is fantastic, not only as an entertainer, but he sits with us on his breaks and he's a great guy. He's Spanish, from Aruba in the Caribbean.

"Kati, you must visit my homeland. I will be going back there soon. Come, why don't you come to visit?"

"Where's home?" I spell to my mom, who asks Mario.

"Aruba. Do you know the Caribbean?"

That sounds like an invitation. Everything I've lived so far has brought me to this point. When I wanted to be a model, I pointed my life towards learning and preparing for it, and then I did modelling. That was my career. But now? I have a book published, but does that mean I'm an author for the rest of my life?

Whenever I'm stuck, travelling somewhere warm helps to get me unstuck. Not only do my muscles relax, but I guess my brain relaxes too, and I can think of new directions to take. A new destination can lead to a new direction. It may sound funny, but new directions can come up from out of nowhere sometimes. We just need to be looking so as not to miss them.

"Let's visit Mario in Aruba."

My parents are willing to travel with me. How long do you think it takes us to decide whether or not to go?

With an invitation to visit a new travel destination that fits the requirements of 'hot and friendly', and with a new friend who promises to help us find our way around, we consider our next trip. There are days when life is hard, and there are other days when we can just go with the flow. I guess it's that way with everybody. So I know beyond any doubt, I'm normal.

CHAPTER 28

Aruba Celebration

Yes, it's the right time to go on another holiday. *In the Blink of an Eye* has just had its first printing and is sold out. I've just completed my high school Italian, which I never gave up on, my parents are ready for a rest and... it's winter in Finland. Isa says a holiday begins at the local airport. He's ready to relax.

Aruba is wonderful. It's hot on my skin and for my muscles. We meet Mario's friends and family, Aruban style, and he shows us all the great beaches and restaurants. My mom is grateful for being able to lie on the beach and I am happy too. It's been ten days of pure sunshine and carefree living. We have just three days left before flying home to face the Finnish winter.

"Kati, here is another friend of mine I want you to meet."

"*Hola,*" says this man, who looks a bit too slick for my liking.

"This is Terry, Kati," says Mario.

I nod.

We've met so many of Mario's friends and family, I don't think even with my excellent memory I can remember every single one. Each day we've spent here, Mario has taken good care of us, making sure we visit a great beach and eat somewhere nice. Sometimes he's working, but when he's not he joins us. He's even learnt to spell a little. The last days of our holiday he is able to spend with us, and his friend Terry has come along too. He's a funny man, and plays a practical joke once on Mario. He flirts with me too; twice he found a flower up his sleeve and put it in my hair. Although he isn't my type, he doesn't seem to mind my chair. Most people I meet don't communicate directly with me, because they are distracted by my chair. So, it's our last night with Mario and friends. I notice Terry isn't with us.

Mario says, "I'm not working, so let me take you to hear another singer tonight." Of course, we all agree to go. It turns out to be Terry, who is the singer at the new venue. He is amazing. He keeps looking at me while he's singing, as though he's singing all those wonderful songs to me. His voice is incredible, very soft and low.

After the show, Terry asks if he can wheel my chair. He wants to show me something. Why not? So, while Mario, Äiti and the others are finishing their drinks, Terry takes me to the beach, to a private spot away from anyone else.

"This is my favourite spot in all Aruba," he says. "I want to share it with you." He kisses me.

It's so tender. I don't mind because he just completely sweeps me off my chair. Wow! I didn't expect this.

"Kati, your mother has said you are returning to Finland tomorrow. But, Kati, you must not. I am in love with you, and I want you to stay."

Of course I cannot stay. But I am pleasantly surprised by his invitation.

"Kati, of course you will say this is not possible, but you must promise to return."

He has seen my face and understood, *Yes, I cannot stay. Do I want to return?* I don't spell because he cannot read. But then he says,

"You think you cannot stay, but you are wondering if you can return. *Si?*"

Yes, that is exactly right. How does he know what I'm thinking when I am not spelling? We must have a real connection. Are we somehow meant to be together?

"Kati!" I hear my mom calling.

"I must take you back, of course," he says.

He gently turns and leads me back to my mom's voice.

The next day, as I'm sitting on the plane, I wonder: who is this man who swept me off my feet last night? I do not know.

Back in Finland, I start to get emails from Aruba immediately. Many people write to say how fun it was to meet us. Mario writes and invites us to come again any time. Terry writes to me too.

"Kati, I awoke this morning and you were not here. I wanted to cry. I miss you, my Kati, and I hope you will return soon."

How charming! I write back. What harm can it do? And so begins our exchange of romantic conversations online, until I can hardly wait to go back to Aruba.

"Kati, please come back to Aruba now, be with me, stay with me, forever, my love."

I can only think of this man – the man of my dreams, the man who isn't afraid to be with me and my wheelchair, the man who reads my face and my thoughts. Yes, we are surely meant to be together. Somehow, he has won my heart. I will go; why not? My body remembers the warmth of Aruba and my heart is ignited by love, and this kind prince is waiting for me. What could keep me away?

I realise if I'm going to follow my heart to Aruba, I must tell my friends. First, I write to Jari. It's natural, I always share my travel plans.

"Jari, my trip to Aruba with Äiti was so wonderful and something completely unexpected has happened. I never could have imagined. I met a man, who loves me and wants me to live with him, there in Aruba. I've decided I will go. I will stay there. At last, I think I've found my meaning, to be with someone who loves me and wants to care for me."

Next I must write to Luigi, "I'm moving to Aruba. I might not be coming back. You and I will always be friends, and I will never forget you, my first love."

Of course I had to tell Jari and Luigi. Jari stopped writing months ago anyway, but I had to let him know my life and my heart are moving to Aruba. When I think about Luigi, I love him too. But he is from the past. I must move forward. The girl he met is not the same now. It has been years and he knew me briefly, when I could walk and talk. I cannot do these things anymore, so perhaps he is only in love with a dream. Terry sees who I am now, he knows me and loves me this way. My future is with him.

"Kati, you are like a sister to me. I want whatever you want. But I don't have any sense this is right for you. Ever since we've known each other, our lives have been in tandem. But I don't see a connection here. This man, this Terry, is a stranger. You will be alone, and I am worried." Irina is like a sister, and it is easy to forgive her for discouraging this love. She cares so much for me, and sacrificed her life in Sweden to help me in those early years. She knows me and cares about me so much. But when she meets Terry, she will understand. She will see how much he loves me, and she will stop worrying.

"Absolutely not. This is *not* a good idea, Kati," says Isa.

Another day, Jukka and Anu are at our house. Somehow, we begin to have a family meeting.

"Kati, you don't really know this guy, and ..." I can't believe even my brother turns against me. Anu stays very quiet. What is she thinking?

"Kati must live a full life," my mother says. "Nothing in life is sure. Yes, this is a chance and it might not work out, but what is life if you don't take some chances?"

"What?" say all the others.

My mother knows me best.

"When Kati was one hundred per cent healthy, she could not be stopped. We should not stop her now just because we can."

After a long silence, my family agrees to help me to move to Aruba. My assistant will come with me, so I am not totally alone, of course. I am so excited!

When I arrive in Aruba, Terry lets my assistant continue to push the wheelchair.

"It allows me to walk beside you, and look into your beautiful eyes," he tells me.

Soon after I settle into Aruba, I start to meet some of Terry's friends. His sister Monica is visiting from abroad, and I really like her. She whispers something to Terry before she leaves for the airport, and then she smiles at me. It's a really warm smile and I know we'll be friends. I feel so welcome here, as if I've lived here my whole life.

Terry's place is a bit tight for getting the wheelchair around, but we manage. When life is right, we can make everything fit.

He's a funny guy. Sometimes little things bother him, but mostly he likes to have a good time. He takes me dancing in the wheelchair and I feel like I'm floating. We get applause and he takes a bow before wheeling me off the dance floor.

We will have to hire a new assistant, because the one I brought with me doesn't want to stay. Alice is a local woman and has her own family. That's good because it means she knows how to be 100 per cent attentive, but it also means that unfortunately, her hours aren't too flexible. Alice is used to raising her own children, and she knows how to anticipate my needs, which is a great asset for all of us.

She learns to spell really quickly. Somehow Terry can't seem to learn. I can't understand why he finds it so difficult.

"Kati, I understand you, we are beyond words. Our love speaks for us." That's very romantic.

Weeks go by. Terry adjusts to having my assistant in the house. Sometimes he asks her to do things for him, which is something I'm not used to.

"Alice, would you please prepare a snack for me. Kati is not hungry, but I am." She does cook for him, but then she comes to me when he's at work at the nightclub.

"Oh, and could you iron my shirt for this evening's performance please?"

"Kati, am I supposed to cook for Terry?"

"No, but I will talk to him."

When I do, he gets very angry. "Kati, do you think you're the only one who needs help now and then? She's here. Sometimes she isn't doing anything, especially when you are on the computer, so she might as well do something for me. Of course your needs come first, but she wasn't busy. What's wrong with her making me some dinner?"

I guess that's okay, as long as Alice doesn't mind.

"Terry, let's do something tonight. You aren't working, so why don't we go out?" I write this to him because he cannot spell.

"Kati, I work in the evenings. When I'm not working, I don't want to go out." Sometimes living with Terry is not easy. But then, I knew that would be true and was prepared for it. Sometimes he gets angry, and his temper startles me, but I guess life with my physical needs is harder than he expected.

"I'm tired, Kati, I didn't know I would have to wake up in the middle of the night."

Someone has to turn me, two or three times a night.

"Kati, I'm exhausted. Can't you...? Oh, no, of course not. You can't *do* anything."

Yes, I can understand he has a reason to be grumpy. But I didn't hide any of this from him when he pleaded with me to come to Aruba.

Our best way of communication is by email. That way I can say whatever I want in detail, and there is no rush.

"Why do you not learn to spell?" I write to him. Sometimes I'd like to be able to talk to him without Alice speaking out my words. I know I'm intimate with my assistants, but some things I cannot say in front of them, so I have to send an email him.

I write, "Terry, please will you learn to spell so we can have private conversations?"

He says to me, "I already know what you're thinking. And I've tried. It's too hard."

Other people have learnt before him, so I'm sure he could, but I don't want to argue with him. He's obviously frustrated.

"Here is a flower I found for you, my sweet Kati," Terry says, as he reaches into his sleeve, just like he did the night we met. Well, the situation isn't perfect, but love conquers all. There he is again, showing me romance.

My parents come to visit after a few weeks, and Jukka, Anu and their daughter, Sofia, will come in a few months. I think it's good for Terry to meet my parents, because he has a chance to express himself with my mother. He has a heart-to-heart talk with her.

"Marjatta, it is harder than I expected it would be," he says. "When she is reading, and self-sufficient it's fine, but I didn't know it would be like managing a baby."

Äiti helps him to understand that I need constant care, and the benefits are my love and my pure heart. I think she helps him to understand this is a life-long commitment and nothing is going to change physically. He seems a little more relaxed after their conversation.

My dad gives me a hug before he leaves, and shakes Terry's hand. They got along well during this visit, and I'm sure Isa is happy to accept I've moved to Aruba, now that he's met Terry.

"Risto and I enjoyed coming to see you," my mother writes after they return to Finland.

Terry and I complete our six-week trial period and are sure we can make it together. I'm so happy. Sometimes, Terry gets very grumpy, but doesn't anyone? Life in Aruba feels perfect. We have friends, we have wonderful weather, and we have each other.

Sometimes, when he's tired, he says things that are not nice. Last night he shouted at me in the middle of the night, "Kati, I'm doing everything for you and you are lazy. Why can't you get your assistant to do more? My life is ruined. I'm tired when I go out to sing. I'm tired all the time. Get her to move your fat ass in the middle of the night."

What is happening with Terry? His anger doesn't make any sense. I cannot make the assistant work more than the hours we have agreed to pay her, and he's said he'd rather have one assistant and him share the work, than pay for two assistants.

The next morning, I receive an email from Äiti.

"Hello, Kati, what is happening today?" Äiti has written to say that Finland is icy-cold. "Nothing interesting is going on here, but it is good to be home again. I am alone right now. Risto has gone out."

"Yes, me too," I write back.

"What? Where is Alice? Where is Terry?" I can tell she is really worried.

"It's all right. He will be back very soon. He just stopped by the market to get some fruit." I am not supposed to be left alone.

I've never talked much about my assistants, but they have always been an important part of my life. They come and go, some are part-time, some full time, some stay a long time, others only a few months. Some become very close friends, and that is good company as well as practically helpful, because the closer we are as friends, the easier it is for our working together; if we are close, the assistant will know better what my needs are and will be able to accomplish day-to-day tasks more efficiently. It takes time to train an assistant, and for us to get used to each other. Not everyone is cut out for this kind of work. Right now, Terry is both my lover and my assistant, and so if he needs to go to the market when the other assistant is not with me, it means I am on my own for a little while. This is not a problem if I am set up at my computer, because I can be busy for many hours. However, it is possible I could lose my balance, if my foot goes into spasm and kicks out. It is unlikely, but it is possible for me to fall, or slide, out of my chair. And, of course, it is important to make sure I won't need to go to the toilet.

Since I am so helpless, it's very frustrating to have an assistant that does not know me or understand what it means to be locked-in. It takes about a year to become close, so we can understand each other. I think this is what is happening between Terry and me right now. Sometimes he is very frustrated, because he doesn't understand what to do or how it feels to be me. But little by little we are improving, and then the other assistant takes over part of the time, so that Terry can observe, learn the spelling, do his work, or rest.

*

"Kati!" Terry bursts in the door.

I wail. I cannot help it. When I'm startled or scared, it's my natural reaction.

"Stop it! What's the matter with you? I've got some great news. What's the matter? Stop that wailing!" he says.

Eventually I am able to be quiet, after the fright wears off. He tells me his news: "We are going to open an art gallery. It's something I've always wanted. I just found the perfect space."

I nod.

"We need the money to rent the space."

We've only just moved into a bigger house, and bought new furniture. I had to pay for it all. I didn't mind because we're moving due to the wheelchair. I understand I need to pay the expense.

I shake my head, "No."

"Of course we do. I know exactly how much we have!" he shouts.

But that money is needed to pay for assistants.

"I've wanted to run an art gallery my whole life. Now I've found the perfect place for us. The money is like a loan. Once we start selling the art, it will all come back. Say yes, Kati, my beautiful woman, and we will be art curators. Would you deny this for your true love?"

No, of course not.

"And anyway, we only need one assistant; I'm your first assistant, and Alice is the other. Don't tell me how much we need; I know what we need to pay for assistants. And I want to take care of you, Kati, so you don't need to worry about anything. This money is only a temporary cost from our savings."

"Okay," I nod. I don't want to argue with him.

"Oh, I liked your hair better yesterday. Today it doesn't look good."

*

Jukka and Anu come to visit with their little Sofia.

"Let's get something to eat in Aruba," Terry says. "We do not eat at home so much. Come on."

We all go out, and while we are out, Terry has a wonderful surprise.

"Kati, for you." He takes, from inside his sleeve, a little ring box. I was expecting a flower.

Jukka and Anu stay for a couple of weeks and we all have a wonderful time. It is so good to have them here. Jukka and Terry get along just fine. Sofia looks at my engagement ring many times. She likes how the little diamond sparkles.

All the time Jukka is visiting, Terry and I do not fight at all, but the day after the family leaves, I seem to upset him. He shouts at me. I don't try to spell because he cannot understand. Today, he just pushes me in front of the computer and says, "Answer me!"

I like the computer more than spelling when I have to explain deep things. It takes time to think of the right words to explain, but he doesn't want to wait.

Today he says, "If you won't tell me what you want, I can't wait around to do it for you." And he storms out, and slams the door behind him.

Alice comes into the room and I tell her I need the toilet, so she takes me.

Later I write to Irina and tell her about my engagement. "Terry brought home a beautiful ring for me. We are engaged! Isa and Äiti will be so happy to know for the rest of my life I am safe and taken care of. You do not need to worry at all, Irina."

"That's wonderful, Kati. I'm so happy for you. When will the wedding be?" she writes back.

Terry comes back after a day at the gallery. Friends are here for a dinner that I have planned, and so I'm cooking with Mario when Terry arrives. He throws his arms around me and gives me a big kiss. Mario and some other friends will spend the evening with us, which is a bit unusual, and fun. Terry is a very silly fifty-year-old man. He plays two pranks on my assistant, Alice, and makes everyone laugh and laugh, except Alice. She keeps losing bets. Now she owes him a total of $25.

"If you want, you can try to win $50," he offers.

She says yes. So, he says, "You have to let me squash two eggs on your head."

$50 is $50 so she says, "Okay."

He squashes one egg over her head and rubs it in. Then he says, "I gotta go to work now." He still does his singing at the nightclub.

"Where's my money?"

"I told you $50 for two eggs. One egg gets you nothing."

Well, she is mad! So she starts to chase him.

"Wait, wait," he says when he's out of breath. "Let me show you how two hairs make love, okay?"

She agrees.

So Terry pulls two hairs out of my head and puts them on a plate. He fills the plate with water and then sprinkles salt on the plate.

"Look," he says.

When Alice leans over to look, Terry flips the plate into her face and she gets soaked. Before she has a chance to chase him, Terry is out the door.

Poor Alice, soaked with a head full of egg, and no $50. Terry is such a joker and makes everybody laugh. I feel a bit sorry for Alice though.

*

Irina comes to visit and I'm so excited.

"Kati," she says, "It's so beautiful here. The house is gorgeous. You have such a knack for decoration."

While Irina is here, Terry takes us out almost every night. It's so good of him to look after us.

"We will get married one of these days," he says to Irina, "and you'll come back, won't you?"

"Yes, of course." Irina is my closest friend. No matter how many miles there are between us, we always stay connected. One moment when we are alone she asks,

"He is good to you. He takes good care of you, doesn't he?"

"Yes." I spell out that sometimes things are difficult, but mostly life in Aruba is everything I could dream of.

"I can see you two are very close," she says. "And he really cares about you, Kati. That's what I want for you."

Suddenly, "Argh!" Someone is leaning on my shoulders. Irina is looking and she starts to smile. "Terry, I think you startled Kati," she says.

"Yeah, that's what's supposed to happen, only she's supposed to jump up, or at least say, stop it!"

He explains his theory, something he's been thinking about for a while, how, if I'm suddenly surprised, I'll move, or speak, when I haven't had the time to process my reaction mentally. Then I'll prove to myself that I can be normal, like everybody else.

"She just needs a shock to her system that will do that," he says.

"Never give up," I spell. It's so nice he thinks about me. Then he gives me a big, sloppy, long kiss right then and there. Oh, he can be so romantic.

Irina sits with me for a long time before the end of the evening. It's our last night before she flies back to Finland.

"I want to know you are happy, Kati." And I am. I have so much to be thankful for: her friendship, a man who loves me, and a beautiful home. What else can anyone ask for?

It's a bit sad when Irina has to leave. But we have the Internet.

I write to Terry that evening, about our engagement.

"We haven't started to plan anything yet. When you talked about it in front of Irina, I thought it might be the perfect time to start planning."

Terry must have read the email because he comes to me while I'm still at the computer.

"No, Kati. This is not the time to plan our wedding. We've got business expenses. Don't you dare put any pressure on me."

The routine goes back to normal after Irina has gone. Sometimes, Terry reminds me of Warren. I sit and sit, waiting for him to come home, and then he doesn't want to take me anywhere. Well, Terry doesn't drink or do any stupid cutting, so he's not really like Warren at all. But sometimes, I feel the same kind of sadness I felt in LA before the stroke. I wish we could go to the beach more often, go out anywhere. At least when I was in LA I could go places if I wanted to. With Terry, I have to wait for him to agree to take me.

*

A most amazing thing has happened today! I met a lady at the beach. Terry didn't want to go to the beach, but in the end, Alice and I prepared and set off on our own, so he came chasing after us and agreed to go. When Alice took me into the water, a lady came up to me.

"Are you Kati Lepistö?" she asked me.

"*Si*, yes, I am."

"Oh, Miss Lepistö, I read *In the Blink of an Eye* and I think it is the most wonderful story... well it's amazing. I mean, you are so strong, you are so determined. It helped me a lot, because I have some problems. You are a real encouragement. Thank you so much for your book and for sharing your story."

Wow!

It's a bit sad though, because later on the beach, Terry comes and asks, "Who was that?"

"A lady who has read my book," I spell for Alice, who tells Terry.

"Your book? You only half wrote that book, and anyway, what's she doing coming up to you, a perfect stranger? She has no right to do that."

Alice gets up, whispers to me, and leaves.

"What are you doing, hey, stay here and talk! Stupid bitch. What's her problem? What did she say to you? Oh, shit. You can't even tell me. Kati, you're so stupid. Why can't you get your assistant to stay with you? She'll probably quit. They all quit. It's so miserable being your assistant. Like being a slave. Well, do you think I'm waiting until she gets back here? You can just sit by yourself. Anyway, here she is, so I can get some freedom from looking after your fat ass."

Alice just needed the bathroom, but I was scared Terry was going to leave me alone in the sun. I'm glad she came back when she did. I think Terry is very tired. Otherwise, he wouldn't say such horrible things. The art gallery isn't doing very well, so I guess he's worried too.

*

The most wonderful thing has happened. A dog just started hanging around outside the house, and Terry has said we can keep her. It's been days since she appeared, and after a while, we started to feed her because she wouldn't go away. It didn't seem like she had a home and we didn't want her to starve. So, Terry fed her, she stays here, and now we've given her a name – Happy. It's amazing because it's as if that really is her name. She learnt to answer to it almost immediately. Now we've made a little bed for her in the kitchen and she's so *happy*, she's made us happy too.

It's incredible how the spirit of an animal can crawl into a person's heart without the person even noticing it. A dog accepts you just the way you are, she does not judge or hold a grudge.

I remember Eetu – my cat when I was growing up – was terrified of me after the stroke. The night of the stroke, while Äiti and I were at the hospital and Isa was at home, the cat was howling and racing around. She knew something was up. And when Isa brought her to the hospital, she was very shy. When I got home, she withdrew, she just wasn't comfortable to be near me anymore. The Kati she knew was gone and a shell was left. She must have felt lost without the total Kati.

Happy only knows me the way I am now, and she is *happy* to have a home with us. She's more than just a pet, she's my best friend. When Terry and I have a fight, and he storms off, Happy is a comfort to me. Her wagging tail puts a smile on my face, no matter how miserable I feel inside. She brings the outside in, and I am happy inside just being around her. She brings happiness to whoever is near. She doesn't choose sides but welcomes Terry home too, when he comes back; Happy can even bring him out of his grumpy mood. She's our little angel and has made the house a happier place.

*

Days go by and sometimes I feel quite sad. A new assistant has come, because Alice had to stop being my assistant. These people don't seem to stay forever. It's very difficult to find and train a new assistant, but we manage somehow. Lately, it's as though the only good thing in the house is Happy. Every human is miserable. Francesca, the new assistant, doesn't talk or share with me anything, so I don't know why she's so sad. She's a mature woman with a family. Maybe she has a family problem. She just does her hours and goes home, so I can't really find out what's wrong. Terry is shouting at me more and more. He says the gallery is not selling anything, so that must be why he's so miserable, but I wish he wouldn't shout at me. It seems the only one around me who is happy, is Happy. She makes me laugh.

I'm taking care not to waste my time on my outfits and my looks. It can be actually very relaxing not worrying about my appearance. I used to think every day was special and to dress for it was important. I don't think so now though. Since I'm only sitting at home at my computer, what's the point of getting dolled up? Well, dressed-up or casual, I do wish we could go to the beach more often, or I could get more exercise. I enjoy the computer life so much, but it would also be nice to go out too, but when Terry gets home, he doesn't want to go out. Sometimes he has his singing gigs at night. Francesca and I manage at home, but for us to go out every day would be too difficult.

"Kati, you look terrible. What happened to Kati the model, Kati the beautiful?" I just look at him. "You're a liar. You made me believe you would be beautiful all your life, but you just sit around doing nothing. Your assistant does nothing. I asked her to do something for me yesterday, and do you know what she said? She said, "I'm here to help Kati." Do you know how pathetic you are? Do you? *Do you?* You don't understand what it's like having to live with someone who is so stupid and useless."

I try to ignore him, as though he's one of those people who would stare at me in public places. But when I ignore him, he just keeps on shouting, as though I'm deaf, not mute.

Francesca and I do a lot of cooking and that's fun. I think she is getting more comfortable with me. She's told me about her family, and everything there is fine. If she has a problem, she doesn't want to tell me. So, we cook. Sometimes we look for new recipes that Terry will like, but Terry even yells about that sometimes. It's very difficult trying to make him happy. It seems like every day there is something wrong and he shouts at me. He interrogates me, but of course he should know that I will not answer. Then he repeats himself, getting louder. It must be very difficult for him, because he works and then comes home to take care of me. But it makes me very sad to have him shout at me.

"Kati, you are useless, why can't you get your assistant to take you out and do something with your pathetic life? Did you hear me? *Do* something!"

"Kati, my life is so boring. I work, I eat, I work, I eat. I have to look after you, taking your fat ass everywhere I go. Don't you care about *me?*"

"Kati, you told me your assistant did everything for you. Well, that's not true. You are a liar! I do everything around here."

"Kati, why don't you dress up now and then? Make yourself look better?" It's as though he's saying, 'Kati, you are a waste of space. Get out of my way!' But he doesn't quite use those words.

Francesca just looks at us. She stares at me. It's so embarrassing. What am I supposed to do? There's nothing that I can do. I don't even tell Äiti too much about this because she will worry all the way back in Finland. What can she do? Nothing. I'm beginning to think this isn't going to get any better. Maybe I shouldn't have come to Aruba.

But then there are the nice times.

"Kati, I sold a painting today."

Terry is happy. We go out to dinner together and he's his charming self. He even makes Francesca laugh, which she doesn't do very often.

Today, 'Brand New Day' by Sting, is on the radio. I think things are going to get better. But they don't. After our nice dinner out, sex is great. We fall asleep comfortable.

"Kati, get your assistant to turn you. I'm dead beat." Of course, Francesca is at her own home, in her own bed.

You are a deadbeat, I think to myself. But I don't like to think that way. There are so many good things about Terry. I'm lying here, thinking, but now I'm getting very sore in bed and I need to be turned. I start to hum. That's what I use to wake him.

"No, Kati." But I have to hum until he moves me, otherwise it will hurt so much in the morning.

"Can't you see I'm tired? Oh, all right." But he's rough and I'm lopsided. It takes longer than usual to turn me. I want to tell him to be patient, but of course he's never learnt to spell, so I can't tell him.

I have to be turned, and any new position needs to be in alignment so that I can fall back to sleep. When we were first together, Terry was very careful to make sure my back, hips, knees are in alignment. Now, I have to hum and hum to make sure he turns me properly. If I'm not persistent, he won't do it. I understand he's tired, but shouldn't he have thought of this before he decided he wanted me to move in with him?

This morning, it's a new day and I'm going to try to make the most of it. Francesca agrees. She is going to take me to meet our Canadian friends over coffee in the Paseo Herencia Mall. I haven't told Terry. We also plan to go to a Full Moon Party at the castle, where the music is great. It'll be fun! I wish Terry could come, but he's working, and anyway, he might be grumpy.

Life goes on, with its ups and downs. Happy is the happiest and she makes us all smile when she chases her tail or a ball, or just quietly lies at my feet. Francesca is adjusting to working with me, and it is getting easier, although sometimes she seems far away, as if she is thinking about other things. I ask her about it.

"I'm fine, everything is okay," she says.

Tonight we all decide to go to Mambo Jambo – a fun nightclub. Fran enjoys going out, and she is very relaxed. Terry and I have fun like we used to, and on our way home, when Fran transfers me from the chair to the car, Terry stares at me. Suddenly he whispers to her, "Damn, I love that girl!" It isn't the first time he's said something like that, but it's been a while. I think we're on a good track now.

But as weeks go by, I have to admit things are not very consistent. Little by little Terry's and my relationship has become a rollercoaster of ups and downs, mostly downs. I think I'm too fat, so I guess another diet will make me happier. Maybe Terry will be happier too. Actually, sometimes I feel so low, but I know I should be enjoying the warm sunshine. Aruba is a place of life and fun, but I don't feel good. Mario hasn't been to visit us in a while. I only see Fran and Terry, and not very many other people. I think it would be good to see more people. I write to my friends and family, which is nice, but every day seems to be pretty much the same thing of computer, cooking, and Terry shouting at me for one reason or another.

When Terry is doing his toxic shouting, I don't respond anymore. Even if I try to spell to Fran, it just makes him angrier, and she hates being with us. I think he likes to make me scared. If I say nothing, and do nothing, which is easy for me, it just makes him shout louder. It's funny in a sick sort of way. I don't know what these lectures are for. I just sit and listen until he runs out of steam or has to leave for some stupid reason.

My daily routine is to sit in my chair and listen while he shouts at me. I can't defend myself and although I know what he says isn't true, it does bring me down. I mean, how often can I ignore being told that I've ruined his life because he has to be with me all the time and drag my ass around? I keep hearing that I'm stupid, that I understand nothing, that I'm fat, that I'm a liar...

Happy is the one creature in the house that is always perky, bright and cheerful. It is impossible to be sad around her. Sometimes, she sits on my lap and keeps my hands warm. Sometimes, she runs back and forth in the house, after a ball. Sometimes, she sits under my computer desk, next to my feet. I don't want to imagine how gloomy it might be without her.

I can tell Fran isn't happy either, but I don't want her to leave. It's so hard training a new assistant. I'm not sure how to make it better for her, because she won't say what's wrong. I only know something is, because she's so quiet.

Another day passes calmly. When Terry comes back from the gallery he says, "Let's go for drinks."

Surprise! We'll do something together. Mostly, we're only together at home when he has to take care of me. So, we get ready and are on our way. At one point though, he pushes me a bit hard and one foot moves, so I hum to get his attention, to fix my position.

"Now I remember why we don't go out together!" he shouts.

He's angry again? Now I don't want to go out. I do not feel his love at all anymore. What's the point of going out? Even if we do go out, and he acts like he's the nicest man in the world, he doesn't know or care that I feel so empty. Without a computer, I can't even tell him. There is one advantage to being unable to speak. When you don't want to, you have an excuse. Does he even know how sad I feel tonight? I doubt it.

More days pass. One evening, Terry comes home from singing at 11.00 p.m., which is my regular bedtime. He's come home only in time to put me to bed.

"I'm here, what are you crying about?" He's staying out later and later because he hates to come home.

I should leave. He hates to be with me even for one second more than he has to be. He only comes home to put me to bed, not to spend time with me. I feel so sad. What has happened to our love? The only thing that brings happiness to this household is Happy, the dog.

As I drift off to sleep, alone in the bed, I wonder what has happened to me. Where is happy Kati? I feel like I can't think straight and I am always cringing inside when Terry is home. What if he shouts? What if he jokes? I don't relax, in case he jumps out at me. He still creeps up behind me sometimes to startle me. He says it's to jolt my muscles into remembering how to work, but it never works. It just scares me.

This morning, Terry tells me that the gallery has gone under, and he has not renewed the lease. The artists are supposed to collect their paintings.

"But it's okay, because I do have another idea," he says. "Kati, I need just six grand to get these watches. I can get lots of guys working for me on the beaches, and the tourists will love these copy watches. You'll see. I'll go to Hong Kong and get these really good copy watches. This is going to be easy money. I don't even have to pay the sellers directly. They'll get some of the money from the sales of the watches. No overheads. So, I just need six grand."

I stare at him for a long time.

"What?" he says. "Come on, Kati. Cough up. You know this will work and we need the money. Anyway, it's a good way to make up for the gallery. Come on, gorgeous."

I nod.

He needs something to cheer him up. What do they say? A man needs work to give him a sense of self-respect. So, he's off to Hong Kong, and I have to hire some extra assistant-help while he's gone, because Fran can't work 24/7.

While Terry's in Hong Kong, we communicate on email and it's like the old Terry again. Every man needs work. He's feeling better, so he's acting better.

"Kati, Hong Kong is fantastic. I've got some of the watches. I'm scouting for different supplies. It's great. They are cheap, but they look like the real thing. You're gonna love them. I'm going to bring you back a surprise too. A little something just for you."

When he comes back Fran is really grumpy and won't talk to me at all. I can't understand it. She just disappears when he comes back.

"Hey, I brought something for Francesca. Where'd she go? Fran? Fran?" He shouts until she comes.

"Hey, why'd you make me shout? Look, I brought you something." It's a pretty, green and purple silk scarf.

"Thank you," she says, and leaves the room.

"What's her problem? Who cares? Now for you," he says, and he reaches inside his sleeve.

Another silk scarf, deep blue, and then he opens it; inside there is a box. He opens the box. Inside is a Rolex copy watch. It's a man's watch.

"You like? I chose it for you. I'll put it on." It's a bit loose but it is nice.

I nod. I'll make a nice dinner tonight.

"I'm going to get the vendors now, down at the beach, and give them the inventory. This is going to work. I know these guys; it's going to go well. That six grand is going to get us going.

"Hey, what's this?"

I bought a set of salt and pepper shakers while he was away.

"Kati, did you pick these? What a waste of money. They're pissin' ugly. You have no decorating skills whatsoever." He laughs. Does he think he's funny?

Fran and I spend the afternoon making a nice dinner, so the two of us can sit down together tonight and relax. Fran has agreed to stay to feed me so Terry doesn't have to. We both decide we'll wear our new scarves, which will keep Terry cheerful.

This is how I cook:

I take a recipe, sometimes it's written down and sometimes it's in my head – either memorised or made up on the spot. Tonight it'll be fish, special rice and vegetables. It's been a hit before. Fran likes it when I cook and she cheers up too as we work together. Happy is racing around with her ball. Fran kicks it back and forth while she's cooking, we've got some rhumba music going and it's a great afternoon. She has become a very good assistant, especially with cooking. She does everything step by step and really is my hands. She reads the recipe out loud, we put in the ingredients, one thing at a time, we work totally together, one chopped vegetable, one grain of salt at a time. She always remembers to ask me, "Is this enough?" Sometimes it is, sometimes we need to add more. She's so careful and I really appreciate it.

"Actually, most of my life is cooking for Terry," I say to Fran. She nods.

I get up, we go to the market or the supermarket for food, Francesca helps me prepare the food, then she leaves for the night in time for Terry to come home to eat it. Food, food, food. It's hard to actually diet when food is your lifestyle. Well, tonight it will be worth all the effort.

But Terry arrives home early and surprises us. He seems a bit gloomy. Well, he'll cheer up when he sits down to a meal he's loved before.

He takes a bite.

"Aargh! What is this shit?" He spits out his food.

Francesca and I look at each other. I feel like I've just been punched in the stomach.

He takes another bite.

"It's too salty. What? Are you trying to poison me?"

I watch as he sweeps his oily black hair from his eyes. He leans his arms on the table and glares across at me.

Terry, don't do this tonight, I plead with my eyes. It's all I can do. But he goes on anyway. "I'm sick of this bull. You know?" He stares at me. "Yeah, you!"

What is he doing? Daring me to speak?

I watch as he takes his knife and fork and cuts another piece of fish. He tastes it. Jeez, he must be hungry if he keeps trying it.

"Aargh!" He grimaces, spits out the food and shoves the plate across the table towards me, as if I'm going to do something about it. Well, you can bet your ass I'm not.

I look at Fran. She looks at the plate. Should she pick it up? I shake my head no. He's ranting, and while he rants I'm thinking...

He's only just got back from Hong Kong, buying watches to sell. I thought he'd come back in a good mood. I gave him the $6,000, but he did the hard work of making the trip, and he'll do the selling. It's a fair deal, isn't it? Before that was the art gallery, which I funded, but it didn't do too well and he gave up after a year.

I missed him so much while he was gone. I thought it was going to be a nice homecoming, but instead he's already shouting insults at me again. Sometimes he's nice – a good lover. Mostly he just abuses me with words. Hateful words. Mean words. Insulting words. Sometimes I wonder, are they true?

"Why can't you get your fat ass to make some decent food? I've taken care of you, haven't I, pushing the damned chair around? I work hard to make us money. But no one should put up with this shit! You're a stupid woman, Kati. Stupid. Useless and stupid. What? You're just staring at me. Can't say a word? Serves you right. You probably used to talk too much anyway. I hauled your ass all the way from Finland, and for what? Salty food? What you got to say for yourself? You gonna apologise? Come on – I'm waiting!"

Do I deserve this? Maybe. But if he wanted someone different, someone who wasn't paralysed, shouldn't he have thought of that before he asked me to move to Aruba? "Ah, you're gonna cry now, I suppose."

I do not cry. Not yet. I look at Fran. She glares at me. She hates it when Terry gets like this, which is most of the time now.

"What? You've got something to say to me? What do you say to me NOW?"

In a flash, it comes to me, one thing I have to say now. Only one.

I look at Francesca, and she looks back. I turn my eyes and start to spell.

"F" she starts quietly, spelling out the letters one by one, like I always do to speak. "u – c – k." I nod, indicating the end of a word. "Y-o-u." I nod confirmation. "Fuck you," she finishes.

Terry goes ballistic. "What? You bitch." He flings his arms in the air. What is he gonna do now, fly?

"What? That's your apology for practically poisoning me? Well, fuck yourself too. I'm done! Salty food? That's it! You take your sorry ass back to Finland, I'm done dragging it around, everybody staring, everybody pitying you. They should pity me. I'm the one stuck with you. A model? You're no model. You're fat and ugly. And homeless! Take off, I'm done with you."

He gets up. "I'm going to work, and on an empty stomach thanks to you. I could faint on stage, bump my head and end up a vegetable like you. Why do I put up with your lousy food?"

He storms off to get himself ready to sing at his two-bit nightclub.

Silence. I look at Francesca, but she's staring at the two

plates on the table. She must be wondering, *Will Kati eat now?* Of course I'll eat. I'm hungry.

Terry lunges at me from behind, startling both Fran and me. He points his finger at my nose. "And you know what? It's the last time I let you cook for me. Francesca, don't listen to her anymore. She's useless. Stupid and ugly! You cook for me from now on."

He turns, "Get outta my house! That's it. I'm done. You drag your sorry fat ass back to Finland."

He mumbles something as he goes out the door: "I could have choked. Then where would you be?" and slams the door.

All the time I'm thinking: *you like my stroganoff.*

He's right about one thing – I must go.

He didn't even notice the scarves we were wearing.

I start to spell. "Let's take off our scarves." She pulls mine from my neck and then hers. They fall to the floor.

I look at Fran. She looks ashamed. Why is she ashamed? Then a surge of energy rises up inside me. She's not ashamed – she's ashamed for me, and Terry's horrible shouting. She's been suffering all along. We have to get out. We have to get away. Not because he says so – it isn't the first time – but because this will never change.

This screaming is over salty food. How stupid.

I spell. "I," nod, "h-a-v-e," nod, "t-o," nod, "g-o."

Yes, she nods.

"W-i-l-l-y-o-u-h-e-l-p..."

"Will you help me?" she says out loud. And then she says, "Yes."

We cry together. Oh, how did it end up like this?

CHAPTER 29

Escape into Darkness

There comes a point when love has to die. I never knew this before, but now I see it. When the best moments cannot cover up the worst anymore, it is time to let go. I must leave paradise for a better life in the freezing, Arctic cold, where at least the love will be warm. This is my secret, well, mine and Fran's. Terry will discover it after we've left.

We want to go. Fran has agreed to take me back to Finland and her husband agrees too, even though he will be left alone for at least a month, while I get new assistants in Mikkeli.

Oh God! For a moment I was excited to escape, but this also means I have to go back to my parents, like a dog with her tail between her legs. Well, we are bringing Happy too, and her tail is wagging, and she's full of excitement all the time, so we will be too.

Planning to leave takes some time to arrange. I cannot leave behind the one thing worth keeping. Yes, I spent a large amount of money to be here, buying furniture, renting a big house, and an art gallery, which failed, and Terry's watches. Well, he can keep it all, but he can't keep Happy. I'm not going to give him the pleasure of arguing about any of it. I will go, Fran will take me, and our plan means one day he will go to work and when he comes home, we will be gone! No note, no explanation. He says he wants me to go, then I will go and take Happy with me. Who knows what he would do with the dog if I didn't keep her?

Tonight, Terry gives me a speech about how awful I am, that I'm such a cold person, and that I am mean.

"That's why all the assistants leave – because of you," he says. Really? This time I let him say whatever garbage he wants to, and all I can think is, soon I'm going home.

It's unbelievable how people change. He used to love me, but now he insults me, and blames me for the assistants leaving. He accuses me of making them do everything. Hello, somebody's paralysed! One thing I know for sure, if I were healthy, I would never ask for help from anybody. But I don't want to be mean. Actually, I want to be sure I'm doing the right thing. Maybe I'm making a mistake. Maybe I haven't given Terry enough time to adjust to my disability. I ask Fran when we are alone. Sometimes, I remember good times. I think maybe I should work harder.

But Fran says, "Yes. It is good you go. He is not a good man." Well that's true; he is not a good man.

I send a message to Äiti. "I'm coming back to Finland. I'm leaving Terry, Äiti. Fran will bring me." I'll send her the flight details once I have them.

"I'll meet you at the airport in Helsinki, whenever that is. Are you all right?"

"Yes, I'm all right. Everything will be fine, when I get home. Love, Kati."

I spend time on the computer writing to myself. It clears this little head of mine; there is a lot of confusion in there.

I was thinking, before the 'salty food' attack, that maybe I should go back to Finland. Now that I am, I admit it is hard to stick with that decision. I don't like to quit. Shouldn't I stay and fight for us? Am I sure it's better to give up and move back to Finland? But he is so unpredictable and volatile. I know I *should* want to go. It's odd though, because as horrible as he is, sometimes it feels hard to leave him. Why is that, I wonder?

Every day Fran and I are a step closer to leaving. One day at a time I am moving forward: yesterday we picked up the airline tickets, a one-way ticket for me; today we are getting some shots for Happy because she is moving to Finland. I'm so thankful to Fran, because I know I couldn't do this without her. I'm thankful to her husband too, because if he didn't agree to her coming with me, this would just not be happening.

There isn't much time now before we go. I think I should be sad, shouldn't I? I mean, we were engaged. I moved to Aruba to the man of my dreams. But was he? I didn't know him really, did I? While I am broken-hearted that I have to give up this love and return to Finland, there is a part of me that is excited, because I am going without telling Terry.

"We are leaving and Terry, that tyrant, doesn't even have a say," I spell to Fran. She laughs.

"Should we call him Terry-the-tyrant from now on?"

She laughs and laughs.

"What do you think?" She nods. It isn't usually good to make fun of people, but I guess the shoe fits.

As we get closer to the day of our flight out of Aruba, I can't wait to leave. Although leaving is very sad, I admit I'm kind of enjoying this plan of ours. What will Terry do when he realises we've gone? I know that even though I have no power to move my muscles, I do have the power to make my life better. And although Finland is icy cold, here in Aruba my heart is frozen solid. I had to freeze it in order to survive Terry's cruel and negative complaints.

"Kati, no one deserves to listen to him. I nearly left three times," Fran admits, and I suddenly understand why, one by one, the assistants left. They came for me, and the job, but they left because of him. I'm glad I realise it now. I don't blame myself, or the assistants for leaving. Now, just like the others before, we're leaving Terry too. The flight is tomorrow and I'm marking the hours until we leave. We have Happy's papers, and we are ready to pack my bags as soon as Terry goes out to work tomorrow morning. We will pack and go very quickly. It is a shame about the furniture, about €10,000 worth of good quality furniture, but my escape must be swift and without conflict, and so it will be. I'm a little bit nervous, but I know it is the right thing to do.

I look at this stupid ring on my finger that Terry gave me when my brother and his family were here. We never decided anything about getting married after my brother left Aruba. It's almost as if it never happened, and yet I know it did, because I have the ring to prove it. I am glad I'm leaving, but I understand now why some women find it so hard to leave a man even if he's abusive. We want love, and we want it to work out. Verbal abuse makes us feel inert. If I was a weak person, he would have conquered me. I'm so glad I said, "Fuck you," that night of the salty food, instead of, "I'm sorry." What a horrible two years this has been. It isn't enough that I'm paralysed, but I had to endure this abuse too. I heard once: strong people must suffer, and the stronger the person, the more they must suffer.

As the time to leave Aruba gets closer, I find I'm watching Terry very closely. This morning he is calm. He takes some fruit and goes out the door. He is fit and moves well. I guess that's what I liked about him, but underneath his humour and sexiness, I can see more now – Terry has been like a cancer, eating my insides slowly but destructively. He's mean. He can't bear the tiniest discomfort. He feeds off me. I used to think, *oh, he's tired,* or *aw, he needs something nice so he will feel more encouraged.* Now I just think he's weak. It's time for me to go, because my disgust might show, and I don't want him to discover we are leaving. Then he'll really go ballistic.

Why did I come here at all? If I'd never come, I wouldn't have had to go through this now. It's a bit like the horseback riding in rehab. It was scary, but it gave me strength. There is no therapy that is useless, and life's like that too. There is always a lesson to be learnt in every little experience. I remember, I came to Aruba because of love. Now I've learnt that love is not enough, and I am leaving... tomorrow.

As I fall asleep on my last night in Aruba, I'm relieved and a little bit scared. What will it be like closing the door and leaving this house? Tomorrow, when Terry says goodbye, I won't let on I'm going forever.

The morning sun comes early, and pours into the room. I'm awake before Terry.

I remember galloping on horseback in Finland. It seemed so irrelevant to getting well and being able to walk, but I learnt to keep my balance when I rode that horse. Somehow, I know I need to keep my balance when I'm on the love-ride too. Today, I need to keep a balanced head, so Terry doesn't suspect anything. I also don't want to give him any excuse to blow up on the day that I'm leaving forever.

"See ya, Kati, Fran."

There goes Terry, out the door. It's like all movement is in slow motion and I see the love-ride is over for me. Maybe it ended the night I had the stroke, but I just didn't realise it. I thought I would have a chance at love; I thought I would get well. I'm starting to cry, not because of Terry, but because love just walked out that door and it's the end of a dream. And there is another reason... it's so damn cold in Finland!

Fran watches through the window until he's out of sight. Then, here we are... packing, talking to Happy so she's ready to leave, and for her it is an exciting new world. She'll probably even like the snow. We check our lists, everything is packed. Fran's husband is taking us to the airport in my car. Terry will not get the car at least. Fran is buying it from me.

As we drive away, as usual, my feelings and how I express them are all upside down. I'm excited, but I'm crying.

It's as hard for me to return to Finland as it is to leave here. How can I go back home? I'm thirty-three. How can I go back to live with my parents? But there's nowhere else. My parents are wonderful. But still, I thought I'd moved past that, twice. Once when I was eighteen and once when I was thirty. Now, I will be with them forever. I can't stop crying.

I am not even sad to leave Terry-the-tyrant. Not sad one bit. But I'm dreading the cold, where my muscles ache every morning. I'm dreading my mother's fatigue, where she gives and never gives up, but has no energy for herself. I'm dreading facing my friends and family who will love me, and pity me. And I'm dreading having nothing to do, no plan, no idea of how to make something out of this prison existence.

"I'm going home," I spell to Fran. She puts her hands on mine. Without her, I could never have escaped. Thank God someone cared about me out here.

As we fly towards Europe, the thought of returning to Finland weighs upon me so heavily, I feel as dreary as the weather I'm returning to. Now I understand what was holding me back, why it took me so long to let go of the Aruba dream. I don't want to live in Finland. I don't want to spend my days decaying in that icy land. I never wanted to live there, not in my whole life. I've seen the world, but is it only to end up where I started?

I'm so scared. Most people when they are frightened, wring their hands, or pace, or talk about it. Francesca is next to me, reading. *Thank you Fran, for helping me to escape from slow death.* I can do nothing but stare at the ceiling. The ceiling of an aircraft is not very interesting. It sits so close to me. It speaks of many travels, and whispers, "This is your last." Can that be true?

CHAPTER 30

Self-discovery

Arriving in Finland is horrible, but it is safe. Sitting in the dark and dreary landscape of Finland, at first I sometimes doubt my decision to leave Aruba, but Fran, and then my new assistant, Jemma, remind me of the horrible memories. I've tried to make fun of Terry-the-tyrant, but living with him was terrifying. I only understand how bad it was now that I'm away from him. It's been three months since I left. He never contacted me and I don't wonder how he reacted when he found an empty house; I'm just relieved it's all over. Leaving was my escape from hell. People might think being paralysed is hell, but truthfully, what I've just lived through for two years was much worse.

In January 1995, I had a stroke, and became almost entirely paralysed with no meaningful movement or speech since. Although I could not move or speak, I was very fortunate. My needs were always cared for. Then I went to Aruba in 2006. I could have stayed in Aruba, and I would have died the slow death of my soul. I was dying and I didn't even know it. I nearly met my match – Terry-the-tyrant was almost as strong as me, and that's scary, because until now I thought there was nothing that could conquer me.

Let me share a little secret with you: I may be locked-in physically, but I don't have to live locked-in. Life is worthwhile, whether I can move or speak, or not. I am a person with passion and a strong will. That I nearly lost it shocks me and it wasn't because I became paralysed. Returning to my family has reminded me of all the accomplishments I've achieved so far. I'd like to find something more to do, but my book, *In the Blink of an Eye*, and the response to it, is proof that I have a meaningful purpose to contribute; I just need to find what that is. I know what it isn't – it isn't to look for romance. I have friends, I have family, and if I never meet another man who looks at me as though I'm attractive, I can live with that.

I do miss Fran. She was like a sister to me; we laughed and we cried together. Of course she had to go back to Aruba. She stayed long enough to help train Jemma. I hope she never bumps into Terry, because he'll probably try to get my car from her.

When I look in the mirror, it feels very strange, having my own hairstyle, without Terry's approval. When I buy something new, I don't have to listen to him shouting at me. I have my own money again, because yes, he controlled what we did with my money.

I left everything behind in Aruba. It cost me two years of my life, and a lot of cash, but what did I say when the stroke left me paralysed? Money is to be used, not wasted, but not stored up either. Moving to Aruba was very expensive, but now it's over and I need to focus on the fact that I escaped with a tiny bit of dignity and my freedom. Freedom is not the ability to move, but the ability to think, feel and live. No one must take that away. As for the bad experience?

Well, we can learn from every experience. What did I learn from two years of living with a man like Terry? I've learnt what abuse is, that it is a bigger, slower killer than cancer or a stroke. It kills the soul of a person, and slowly, slowly takes away dignity and self-respect. That's the worst kind of being locked-in.

I could have spent my entire life there. When I imagine that, I burst into tears again. I would have wasted away. Where was Kati? Where was that spark of life that can't be told what to do? That can't be stopped, even though totally paralysed? Never again will I allow myself to love someone who just says romantic things. Love is a lot bigger than words. I won't hate him, because that's another kind of cancer, but I do have to remind myself how much he hurt me, so that I never let that happen to me again.

Today, Äiti brings me a letter. It has a postmark I don't recognise. She opens it and reads,

"Dear Kati, I'm sorry you had to leave Aruba, but it's all right because I know you suffered. I have something to tell you.

Before Terry met you, there were other women. All of them had one thing in common: they needed help. You were paralysed. But before you, he had a woman who was an invalid.

Why Terry always chose women who have special needs, I do not know. But it is not because he cares about them. He is not able for that. Now that you are gone, I can tell you without interfering in your relationship, Terry is a narcissist. This means he cannot recognise other people have feelings..."

I start to howl. I don't want to, but it just pours out of me. Happy comes to my feet and is staring. Äiti stops reading.

I howl for a while, but finally, I'm able to stop. I nod for Äiti to continue. She is crying now too.

"... This means he cannot recognise...

He also doesn't want to work for reward, but he does want other people to admire him. I have to let you figure out the rest yourself.

When I was visiting Aruba, that time I met you, I really liked you. I told Terry to take care of you and not make you take care of him, like the last woman. Well, I'm glad you left. You don't need to tell me, but I guess you finally figured that he was not going to take care of you.

I hope you find happiness.

Sincerely, Monica"

Monica. That's Terry's sister. She wrote me a letter? And she explains a lot. Jeez. He is a narcissist. That explains everything! The control, the big show of affection in public, the yelling and shouting, and even how he treated the assistants. Oh! Now I literally want to shoot myself in the foot, for being so blinded by love and sweet words. I didn't see the tyrant in Terry before I went to Aruba. Why didn't I see it sooner than I did?

I'm wailing a little less now, and my mother has put the letter back in its envelope. She puts her hand on my knee. I can't talk about it, she knows that, but we cry together, and that's okay.

"Kati," she says. "We didn't know."

Of course she didn't. How could she? I cry and cry. Whenever I think about him, I cry. It isn't because I miss the b******. I don't miss him at all. I cry because... I don't even know why. It's horrifying, I know that much! Maybe it's because he stole my life for two years, and if Fran hadn't helped me to leave, he might have stolen it forever. That thought makes me wail some more. How could I have been so blind?

When I've calmed down, which takes a long time, I start to think about Terry and how he operated. The first time we had a fight, I should have known, I should have seen it then. How could someone get angry just because his girlfriend wore an outfit he didn't like? But now I get it! Everything was about *him*. And how *he* looked. So if I looked really nice, as I usually did, it took attention away from *him*. When I stopped dressing up, so he'd stop shouting at me, he shouted anyway. At the time I made excuses. I thought it was our age difference, cultural differences, my paralysis, a personality clash. I mean we were both feisty individuals. But all along it was nothing to do with us, not even with me. It was all to do with him, what suited him, what made him look good to other people, what gave him attention. Ah! That must be why he gave me that little engagement ring when Jukka was visiting. It was all for show. No wonder we never talked about it again after Jukka left. I tried, but he just got angry. The whole relationship was fake, a losing battle right from the start.

As I scan my mind over many memories, a power sweeps over me, and I'm stunned by a realisation – my life was over when I went there. My life was sucked into his. If I had stayed... Oh, if there is a God, he's done well to get me out of there. All because of salty food; how ridiculous is that? I couldn't see it, but I see it now. I see it and I'm so relieved.

They say time heals. Good! I shudder to think how life might have been if I'd stayed with Terry. Instead, I am going to start to live again, to be my own person, even though I have appendages that don't work and need people to be my appendages. I don't need a man to have a romantic life. Love for life and for other people is what matters.

Funny, it takes all of the life to get sucked out of you, before you realise you have a life to cherish and treasure and take care of. If you love your family and friends, that's good, but you've got to love yourself too. And for me, that is being independent, because that's how I live best. What can I do with all my energy? I know and I'm smiling now, because I have the answer to what will bring me happiness. I will keep doing what I do best. I will write. It's the one thing I can do that I don't need anyone else's hands for. I can do it myself.

I write to myself: "The present and future are in my hands. It's a very powerful and exhilarating moment to understand. I've changed from a lost ship adrift at sea to the captain of my ship, the deliverer of my destiny. My sails might be a little broken, but I have the power to sail that boat anywhere."

Yes, I can keep my own company in this dreary Finnish weather; I have a lot of time to think. Irina is working; Jukka and Anu have their little girl, Sofia, to raise; Isa and Äiti do so much for me, I try to ask as little as necessary; the assistants do all they can. They are new, Jemma and Ina, and we don't know each other very well. None of us talks very much yet. But as I stare at the ceiling, I find my answers there.

Finnish people are bad at talking about their feelings. I did not know how to tell Terry he was hurting me. I put my feelings on hold with Terry-the-tyrant. The more he shouted, the more I locked everything inside. In fact, I am more locked-in emotionally than I will ever be physically. That is pretty funny. But now that I'm home with my computer, I can say what I feel. Nobody will see it, but I will see it. And as I learn to love my situation, I can share with me. I am a good audience.

Every time I think about Terry and Aruba I cry. I don't miss him. I don't even miss Aruba, although I did like the warm sunshine on my skin and it was so good for my muscles. I cry because I might have lost my life forever. As

I crawl out from under the dominance of that mean and hurtful narcissist, and my wings open up and I fly from my cocoon, I am able to feel free in my mind and live again, like the Kati who was stubborn enough to tie my own shoes, to buy my own boots, and to fly myself back from Italy all alone as a young girl, I am free. As I'm writing all of this down, instead of stopping myself from crying, I am letting myself. Why? Because I can. Because there is no one to stop me. Because there is no one I must explain to. Because the more I cry, the less tears there are inside me, and one day, I won't cry anymore out of sadness, I will only cry out my joy. I am letting myself be sad because I was stupid, and desperate, and hopeful, and in love. But no more stupidity, no more desperation. I can hope, and I can still believe in love, but I don't have to believe some prince will come and rescue me.

All my life I have wanted to do what I wanted to do. Now I can, because what this prison of my body has taught me is that freedom is not a physical state, but a state of mind. Peace comes when we have no worry. Worry goes when we do not want something, but instead cherish and accept what we have. There is no point looking back and blaming. The only point is to look forward. Once there is no more grief, we can move forward. And that is what I am doing.

Inside I am crying, but I am also shouting and singing, and more than anything else, I'm dancing. Happy is dancing with me. Life is good, not because of where I live or who I love, but because I am free to think and be as I want to be.

As I gaze at the ceiling, I smile at the cracks and paint smudges. Not everyone in the world gets to see these bits of reality. Not everyone notices. But I do. And that is my little bit of peace. I don't know what's next. But for the first time in my life, without a plan, I don't care. Whatever comes will be good, because the people around me are good, and life is good, and worth living. I have a secret – to be alive is wonderful. Now, I'm going to live without knowing where life is taking me. All my life I've had ambition. Instead of pursuing my goals, now my ambition is to discover what life has for me.

The unknown is scary. And exciting.

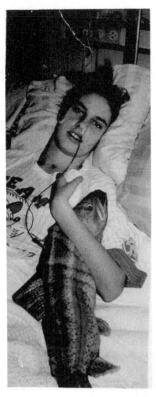

In hospital after the stroke

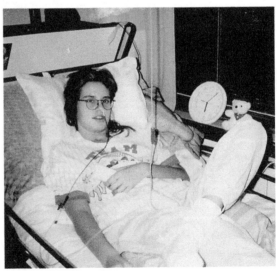

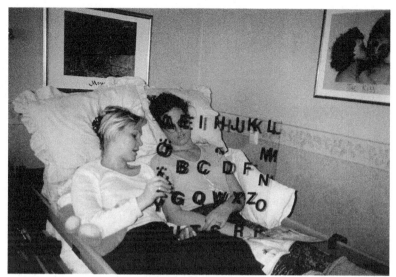

The Spelling Board

Learning to use the computer

KATI LEPISTÖ EI LIIKU
MUTTA UINTI KUULUU HÄNEN
VIIKKO-OHJELMAANSA.

24

Swimming and standing therapy

Kati around the world

Part 3: Learning to Float

The worst possible outcome of any situation is that you gain experience, and you lose ignorance. That is not bad at all. I say go for it!

Kati Lepistö van der Hoeven

CHAPTER 31

Surprise Encounter

I spend most of my time at the computer. I'm meeting new people and making new friendships. Romance is dead but Facebook is amazing and brings me into contact with friends, and people who become new friends. Of course, there is still reliable email, which has served me well for so long; it gives me a great way to communicate deeper, private things with people close to me.

There's a way to stay connected with friends in Aruba as well, it's called Tagged. I left abruptly and no one knew I was leaving, so with Tagged I can reconnect with Mario and all of the other friends I made, and I avoid Terry-the-tyrant. It helps me find people I already know, or who are connected to Aruba. I'm not looking for anyone or anything in particular, but I'm open to anyone who wants to connect. There are a lot of lonely people, and a lot of creative people on the Internet. Whether it's Facebook, Tagged, or some new platform yet to come, I reach out to meet new friends. Life doesn't pass me by. And when I don't have someone to write to, I just write to me.

My dream is to have a happy and fulfilling life. Expectations that are based in reality give me a great boost, a reason to wake up every morning, a sense of meaning. On the other hand, wishes that will never be achievable make life a series of delusions, like living in the past: a world of could have, should have and would have if only.... I don't have an endless hope for a miracle cure, nor am I waiting for life to come to me. Daily, I'm enjoying what I have: a devoted dog, a wonderful family, an extended world of people who drop in and out of my life, offering and receiving a connection that is meaningful. That's life. It's worth living.

One thing in my life that is really odd is that even after more than twenty years of being paralysed, in all my literal dreams, I am able to walk and talk. While I'm sleeping, I have the real opportunity to live a 'normal' life.

There are some people who do get a miracle cure, in spite of what doctors have told them. What about them? I think that people who have had a miracle would reveal that it has come after daily improvements over years, even decades, of hard work and perseverance. I don't think it happens suddenly. The final outcome is what gets the publicity, but just like an acting, or modelling career, exposure comes only after years and years of hard work and dedication. There aren't quick fixes and supernatural miracles. Life is the miracle. We can miss that looking for something that isn't going to happen, or we can embrace it, knowing we're living our miracle, as we live, breathe and love.

Talking about love, I believe it is unending, but the object of our love must be deserving. Everyone deserves love, but some can't give it back. If you're tied to one of those people, you have to let go. Otherwise, you'll be devoured, and you'll end up with nothing left to share. Emotions have to be expressed, or else there's no real connection between you and someone else. Life is about connections, otherwise it's an isolated and lonely existence.

I write this stuff to myself, but sometimes someone comes along on an Internet chat group, and we start talking. I meet a lot of new people that way. I have a static website that I created after *In the Blink of an Eye* came out. Sometimes people look me up there, to learn more about me, after we've 'met' on social media.

Usually men see my profile picture and want to talk. "Hi, Gorgeous, how are you today?" or "You are so beautiful. Will you be my friend?"

Some women write to me too: "Oh, I love your make-up. Can you give me some tips?" or "Oh, you're in Finland. I'm from Canada and I am part Finnish. Can I practise my Finnish with you?" These sorts of topics don't go very far. I'd prefer to talk about deeper issues in life.

Sometimes I think about random things. For example, what is prison? Let's take a person who is sentenced to life imprisonment. His worst enemy will not be the walls that surround him; his worst enemy will be the thought that those walls are going to be the only thing he will see for the rest of his life. Usually, things are not as bad as they first seem to be, but in the first moments of a situation, we think something horrible will be that way forever. Don't people tend to see the worst as though it will be that way forever? That's what makes it seem so bad. Also, if the surrounding people see it that way too, they reinforce that thought, making it even worse for the person living the nightmare. Instead, I like to make myself remember that nothing stays the same forever.

Life is a series of peaks and valleys. Bad situations will always improve. That gets me through difficult times and I think it can help other people too, if they realise it. Perfect situations change too, so we enjoy the high moments and persevere through the low moments, while they last.

As I'm writing on the computer, I receive a message on Tagged from someone new.

"Hi, I found you while I was looking for some old acquaintances. It says you live in Aruba, but you don't look Aruban. So, I am wondering who you are?"

This message comes from a man, but it's unusual. He isn't flirting. There is some music in the background; it's the song 'El Amor', aka 'The Love'. It's a Latino song I know well. It draws my attention. It makes me think of dancing, and so I decide to write back to him.

"Yes, I'm Kati Lepistö. I lived in Aruba for two years, but I've moved back to my home country, Finland. How about you?"

"I am from Curaçao originally. I now live in Amsterdam. So, you lived in Aruba? That's odd. How did you get there?" he asks.

"Ah, love took me there, but it didn't work out. Well, I miss the sun, but life moves on, you know?" I reply.

"Yes it does. So, will you stay in Finland? Are you working there?"

I'm surprised he doesn't ask about love, or what happened to it, not: don't I miss Aruba? Or, when will you go back? Most men would have flirted and asked about my broken heart and how he can imagine how lucky any man would be to have me, and what a tragic loss I must have overcome... Blah, blah, blah. Flirt, flirt, flirt. Then he'd say, "But I can help you overcome your loss. Be my friend..." But this man does not. He talks to me as if he's interested in my life now, not in what happened in the past. He sounds like a good guy to talk to.

"My work is my writing, I guess. I'm surrounded by wonderful friends and family, and this is home for me. But I do like to travel, especially to hot countries, because the sun is good for me."

"How did you end up in Amsterdam? Do you like it there?" I ask.

"I am meant to be in Europe. It just happened that way." We chat back and forth for a few days. I find myself intrigued by his messages and look forward to them. Sometimes he shares his philosophy, like we're all here for a purpose, and we need to live that purpose if we want to be truly happy. I totally agree!

"Sometimes people seem to be too busy and miss the real reason we're here," he writes.

"And what's that?"

"To be kind to each other, to dig deep into ourselves and get to know ourselves; to be the best people we can be."

It stuns me the first time he writes like this, because he could have been stealing from right inside my own brain.

Then, out of the blue one day, he says, "I have this feeling that you are a very special person."

Ah! There it is, finally. I'm sure he's hinting at my wheelchair and is wondering if I'm disabled, but he's not asking directly. Why not?

I write back immediately, "I guess you noticed the wheelchair. Yeah, I had a stroke when I was twenty and I'm paralysed. That's why the sun is especially good for me. It soothes and relaxes my otherwise very tense muscles. So, now that you know that, do you want to continue our correspondence, or do you want to quit?"

I think he'll probably write a polite email, or we'll have a couple of exchanges and then he'll fade away. He seems like a nice man, so I don't think he'll be rude, but like so many people looking for something from me, since there's no prospect of any heavy relationship, he'll fade himself away.

I guess I'm a little disappointed, since it was nice to meet someone who talked about philosophy and abstract things, not just what they had for lunch, or their neighbour whose dog wrecked their fence.

The next moment he writes back, "Are you crazy? I think you're a really interesting person. You've got my complete attention. Now you ask me if I want to stop writing? Of course not. Look, here's my email address... If you write to me, I'll write back. Okay?"

Wow! This guy's got stamina! Okay, I'll write him an email. I'm not sure how this is going to go, but well, I learnt a long time ago to go with the flow. I've got no choice in my physical life. I might as well let go and see what happens in my social life.

I write an email that says, "Hi, it's Kati, I'm surprised you didn't decide to stop writing. Here's my email too."

Our exchanges intensify once we're on email. This guy, Henning, must be crazy! He writes to me every day as soon as he gets home from work. Soon we're writing in the morning too, even before he goes to work, and when he comes home at night, and on the weekends we chat at least three times a day, sometimes for an hour or two at a time. Doesn't he have any friends?

"Yes, I have friends," Henning writes. "I've got family too, but they're spread out around the world. I've told them about you."

Oh yeah? Really? He's told family about an online friend? That's interesting. "What have you told them about me?"

"That you're unique."

"Well, that's obvious."

"No, I don't mean the wheelchair, I mean what's unique about you is that you don't complain about it. That's unique. Do you know how many people complain about tiny things?"

"That's true. I don't complain about being paralysed, that would just be a waste of energy. But why would I complain about it? What would be the point of that?"

"Nothing," he says, "but you see, your attitude is so different. Unique."

"Well, everything that happens to us happens for a reason, and the best things come out of it."

"I think so too. We're here for a reason, every one of us. When we accept our experiences, we can find that reason. If we complain about it, resist it, we might not."

"Yeah, I think so too. I think I've learnt a lot from becoming paralysed, stuff I'd never have learnt without it."

"Like what?"

"Like I can be free in my mind and in my soul no matter what physical limitations I have. I'm not sure people realise we can be trapped by the way we think. We put limitations on ourselves and act trapped, like we're in a bad situation we can't do anything about."

"Yes. And then we complain about it..."

"... because we don't know what else to do."

"Exactly. You'd be surprised how many people complain about their situation."

"I wouldn't actually. It's funny. Sometimes I'm in a restaurant and I hear people complain about this person or that job. Then they whisper, and I figure they're whispering about me, because they glance over. It usually happens when I'm being fed."

"So, what do you do?"

"Nothing. I can't."

"Oh, yeah."

Then I tell him about some of the crazy things people do in restaurants, because they don't know how to behave with me.

"One time, a waiter started to shout at me, like I was deaf. My friend Irina and I had to stifle our laughs. But of course, I can't stifle anything, so I start sounding like a donkey and he asks if he can get us anything else, meaning – 'Are you finished? Can you go now?' It just makes us laugh even more."

Henning replies, "Can I take you out for dinner sometime? It sounds like a lot of fun!"

Wow. That's a date, I think.

"Yeah, sure, but you'd have to come to Finland to get me." We have a good laugh about that too.

We have a lot of good laughs, and a lot of serious talks. Then, all of a sudden, something unexpected happens. I'm going to LA to visit my friends. When I book the flight, guess what? The best flight just happens to stop in Amsterdam on the way over.

"Henning, I am coming through Amsterdam to fly to LA. Let's meet."

"Yes, let's meet."

Oh, what just happened? I've got butterflies and I think I'm in love all over again. How did this happen? I didn't see *this* coming. But he's willing to meet me and now it's time to discuss the practicalities with Äiti.

The whole family knows I'm going to LA, and they know I'm stopping in Amsterdam, and they know it's to meet some man I met on the Internet. I'm sure they think I'm crazy, but they don't say anything.

*

I almost can't believe this. Today, I'm going to meet this mystery man, Henning van der Hoeven. Of course he's not a mystery, but because we haven't met face to face, there is some information I don't have. We've never kissed, for example, but I'm getting way ahead of myself, aren't I? I said there was no possibility of that kind of romantic love anymore, and I really believed that after I came back from Aruba. But now? I feel like I know what's inside Henning's brain (at least he has one, unlike Terry-the-tyrant), and I guess that's the most important thing I need to know about, at least for now. As for romance? I want to take things easy, but on the other hand, I have to be practical. We live in different countries, and it's not as if I can meet him for coffee, or go dancing, any time I like. Well, we have sort of had coffee, or he has, while we've emailed back and forth. And there was that crazy song on his Tagged page; 'El Amor' was playing in the background. It isn't a sign that he's a love for my life, but it does mean we have the same taste in music.

The flight feels like it's taking too long, but of course it lands right on time. I'm nervous, only because I'm so excited. I know we'll be compatible. And Äiti has arranged the rooms for us, just like I planned. She, and my assistant, Sanna, will share a room, and Henning and I will. I think he'll like that. What man wouldn't?

When we exit the gate at Amsterdam airport, I see him standing several metres away, in profile. He told me he is short, but he isn't really. He doesn't see us, because he's looking through the glass at the baggage claim. We move towards him.

"Do you want me to call to him?" Äiti asks.

I shake my head. He'll turn around eventually. And when he does the look on his face when he recognises me is priceless. I send him a huge smile and he practically runs to me. I can see he's bursting with the same affection, energy and excitement I'm feeling. I can't help it: I start crying.

"Am I that ugly?" he says, smiling, and we all laugh.

Remember I said once that all my tears of sadness would eventually run out, and I'd only have tears of joy left inside me? Well, I think that time has arrived.

"Kati, Marjatta, Sanna it is so nice to meet you all, face to face," he says. He shakes their hands, and picks up mine.

Oh, it is good to meet, face to face, and my romantic butterflies can't help themselves. He already knows me so well; we've talked and talked on email so much. He knows I can't control big emotion, so he doesn't fuss that I'm crying. He just takes it in his stride. We all go to book into the hotel; he smiles that we will share a room and a bed. Nothing seems to faze this guy. I'm impressed.

"While you two settle in, Kati and I will go for a walk around the airport," he tells my mom.

We walk through the airport and to a market, see gorgeous flowers and just enjoy each other's company. We both feel like we've known each other our whole lives. And he's already learnt to spell.

The four of us have dinner, and then my assistant, Sanna, takes me up to my room – our room – to prepare me. Äiti and Henning chat. Why do I feel like we're married and this is our wedding night?

"Your mother is a very special lady," Henning says when he comes into the room." But after that we don't talk about anyone else.

Sex with me is very complicated. There is nothing wrong with my biology and I feel. I have to be put in position, as when I'm sitting down or sleeping, but everything works. First, my body has to be prepared so that I don't cramp.

Slowly, one arm at a time needs to be stretched, then each leg. It helps the muscles to relax. Even with preparation, my body reacts involuntarily sometimes, because of excitement. A leg jumps or my arms can close as if I'm squeezing a teddy bear. But nothing fazes Henning. Everything works for Henning too. And he's a perfect gentleman. I feel like I've been waiting my whole life for a man that leads, loves, and responds to me. We have a perfect evening, a wonderful night, and Henning doesn't mind waking up in the night to turn me.

"Kati, just tell me what you need, and we'll fall back to sleep together."

We actually talked a lot about my care in our emails, so there is not really any shock or surprise for him, and our relationship feels totally natural. Come to think of it, during love making, how much do any of us actually speak?

When I wake up in the morning, I can't help thinking: *can life ever be richer?*

The trip to LA is fun, but honestly, I'm thinking just as much about the stop in Amsterdam, and that we're stopping over on the return flight too.

Äiti tells me, "I like him, Kati. I feel very comfortable with him."

While in LA, we stay at Jamie's and I mention Henning to him. Jamie's been a long-distance rock through the entire stroke trauma. I don't want to keep a good thing – meeting Henning – a secret.

"You met a guy, Kati, after all this, and he sounds really solid. There's nothing you can't do."

Henning is the man for me. After Aruba, I accepted I would not have the love of a man in my life, but here he is: a breath-taking surprise from heaven.

While I am in LA, Henning and I continue our email correspondence.

"Are we a couple now?" I ask him.

"I feel that way too, but let's talk more when we meet again in person."

When I see Stephanie, my long-time friend from Milan who has since moved to LA, she's ecstatic.

"Kati, this is fantastic! Got a picture of the man?" Stephanie always encourages me to dig deep, discover more about myself and share it with other people.

*

Henning and I have another wonderful overnight visit in Amsterdam on our way back to Finland. Spring has sprung in the world and my heart is also in bloom. What more can I say about our happiness? I know Henning feels the same way.

The emailing continues when we're both in our own homes.

"Yes, Kati, I promise I'll come to Mikkeli for your birthday in June."

We continue to get to know each other over email and discover more and more how we think alike and have the same perspective on life: to find and live the life we're meant to live, whatever that might be. Then one day, I receive a gorgeous message. This is just part of it.

"A new password has been created that opens happiness into my life, a four letter synonym for the word love. It starts with a 'K' and ends with an 'I' and beauty and magic and wonder lay in between. You are the food of my soul, and I would sell my tears to the devil to be the reason to make you smile. I would bow to my knees if I were to be caught in the shadow of your eyes. As I think of you, I get this urge, this need to feel your lips melting on mine. Wherever you are, whatever you feel, just know that somewhere between heaven and earth, a lonely heart beats at the rhythm of love, just for you."

Jeez. He's never written like *that* before.

I'm not nearly as poetic, but this is my reply: "Many people think they really know me... but I think it is only you (and Mom) who truly know me. And still you love me. Then you must *really* love me. You have shown me what love really means."

In my own private thoughts I've realised: God wants us to meet a few wrong people before meeting the right one, so that when we finally meet the right person, we will know how to be grateful for that gift.

We email like two crazy persons whenever he's not at work. He has a holiday coming up.

"Oh, you can come here!" I write.

"My mother and my sister are coming over from Curaçao and will be here for most of the time I'm on holiday. I can come after they leave for the last few days."

"Well, I'd like to meet them," I tell him. "Why don't I come to Amsterdam during their visit?"

He says he can see I won't take no for an answer.

"Okay," he says, "for the last two days."

His mother, Sheila, is a nice person. She is immediately comfortable with me, and learns to spell. So does his sister, Dianthe. I feel like I have a brand new extended family. We all have such a good time in Amsterdam, first with lunch, then walking around the city and relaxing in the park. All the time we are getting to know each other, and Henning's family is very relaxed around me, just like Henning is. In the afternoon, some of his cousins find us. It's so wonderful to be around cheerful, happy people.

After his family departs Amsterdam, Henning returns with me to Mikkeli, to spend time with my family.

"Now, here is a good man," my dad says, giving his immediate approval. With Aruba behind us, my family has learnt some things that cannot easily be unlearnt. They have experienced how a person can take advantage of my situation. They want to make sure that never happens again. Their acceptance of Henning only speaks more of what a decent, kind and sincere person he is. Although I never seem to stop surprising my family, they always rise to the challenge, accept my choices, and allow me to shape my life, rather than to be a victim of my circumstances.

Henning is eight years older than I am. Considering other men in my life have been older, eight years is not much. Unlike Warren, or Terry, he does not carry baggage that brings him down. He once married a woman, who was filled with grief, because she needed him. When circumstances changed, they agreed to part. But his kindness to her, and his lack of selfishness, fill me with respect and peace. There is much I could say about him, but I will say only this to try to capture the essence of the man: Henning has the confidence of a cat and the loyalty of a dog, the mind of a philosopher and the heart of a lion. And he is sexy.

How did I manage to find this man? Well, I didn't. I simply responded. I'm very different now from when I was twenty. Before the stroke, I was master of every detail in my life. Since the stroke, there is no spontaneity possible. Every activity, every moment of every day, has to be planned, because I need assistants' help and they have a life too. But in my attitude I've become completely the opposite – instead of control, I've learnt to accept life as it comes and to embrace the good in people and situations. Henning is the best surprise, in every way.

We both know we are meant to be together. Henning leaves his job in Amsterdam and moves to Mikkeli. He arrives on Christmas Eve. This Christmas, 2010, is the best Christmas ever, even better than the year I gave all my family and dear friends presents of thanks, and even better than the years when I was a child and received all my dream presents, like any child. It is even better than when I was 100 per cent healthy. I have my dear family and I have found true love – all the better because I didn't expect it, search for it or plan it.

One of the qualities I like so much about Henning is, I cannot persuade him to do what I want. He has boundaries. He's a very giving person, but I can't get away with demanding, which – to be honest – is something anyone in my position might be prone to doing. I want him to move to Finland right away, but he is more measured. Just like I wanted to visit him in Amsterdam the whole time his family was there, he agreed I could visit but made me wait, so that he could first have the family time already arranged. We are both people of clear, strong minds, who just happen to think a lot alike. (Good thing!)

Once Henning and I decide that we want to be together, the best and easiest thing is for him to move to Finland. I buy a one-storey townhouse, but it has to be renovated and made easier for a wheelchair. I design everything myself. Henning is very easy-going about this. I do have some discussion with my mother, before Henning moves from Amsterdam. The way it is designed, it is not obviously to accommodate a wheelchair. The house has no handicap toilet or shower, just big space. In fact, the whole house has wide and spacious rooms and hallways, so it's easy for me to move around. The wall between two small bedrooms has been taken down to make one big bedroom. The kitchen walls have been taken down to make an open kitchen/dining room/living room area. As in every Finnish home, this house also had a small bathing place next to a sauna, but I'd rather have a spacious bathroom, so we removed the sauna and make a big spa-like bathroom. I just love our terrace and garden. The back garden has been transformed into an easy-to-keep Japanese feng shui garden, with water running down a little layered fountain. I did have some professional advice for the landscaping.

One day we will move to a bigger home, but I will never stop loving this first house of mine. This house is a very important part of the beginning of a new, great chapter in my life. It shows that with pure will you can make impossible dreams come true, without even lifting a finger. Maybe one reason I did this on my own is to prove I could.

Henning is happy with the house and everything I've done. We talk about it, as with everything, but the downside to spelling is that sometimes it's just hard to keep up. When I'm planning and running around he says, "There must be a Broadway show going on in that head of yours."

It's true. Sometimes there is so much to share, and spelling and explaining is just too slow. We communicate about everything. At first, this is very difficult for me to get used to, and I don't even know why. It should be wonderful to have a partner you can share everything with and who wants to share back, right? But on the rare occasions when we have a disagreement – and let's face it all couples have some – I get even more upset when Henning says, "Let's talk about it." I mean, when you disagree and someone says, "Let's talk" that should be good, right? But I start sobbing even more. Why? It's a mystery, but one we have to solve.

So starts the opening of a big dark black hole in my head. Oh, no one put a bullet in me, but it might just as well have happened. The sobbing proves to be all about Terry, and the fact that he never wanted to hear from me.

I never had a voice at all. Henning saying, "Let's talk about it" triggers two horrible, parallel, competing, nonsensical thoughts.

One: Man talking equals Kati being verbally abused.

Two: Couple talking equals reminder of how Kati never got to communicate with Terry at all.

Henning says Terry's ghost is on the rise and we need to get rid of it.

That'll be great! Realising how much pain is underneath my smile, I start to feel really happy – even when we disagree – because it means we can talk and talk until problems are resolved. Now you can't stop us! We share about everything. My favourite time is at night, when we're in bed. You know, you only need a little bit of light to be able to air spell.

The ghost of the past overcome, we start to think about what we can do together with our life. For Henning, being together is more than a matter of love and companionship, although they are important and to be valued. There also has to be a reason, a purpose for our life together, a contribution we can make for the betterment of our world around us. We need to discover what that purpose is. In time, we will discover it.

Life with Henning is natural. It's evolving without any hitches. He does not get angry, but he knows when he needs time to himself and he takes it. I'm fine with that. He knows himself like I know me. It's a perfect match. When he first arrived, Henning was really happy just to be here with me, and then it got a little bit difficult for him. Getting a job was hard (his Finnish is excellent, so it should have been easy) and the long dark winter days were something he was not used to. I couldn't cheer him up, but when spring came, he cheered up on his own.

When the second winter came around, and he felt gloomy again, we both realised that he needs an escape to cheer him up.

"I think I'll go to Curaçao every February," he says. And I agree with him. He can see his family and enjoy sunshine.

Henning and I do not argue, but sometimes I do try to see what happens if I push a little.

"Why don't you just admit you're cross, for once," I spell.

"Nope."

There are some decisions we take to ensure our life is as normal as possible. For example, Henning will not play the part of an assistant, like my mother has sometimes had to be, but he will oversee everything. That way, he is my lover and my friend, but not my carer. We agree this is the best balance. Day to day and moment by moment, and through the night, he makes sure I am attended and have whatever I need, but he has said we must separate the care from the love, and that works well. It does mean I have my two assistants, and their schedules rotate. When neither is available, then Henning takes over. This is an excellent balance.

And my mother? She is so happy. She even allows Henning to take charge of managing the assistants when one needs to leave and we need to hire a replacement.

Recently she said to Henning, "All is well now. We are on the winning side. Kati's dearest wish has been realised. Both my children are near, and I finally feel that I can relax, and know she is cared for."

Here's a typical day for me:

At 8.00 a.m. when the bedroom door opens and the assistant arrives, is how my day starts. For the assistant, it's just another day of work, but for me it's life. Blinds open and sun hits my eyes. Happy, my little white dog, continues her sleep next to me like nothing's going on. She's used to my morning routine, and the coming and going of the assistant does not disturb her at all.

It's time to start making ourselves up for the day. Getting ready when you can do nothing by yourself isn't fast or easy, but even so, by pure determination I have kept my old habits of always looking good, no matter what it takes. You could say that this is my way of fighting back, refusing to give in to depression and sombreness. Actually, before the stroke, being pretty was my work, so hair, make-up or dress-up was the last thing I wanted to do on my days off. I think that I got about 80 per cent more determined in the dressing-up game after the stroke, except for the time in Aruba when I let it slide. But I let it slide for the wrong reasons, and now I get dolled up for the right reasons – I love it and it's fun!

Oh, there are rare days when my face is all natural. Henning loves those days. "Kati, you're so beautiful you don't need anything on your face," Henning tells me as he leans in the doorway while my make-up is being applied. But I don't listen.

Isn't it funny? Don't men usually complain if a woman doesn't take care of herself and how she looks? As a former model, you may think that I'm always fully covered with make-up, but no. Make-up is just about enhancing what you already have with some powder, eyeliner, mascara and lip gloss to do the trick. To be honest, make-up time can be a nightmare moment for me, and the assistant. It drives me up the wall if she can't get it just the way I want it. How many times have I thought to myself, *if only I could move my hands*? It's as bad as having an itch you can't scratch when you want to get your hair, or eyeliner, just right and you can't. Ladies, you know exactly what I mean, right?

Next comes the time for my grand breakfast, which is usually a little bit of porridge, generally with a lot of cinnamon. Breakfast is followed up with a day that I mainly spend at my PC. Writing, writing and writing. To my friends abroad, my online friends, and to myself. As well, I am still the locked-in spokesperson and like to stay in touch with COGAIN and other people, who champion locked-in and other disabled people. Of course, my days vary depending on what kind of day it is, but if there is no physiotherapy, no household chores, no appointments, or hanging around in the city, then the PC is my main occupation.

We usually eat dinner around 5.00 p.m. The assistant helps me to eat, so Henning and I can eat together. Then at 6.00 p.m. the assistant leaves for her private life, and ours begins. We don't have that much time alone together, so we really appreciate it when we do. We don't want to waste it arguing about some stupid little thing; we discuss things, but we never argue. One of the things I really love about Henning is that he really can talk. Communication is key to any relationship, and ours works well, especially because we talk so much. It's ironic isn't it? I can't speak but I guess Henning and I talk together as much – maybe even more – than any other couple.

The assistant returns between 10.00 and 11.00 p.m. for the night shift, which starts with a midnight snack and a cup of coffee. Then it's time I hit the shower, which is more like a shower/happy-hour event full of silly information exchanges, and laughter with my assistant. When someone else showers me, how do I cope? Isn't a shower very personal? Practically speaking, this is not a romantic or sexual activity. Out of necessity, the assistant is touching me everywhere and I blank it out. It's the best way to deal with the lack of privacy. Most nights an assistant prepares me for bed. But once or twice a week, Henning and I take this time together. With no one else in the house, we have real privacy. It's precious. Before sleeping we watch some TV, cuddle and talk. I love our pillow talks. They are the best foreplay for a good night's rest.

This seems like a routine, and it is. You can see how spontaneity is impossible with my condition. But we find our intimacy, we plan our privacy, and life runs smoothly, most of the time. Some days things don't quite go to plan. Remember Henning learnt to spell even before we met? Well today, when my mother is with us, things get a little confusing. Äiti and I are making a grocery list. Henning is writing down what we need. As I spell, my mother verbalises what I'm spelling, and sometimes my mother says one thing, but Henning is writing something different. For example,

"*Porkkana,*" my mother says.

"No, carrots," says Henning. I start to laugh.

They both look at me.

"What is the idea?" Henning spells.

"I'm not an idiot!" says my mom.

I can't stop laughing so I can't spell to them what is so ridiculous. I just want some carrots!

Here's where the confusion was. I'll let you work it out: In Finnish, the word for carrot is *porkkana*. In Finnish the word for ideas is *ideoita*.

What is so complicated about a grocery list? I realise there are two alphabets operating and two languages, the Finnish and the English. There is a lot of overlap, but there is enough difference that, if I buy what Henning is thinking, translated from English to Finnish, we will have a very strange vegetable dish, and a mildly offended mother-in-law. Sometimes there are disadvantages to knowing several languages.

Spelling can also get overcomplicated, not because of duel languages, but just because people are trying too hard. There have been times when I'm just gathering my own thoughts, not even spelling, my eyelids are closing, or I'm just looking around while I'm thinking, and someone starts to spell out what I'm saying... but actually, I'm not saying anything!

""No?" Kati, what do you mean "No", you haven't said anything yet."

"I-a-m-n-o-t-t-r-y-i-n-g-t-o-s-p-... Oh, you are not trying to spell! Sorry."

We have to laugh, and start again, or stop completely. I admit there are times when Henning and I do get angry with each other. Maybe we haven't had enough to keep us busy, or maybe too much? Anyway, finally we have our first fights, one when he's angry and one that's my turn.

The first – Henning's turn: We're on our way to a special lunch with friends; but the car has a different idea. Henning gets mad at the car, and mad at me for (the assistant) sending a message on the phone, to my dad saying, "We're on our way!"

Another time, I get mad because Henning is driving too fast. It's important to note that, in a car, I can't auto-adjust like most people. Instead, if there are jerky movements, fast turns or bumps, I'm shifted forcibly in my chair. Sometimes my head rolls around on the top of my neck. I'm completely floating with no way of controlling where or how I'm moving. On this occasion, it's too much, and I get scared, and start to howl.

Then there's one time when both of us are mad at the same time. Yeah, it's a real fight! Although he gets mad first, he keeps his cool as usual. Honestly, I think I get maddest when he stays super-calm.

We have a difference of opinion; of course now I don't even remember what that is about. He leaves the room to watch TV in peace, then all of a sudden, he decides to take Happy out for a walk without saying a word (now, just thinking about it makes me mad). Humph! We're supposed to have a nice movie evening, and instead he walks out. So I think – well, two can play at this game. I had put a plate of gingerbread, grapes and cheese out (I had the assistant do it on my behalf, which in my life is exactly the same thing) for us to share during the movie. But he's left, so I change my mind and I decide to spend the next four hours at the PC. In fact, if I could, I would throw the plate at the wall. (I don't ask the assistant to do that on my behalf; that is going a bit too far!) Actually, I think this is the first real anger I've felt since the stroke. You might think I've felt this anger countless times before. Nope! Not this kind of anger; it's like a burning sensation in my heart. Well, it's good writing material; writing is so much easier when I'm angry, and this is infuriating. It's rare that we have time totally alone together, and why do we have some ridiculous fight to ruin it? Well, we are both very stubborn and I'm not about to give in. Later, Henning returns and I stay at my PC. I just ask for water and Henning acts like nothing is wrong. Humph. He's just trying to cover up his stupid behaviour.

The next day comes and I feel so sad because of the fight. We just wasted our evening. Of course we talk about it, but at least for me, that is not resolution enough, so I also write to him about it. Eventually, we make up, otherwise I would not be here telling the story.

Henning has to have a portion of his life as his own, even in Finland, and in the early days that brings with it some problems. When he goes out with his friends without telling me, I get mad. The worst, for example, is over a weekend, when he decides on Saturday to relax at the PC and sleep, because he'll be going out in the evening. On Sunday, he sleeps because he's tired after going out on Saturday. Well that's a no-fun-filled weekend for me. When it happened, I didn't say anything to him over that weekend, because I'm learning from him. Sometimes I get annoyed, and it's really over things that shouldn't annoy me. Being left alone reminds me of other painful times, such as when I lived in Aruba. There I felt abandoned a lot of the time, and a memory is not Henning's fault. So, I'm learning not to explode until I've had time to think about what's made me mad. Usually, it isn't really about Henning at all. The only thing that's making me cross these days is that I'm dieting, and after three weeks of strict diet, I've lost only 500 grams. Grrr! (Sometimes life is like this.)

Henning is very sensible, and has convinced me that getting angry isn't worth the struggle and the pain. He's amazingly wise, teaching me to roll with disagreements, rather than to punch it up with my fury. I guess, up until now, that's always the way I've been, but I'm changing.

I'm learning to think about him more and more, and a little less about me. For example, Henning has finally got a job in a school and it is something for him, but it isn't his dream job. It isn't easy for him, in many ways. He's given up a lot, leaving his home and his work in Amsterdam to be here in Finland with me.

Today after work, on this sunny summer's day, he comes to me and kneels down. Although I'm always in a chair and to kneel puts us at eye level, he's never actually done this before.

"Kati, my life is to be with you. Will you marry me?"

I blink once – no need to spell, it's such a nice moment.

Soon, we find an engagement ring and have a party. I've planned parties before, but never an engagement party for myself. If this occasion is a foretaste of our wedding, it will be a day to remember, let me tell you. I mean, this is really something to celebrate!

Of course, with an engagement must come a bridal diet. Isn't that right, ladies? I guess I drive Henning crazy sometimes with my mood swings. It'll be worth it when I wear my gorgeous wedding dress though.

The bridal diet started officially on 1 January 2012. Imagine this: the first time I go swimming, I swim like a crazy person with a taste of blood in my mouth. I swim for nearly an hour and I manage to swim... only 300 metres! Aargh! That's bad, but I keep going and with each visit to the pool I improve by 500 metres, until I finally reach 1,400 metres, twice a week. A couple of times I make 1,700 metres. And do I slim down? You betcha. With the eating discipline of a model (when I decide to turn it on) and regular exercise, I shed the weight just like I'm meant to.

Stephanie writes from the States.

"Engaged! That's awesome!" Then she reminds me to keep journaling. "We need lots of new material for Book Two," she says. She's a number-one cheerleader for me. She even put my name into the Oprah circle. Apparently, Oprah doesn't go with the direct approach. She has to find the person, or the book, or whatever, on her own. I didn't get onto the show, but Stephanie's effort was amazing, and it did give me a boost to keep writing.

The weather is fantastic this summer and it's a great time to plan the wedding, and to get out, to do things and go places. It's the last summer of our singlehood, so we discuss ideas and possible projects. One crazy idea is to make a documentary about my life. Why not? We've already got footage, and we enhance it to create a reality TV insert. Henning has a background in film production, I love to write, and so we're always thinking of creative ways to get our message of encouragement across.

Our message is evolving all the time. It's really simple. Henning has always wanted to encourage people to do, and to be, their best. In a way, that's the reason he got married before. Although he didn't exactly realise it at the time, he just wanted the best for a young woman who was really struggling. He loved her and wanted to help. Now, he still wants to help people. He's not marrying me for that, but since I am a 'champion for locked-in people' and he is a believer in helping people to become the best they can be, together we have work to do to make a difference with what we know.

While we're having a meal with my brother and Anu one day, Henning says, "Kati, you don't seem to realise this, but you have an amazing, positive attitude, unlike anyone I've ever met. You have a gift to be shared."

"Really?"

"That's true," says Jukka, "it's impossible to make Kati stop if she believes she can do something."

"She'll go through a brick wall. No one can stop her," Anu says.

So we will pull down the brick walls that separate us from other people who need inspiration and hope against huge physical or even mental odds. But how?

Summer brings with it a lot of wedding-planning time and family time, but we also share some amazing fun time. After years of adoring Prince, I finally go to a live concert. Man, it's worth the wait. The highlight is 'Purple Rain', of course, when the confetti pours down and the music fills the stadium. Ahhh! Henning laughs at me, I think, to be so crazy for this singer. But it's a good laugh.

Then Henning and I take a trip to Barcelona. Oh, it'd be so great to live in Spain; not too far from family but far, far away from the cold, and it would be a wonderful place to raise children. Yes, that is why we will one day need a bigger house – for a family.

Sometimes, I look over at Henning and I wish I could run my fingers through his dark, curly hair. He is so thoughtful. He anticipates this. He massages my hands and fingers, and then puts a hand onto his head after we make love. I adore his wavy hair, and it makes me feel like I am giving something to him.

With the cool autumn air comes some frosty news. When we got engaged, we started to discuss having a baby. Recently, after meeting with a doctor, I can sum up the verdict in his few short words: "Blood thickens during pregnancy, and that could trigger another stroke."

Conclusion: no baby, it's too dangerous for me. There it is: another crushing blow, another life sentence. I feel so empty, like half a woman. I'm crying in the doctor's office, stunned, with no desire to communicate. Henning is wonderful, kind and gentle, but I know he's hurting too. I saw him wiping his tears, before he took my hand and held it.

Our relationship is not built on false hopes. Henning accepts me as I am. To a stranger looking on, our situation may not look good, but appearances can be so deceptive. They say communication is the most important thing in marriage. Well, I cannot speak, but Henning and I have so much dialogue, I can't believe anyone has more than we do. We communicate on every matter, without reservation and without judgement. Sharing our thoughts and feelings is, perhaps, our secret weapon for the strength and health of our relationship. Yes, we both feel crushed by the doctor's news, but we share our feelings with each other, and this makes our relationship even stronger.

In our society, outer victories are celebrated, but we all know deep down, that the greatest and most important victories come from the challenging battles we fight and win deep inside ourselves. People look at me and say they are surprised, and in awe, of what physical challenges I've overcome. But the biggest challenge by far was my desire for romance, a deep and loving relationship with a man. I always wanted love, but after Aruba I finally had to give up on it, after being so hurt and emotionally bruised and battered. Then along came a quiet, confident, wise man. Quite unexpectedly, romance came knocking on my door and I opened it.

People ask, how do I live with paralysis? The answer: I live day to day. I never expected to be paralysed at age twenty, and I certainly never expected to meet a prince at age thirty-five. Life is full of the unexpected. We learn to embrace it in order to live life to the full.

I see Henning, sitting patiently in the doctor's office, waiting until I'm ready to be wheeled back out into the cold world. I'm reminded of something he said before we left the house today, about our future, no matter what the doctor would say,

"On the porch of a small cabin in the middle of the Garden of Eden there sits a couple, who met long ago on the Internet, a place where all thought is fake and cold. They sit there as proof of the miraculous ways of the Lord, who can create life and love, no matter what the circumstance or place."

CHAPTER 32

Wedding Day

Henning and I have a civil ceremony at the registrar's office on 20 December 2012. If this was our wedding day, this chapter would finish here. But this is only the day we got married. It was a nice enough day, but not special.

However, like any sensible, romantic bride, I have made plans for a grand affair to be remembered by every family member and close friend in the Lepistö/van der Hoeven clan. And so it will be.

"Kati, I am so glad I found you. Life is full of challenges, I am so happy to share them with you." That's what he said after the civil ceremony. That's my wonderful husband, Henning.

One key I've learnt about relationships is this: in a normal, everyday relationship, as well as in marriage, nothing is more important than listening to the other person and trying our best to understand without judging. If we truly listen, without defending ourselves or offending the other person, life is so much easier.

*

December in Finland is freezing, but with the snow glistening in the sunshine, it can be strikingly beautiful. Today, 23 December, it's perfect, and it's our wedding day. I've been awake since 3.00 a.m. when beautiful bridesmaid Irina went to the bathroom. Her getting up woke me and I haven't been able to get back to sleep. How could I? It's like Christmas and New Year, and a sixteenth birthday all rolled into one. How could I sleep any more today?

Well, at least you can't say I was tossing and turning.

I finally get up at 6.30 a.m. and drink coffee. I won't eat or drink once I'm dressed, because it would be an ordeal to try to pee wearing my wedding dress.

I spent hours on the PC planning this day. Every detail of the wedding has been arranged. Photographs will take place before the ceremony, while there is some daylight. It's so cold; the outdoor photos will be only of Henning and me. I have a fur coat that will help to keep me warm.

When I look outside, I see that nature has cooperated fully. The snow covers the land and the trees, as hoped. It's a frosty white wonderland, and I am Alice looking into a new world full of wonder. Irina and Stephanie, my two dearest girlfriends, are with me for this incredible occasion.

"It's so beautiful," Stephanie says. "I never imagined it could be this...Well, girl, this is it! You made it through everything and now the best is yet to come. That's what they say, right?" Stephanie is funny and confident, and I can tell, underneath that super-cool girl is a woman nearly crying. She's been a rock and I'm so glad she's come from California to share this day with me.

Crazy Stephanie from New Zealand, and Irina the Finnish free spirit, will stand up with me. I am so spoilt! (Of course they will flank me in my chair.)

I'm so excited. How did this day come to be? It's not the first time I've been engaged, but it is the first and only time I will be married, and it has been such an amazing experience to meet Henning, and worth the wait for the right person. We respect each other totally.

Last night he reminded me, "Kati, I love your attitude to life. You have the most reason to complain of anyone I know, and still, you do not complain."

I've told him, "Henning, when other people would cave in and give me what I insist, you do not. You give me what I need."

All the usual things that happen to a bride on her wedding day will happen this morning: hair, make-up, dress. When it is time, six women, myself, my bridesmaids, my mother, my assistants, make our way by taxi to the wedding mansion. I am breathless, and the joy and chatter of everyone fills the car. We arrive and my prince comes to meet me.

Henning braves the cold in only his suit. It's -30°C. He shivers and shakes, but his smile warms the whole shoot and we finish with jaws frozen in a smile. He will tell me, even years later, "I never felt the cold."

The photographer snaps away for almost an hour, his fingers freezing, I'm sure.

"Okay, look this way," he says. "You all right, Henning? You're shivering."

"Our hearts are warm. This is one day in a lifetime. Let's not miss a single moment wishing for something else," Henning says.

Henning is only wearing his wedding suit and no long underwear underneath. I wish I'd included that detail in the planning.

The string quartet plays 'Sleeping Beauty' as my father wheels me to the priest. I am wide awake, ready to live with the down-to-earth prince who has come. Henning holds my hand as the service is carried out, and I cry surprisingly little, and quietly.

Irina reads the classic piece about love from the Bible, (1Corinthians, chapter 13), which makes the floodgates open up more. She is so loving; it's the perfect piece for her to read. Love has been patient and oh, so kind. And as I look into Henning's eyes, I know we will keep no record of wrongs.

After the official service, when the whole audience comes to congratulate us, I finally lose it big time. Laughing and crying are so close to each other on the emotional spectrum and I manage both, simultaneously. Who says a tetraplegic can't multi-task?

Isa makes his speech at the wedding, and the most memorable dinner-moment is when he says, "Henning, welcome to our unbelievable family." Everybody laughs.

Henning's mom, Sheila, speaks and then my bridesmaids, Irina and Stephanie do a double act. It's all wonderful, including Stephanie's stand-up, which is hilarious. From that moment we will always be called The Katings. Then Henning's best men, Leontios and Darrick, say their pieces. Jamie and my mom were close by, silent supporters enjoying their time to soak in our happiness. We should have had flags from all the countries the wedding party represented, never mind all our guests. From America to New Zealand and many points in between, our guests speak the international languages of love and joy at our wedding. I planned it, and worked hard, but the wedding is even more wonderful than I could ever have expected.

We are both so happy, and so pleased that everyone else is happy. It's a day that angels must have been singing: "Finally, Kati, you have made your match" – or is that "met your match?" Both are true.

The beauty of the wedding day is etched into everyone's mind. Anu, my sister-in-law, whispers to her little girl, "It is like a beautiful fairy tale." And even better, it is all real. The love in the room is profound. The food, the cutting of the cake, the wedding dance as Henning takes me around the room in the wheelchair to the music we met by, 'El Amor', is full of laughter, and I know this is the day of the beginning. He wiggles his toosh and makes me laugh. Sparklers, and then good luck lanterns are lit. The night becomes alight with star-struck beauty, represented perfectly by the expression on my niece, Sofia's, face. Colours of pink, orange and yellow light the black sky and the freezing cold is met with warm glows that ascend high above the trees until they disappear in the distance. The dancing carries on until very late, in perfect Latino style. Finnish thoughtfulness meets extravagant happiness. Our family is perfectly balanced.

The morning light, which in Finnish December isn't very early or very strong, brings with it a sense in me that life is just beginning. I'm very lucky to have Henning. Usually, we have our most handsome boyfriends when we are young, but at thirty-six, I can say I have the most intelligent, romantic, funny, sweet and handsome husband ever. At the wedding, the priest said that I thought Henning is my angel, and no one can tell me this isn't true.

If anyone asks me what I have that other women don't, to bring me such a wonderful husband, I say, a positive attitude and a smile. He said that's what drew me to him; I've never complained about any situation and I have a goddess-like smile.

Sometimes, I've been asked if I'm hoping for a miracle. To tell you the truth, the answer is no, because I already have my miracle, and he is called Henning. A woman doesn't need a husband in order to be happy, but in my case, to have a husband at all is a miracle.

As a thank you to cyberspace and all technology available that has brought two lovers together, it seems right that, since we met on the Internet, I should add the wedding video here:

https://youtu.be/fRPy44KnXRY

A short time after the wedding, I read my journal spanning the year before we got married. It's joy and fury, angst and excitement. It's life with a tetraplegic! That Henning sticks by me, through all the ups and downs, is amazing. That I persevere through my temper and dissatisfaction with others is astounding. In truth, I am learning to keep my cool – thanks to Henning. Sometimes, he can be annoyingly wise, and we are the better for it. Yes, sometimes his cool infuriates me, but actually, his is the better way.

CHAPTER 33

Ultimate Purpose

Henning is not bossy, but he is smart and for the first time in my life I've found someone I'm willing to follow. It's harder though, to work with someone else rather than to make my own decisions. Better together, but harder.

He shares with me an idea he's got: "On our wedding day, as we were strolling up to the altar, everyone's eyes were on you. I raised my head and looked at the priest as he was wiping a tear away from his eye. I'm sure he doesn't cry at most weddings. At that moment, I knew that our union is not just the biggest thing in our lives, but it touches others too, and we have to share this. Kati, we need to share with the world, that we have something very special."

"Yes," I spell, "of course we do." But it isn't until a little later that I understand the full scope of what Henning is suggesting.

The priest's tears simply confirmed what local press had said before the wedding. I'm a bit of a local Finnish celebrity, and reporters arrived before our wedding.

"Ms Lepistö, your story is so inspiring," one of them said.

"Mr van der Hoeven, will you continue to encourage your wife to share her experience so others will be inspired?" another asked.

We said, "Yes," but to be honest, I thought they were complimenting us in order to have better access for pictures. Henning is perceptive. He saw there was something more to it.

"This is not just about love," Henning says now. "Love is good, but we have even more to offer. We have insight into what other people need in order to thrive, and we can share this insight. In fact, it would be selfish to keep it for ourselves. Think of the people we can encourage. You wanted to die..."

"I don't want to think about that," I spell. "That is in the past." Thankfully.

"But there will be other people."

I begin to understand.

"Oh yes, of course, we can help others to push through the difficulty." Yes, I understand what Henning is saying. Our life together is an inspiration to others, for what is possible when you face the odds; there is no border between the possible and the impossible, if we push through.

We can share our story together, so that people can learn how to cope and to believe anything is possible no matter how bad the odds. It is enough that I have suffered. That gives me credibility, and even wisdom, on how to cope with being locked-in. I can go back into history, to share what I went through, so other people can understand. I have been a representative for locked-in syndrome in order to raise awareness, for families of those locked-in, and those who have suffered themselves. But now Henning and I can be spokespeople for living positively, to overcome the barriers we are faced with.

"There's something else, Kati," my husband says. He has my full attention. "This will be painful." Immediately, I start to cry, but he continues. "As you share your fear and frustration, it will not be a romantic look at our happy ending, but it will be a real look at your pain, to share your experience and wisdom. That's the way we can make a difference." I'm scared, but I also know he's right. If I am going to be the biggest help I can be to other people, I *am* going to have to recall my story and share it so that other people can connect with me, and trust I know what I'm talking about. My story does have a happy ending, not only because I got married to a wonderful man, but more importantly because I'm thriving as a very handicapped person. I will have to relive some of my pain as I share my story with others, in order to help them through theirs. *In the Blink of an Eye* was journaling, but from now on we will go much deeper – we have to. And in a flash it's all come together: Now I know why I've been writing all these years – it's to encourage other people, not just those who are locked-in, but all people who are looking for the way to live a happy and fulfilling life.

"Kati, you have your website about locked-in, and we can use that to start, but you need to blog." And that's what I start to do.

Henning and I set up the blog platform on the website, which already accesses translations in four languages. As I start to think of what to share, I'm overwhelmed with the sense that this is what all my suffering has been about, this is what all the writing (practice) has been about, and this is what my life has been about – sharing my suffering so that others can overcome their own tragedy. This stubborn, beautiful supermodel overcame total devastation, and if we can build a platform from this, we can share the message: if I can, anyone can.

Henning and I understand some secrets about life. It isn't about what you have, or even what you achieve, life is about making the most of whatever comes our way, so that we can be truly alive, and make the world a vibrant place, full of love. I'm looking at my dog right now, sitting quietly, gazing at me. The secret to happiness is contentment with the situation you find yourself in. I need to write that down, and explain how I know that and how to live it. I really want to make a difference, to impact the lives of others who are struggling. Telling my story will help. *In the Blink of an Eye* was a start, and now together, Henning and I can engage with people around the world who need inspiration to carry through their difficulties. This is our mission.

I begin to write.

"Our words that we keep saying to ourselves are extremely important. Are we aware of our unspoken thoughts? Our feelings follow those thoughts, and they will lead us to action. When I'm feeling low, I deliberately think happy thoughts and act happy, and I find myself feeling happy." I show Henning. "How's this?" I ask him.

"It's okay. There needs to be more," Henning says. I try again...

"Some people chase happiness while other people choose happiness. That makes the whole difference in our lives."

And another: "Happiness comes from the progressive realisation of a goal. My first goal was to survive. Now, having done that, it is to enable others to survive, against any odds."

"This last one is getting better," Henning says. "It's a good start."

On another day, another entry...

"Kati, you can't say this!"

"Why not? It's what I'm thinking."

"It's not polite."

(Sometimes I write four-letter words.) Grrr. I don't like being told what to do.

Another day comes and Henning reads another post. "Kati, you must tell them more, not just keep it shallow or superficial. You must tell them what's deep inside your heart. How you have learnt from the stroke, how you have changed."

His words hurt me. I'm sharing, I'm trying, but is he just criticising? Or worse, is he telling me what to do?

"Kati, we need to be real. People are suffering. We can help them to learn how to battle through the hard times, while they adjust to their trauma, whatever it is."

But I don't want to dig too deep.

"This is not for you, this is for other people who need our help and inspiration."

He's pushing me and pushing me. I cry, I howl, I fume, but deep inside, I know he's right. I can't avoid it indefinitely. I have to dig in, although it takes me longer to admit it to him.

It's easy for Latinos to express themselves with warm words and big hugs. They do not hide their feelings, good or bad. They express everything. Finnish people are different. We are very reserved, not open with our emotions. Oh, I am outspoken, and confident. Before the stroke I had a loud and clear voice. But never have I been one to show how I'm feeling. That is private. The stroke caused me to cry or howl, but without that, it would not be obvious how I am feeling. And anyway, my howling is nothing to go by, because as I've said, sometimes I show the opposite expression to what I'm actually feeling.

He's pushing me, and I'm getting angrier and angrier. But the more I resist the stronger I feel deep inside, that he is right. I am still healing from my own past, from the brokenness I felt in Aruba. I'm resisting memories of the helplessness and cruelty I suffered, of the disappointment and shame and misery. It also goes back further, to the dark days after returning home from rehab. Damn! I'm trapped by my own emotions even though I have love and family and so much good on my side. If I'm still trapped by history, what about other people? Henning is right. Oh, of course he's right. If I'm going to be any help to anyone, I have to be willing to share my struggles, to show others how to pick themselves up and carry on. I need to deliver what is needed and not hold back. Like the people I'm writing to, I need to dig into the emotional pain, so they'll trust what I say works. If someone is suffering paralysis, I'm a safe adviser. But how can I help others with the emotional baggage attached, unless I open up and share myself? It is hard to go against our own personality and culture, but when it's for a good purpose, we have to.

"You're right, Henning."

And now our mission begins.

Henning has wisdom that goes beyond his experiences, and he has a strategy to fulfil our purpose together. What attracted me to my husband, and him to me, was far more than physical chemistry, or even the song, 'El Amor' ('The Love'). We have a like-mindedness; we are pragmatic, and want others to live fulfilled lives. I am the brand and he is the voice, and together we are helping others to see their potential. In all of this, we've wrestled sometimes, because we make each other grow to be the best we can be.

To be honest, he's perfect already, but he's taken me closer to perfection too, guiding me to be more even-tempered and more giving. All of a sudden, I even see an advantage to being in Finland: *Sisu*[2]. Maybe it's the only one for me, but it is making all the difference to my life, because I am making a difference to others.

"We need to work; write and promote what we write, Kati." I nod.

As I start to blog, it isn't like my *Blink* journal entries, or my private writing. I'm improving my writing as I imagine the people I'm writing to, and learn how to open myself up. Sometimes I feel embarrassed, so there are some things I don't talk about. Maybe I will one day, who knows? As I write, Henkka (Henning's Finnish nickname, which he doesn't like very much) coins the phrase 'Inspirational Model'. I love it. I can't walk down a catwalk, or pose for magazine shots, but I can inspire others to face their challenges and to overcome them. My experience is my credential.

---

2. *Sisu* is a Finnish concept I will share with you in some detail on page 438.

CHAPTER 34

Beginning to Blog; Sharing a Lifestyle

Here are my inspirational points:

» Never give up!

» Do for others.

» Have a purpose. Everyone has a reason for being here. If you don't know yours, find it!

» Self-pity is only an energy drain. Dump it.

» The answer to every interpersonal problem is to communicate.

» Everything happens for a reason. There's no point moaning when something bad happens. Find the reason for it, rather than fight the problem.

Before we were married, I gave interviews and speeches (of course someone spelled out my words for me). Now something is different. Henning is like a part of me, or I am a part of him, or both. We have the same purpose, which is to inspire others to achieve everything they can, no matter the odds against them. That's how I've lived. That's what

Henning believes in. Our union is not just only because we love, but it has a purpose, and together we are better to fulfil that purpose. Better together! By the third blog, I'm becoming quite relaxed with sharing openly.

Blog post:

Making a Difference to the World:

About a year after paralysis, I began to think seriously that life has to be more than just the disease. Out of the question that I would expect the rest of my life to be idle, like death.

I could no longer continue as a model, and I thought that no one would hire me to work. I decided to create a name just for myself, Kati Lepistö, so I could get a job. I was thinking that I need public visibility.

I thought that maybe I need to be a role model for others in how to live, even though there are physical limitations. I realised that it did not make any sense to fight against my situation. Better to accept the new one and enjoy life.

I began to give interviews...

Another Post:

On the Road:

Nowadays, being spontaneous means planning something at least twenty-four hours in advance. I cannot just jump into the car and go anywhere. This is one of those things I envy – people who can just go wherever and whenever they please...

I have to check at least three other people's timetables before I can decide what is feasible, and only then can I do the rest of the planning.

Often families with disabled members are afraid to travel. Family Lepistö is an exception. We have visited the Caribbean, Mexico, USA, Asia and different countries in Europe, all from Finland. My parents almost never travelled before I became paralysed.

When Henning was moving to Finland, he insisted we get a wheelchair-accessible car.

My parents always had just a normal passenger car....
You cannot imagine what kind of heavy work it is to lift me to the car. One time Mom was counting that she lifted me ten times a day, in and out of the car. You do not need a gym after that!"

If readers learn the practical side of things they can prepare themselves and know they are not alone in facing difficulties.

And opening up myself:

Still, after years, I felt like a major loser, although I had beaten a life that had left me paralysed. To see friends with boyfriends and girlfriends forming families, and here I was, thirty years old and still living at home. I'll never forget the day I turned thirty. Sure, I was happy on the outside, but man did I feel like the biggest loser ever! Friends were having great careers, making money. And what do I do? Sit at home and get very little money from the government.

When people read this, I hope they'll recognise the shame, the pain and struggle they are facing is what I faced too. They don't need to feel ashamed, or guilty. It's all part of the healing process and getting on to live from day to day.

And:

We were pretty sure that doctors would not show a green light to getting pregnant, but when the doctor said out loud that they don't recommend it, I was surprised how hard I took it. I was crying very much. I felt like I was not a woman if I didn't have children. It hurt so much for a month. But then I pulled myself together and understood that you don't need children for a happy and fulfilled life. I was not ready to take the chance that I could have another stroke, or even die. Adopting a child is exactly what we'll try to do – to help another person.

Although:

Sometimes when I look at my niece I thank God I do not have children, because I can only imagine how horrible it would feel if I could not touch them.

This is raw and real, Henning says – and polite. I laugh at myself for how rude I can be, because yes, well, admittedly, sometimes in my mind, and in my writing, I swear – like a trooper. It's a long-time habit, which I cannot blame on the stroke. The swearing came long before that, and is a piece of me that didn't malfunction. Perhaps it should have. Now, I leave it out of my writing.

So here we are, newlyweds. For Henning, compatibility has always been the big issue for him in marriage, not mobility. When he recognised how compatible we were, the physical issues didn't faze him. As we begin to work together, it's obvious we are connected: I'm the brand, Henning is the manager. We both write and are determined to fulfil our joint purpose, which is to make the world a better place by engaging with people so they will see the possibilities beyond their challenges. Our passion is to inspire others to live life to the full, regardless of circumstances. I'm living proof that this way of looking at life works. Until now I have been a face for paralysed people. Together our aim is to get our life-fulfilling message out and to be available to help anybody who's open to our way of thinking.

In our life together, we mostly try to keep life light, without conflict, and save drama for movies and TV. Humour is better than drama in difficult lives. We take tension, convert it into passion, and save the 'oohs' and 'aahs' for the bedroom and under the covers.

*

There are all kinds of blogging. Sometimes I share inner thoughts; sometimes I write about practical living.

Home: organised.

Along with our trips around Finland and across land over Europe in our wheelchair-accessible van, there is day-to-day life to be lived. Sharing this publically can give people a sense of how I cope. Some things will resonate; nothing is weird or incorrect; everything is to help manage the challenge better.

First, remember I dress up every day? I choose my daily wardrobe, accessories, matching shoes, add my hair and make-up, and perfume. I think I drive my assistants crazy, because I look in the mirror to test whether my collar is best up or down, how to fold the sleeves just right, and so on. My clothes are stored by colour, making it easier to explain what I want to wear on any given day. Someone else may think this is eccentric, but it's a deliberate strategy. Dresses are stored by colour in the closet, sweaters and tops too, stacked on open shelves. Even my jewellery is organised this way, so it makes it more efficient when I have to ask someone to find something.

My food is stored in an orderly fashion too, which simplifies any explanation about how I want to do my cooking. When my assistant is my hands, every single step is initiated and checked over by me. First, the recipe is chosen. The ingredients are taken out of drawers, the size of veggies is discussed, the amount of spice – I like my spices, which I discovered on my Asian travels and especially since Aruba – herbs, salt and pepper, grain by grain, are all gauged by me, just like any cook or chef would do. Jovy, my current assistant, is perfect at this. My mother is not as easy-going; we have our fun disagreements when she comes to visit. Sometimes, we do the cooking together, because she likes to have her say too (that's my view, although I doubt she'd agree with me). That's what mothers are for, and she's the perfect mother in every way.

My kitchen is ordered and there is no clutter. This makes for very easy access, and to find things. I don't need to explain to someone else as to where to find or put something. We need few words before getting on with the recipe.

The whole house is tidy, white, clean, and pristine. I don't leave the house to go to work eight hours a day, so I think if you're going to spend a lot of time somewhere, why not make it pleasant to look at? Oh, and I'm girly too. I've still got a stuffed teddy bear on a bedroom chair. Henning doesn't seem to mind.

Garden:

The small cherry tree in the corner blooms in spring and is perfect. There's a trickling rock fountain, white woven furniture with soft cushions, chosen as much for comfort as elegance. I won't sit on the sofa, but others will, and I want them to be comfortable.

In my spare time, I keep up with my scrapbooks and photo albums, which track my public life. As a child, I may not have liked being photographed, but I trained myself to like it and even since the stroke, I've not avoided it. I'm always keen to pose or be filmed, in order to communicate with others what is possible in a seemingly otherwise impossible set of circumstances.

For male readers, this information may seem irrelevant to you, but you know what? It is not so different from your shaving daily, cleaning your nails, looking after all your grooming and attire.

A friend of mine once told me a story about visiting a war-torn country. In spite of all the turbulence and fear, the women still dressed well, neat and tidy. Why on earth? Because it was a way of showing they were not giving up hope, but were carrying on with life.

Those horrible days in Aruba, when I didn't take care of myself, were dark days, and that was reflected in my lack of interest in personal care and fashion. We all have different ways of expressing ourselves. What matters is that we are true to ourselves, which lifts our spirits and builds our self-respect.

Exercise: essential.

"One more lap, Kati?"

Swimming is my favourite way to exercise. Always, yes, one more... one more. And I want to go further than the swim before, and last longer. Anyone working with me has to be fit.

Natural adrenaline gives a boost to anyone's state of mind. I have a routine that keeps me afloat in times when I might be feeling unproductive or low. Swimming is one of the most delightful rituals I have. I go to the pool not just to swim, but also to push myself. I aim to break my record each time I go. I've tried many different kinds of therapies, and continue to do so even though it isn't going to lead to a cure. Cold and stiffness are my enemies; sunshine and activity are my friends. Swimming is the one exercise I can do somewhat on my own, and I get a dynamite workout from it. I work with what I can, going twice a week to burn calories. Twice-weekly physiotherapy sessions stretch my muscles and keeps them warm, but swimming lets me actually do the activity myself – and I love it. My fighter mentality kicks in when I'm in the pool. I work up a sweat, swimming two kilometres in under an hour. Each time I increase my distance, and I feel like I've swum a marathon after that hour. Sometimes it hurts, but it's a good pain, not my enemy. I'm burning calories and the ache tells me "I'm alive!" Sometimes I – or my therapist – take a holiday. Even when I return to it and feel sluggish and stiff, I love the challenge of getting back into shape, and I advance pretty quickly in the pool. Whether you're 100 per cent healthy and mobile, or zero per cent, swimming is great exercise. For me, it's the one place where my body is light and has some flexibility and freedom.

Cold is my body's worst enemy. The cold puts stress on my muscles and makes them very stiff. Lately, my spine is twisting as a result and I have been told to wear a corset. It's very uncomfortable, but I do wear it as much as I can. Physio is important. I have it twice a week, to stretch out my muscles.

"Hi, Kati, It's good to see you. How are you today?"

"Stiff," I spell. My muscles cramp at will, in the cold more often than in warm temperatures.

"Well, let's give you a good workout."

The physio is slow and careful, but it does hurt in spite of her care. If it didn't hurt, I wouldn't be getting the workout my muscles need. Legs first, then arms, neck and finally the back. Lying on the bed while my limbs and body are moved around, the routine never changes, but the aches and pains are sometimes more here, sometimes more there. The routine is always the same: I am put on my back, each leg is manipulated and massaged, followed by each arm (sometimes I can bring down a raised arm all by myself), then my back is lifted forward, then moved from my waist down through my spine until I'm lying down again. The therapy is to stimulate the muscles to keep them from tightening. Against all odds, I continue my routine physiotherapy to keep my body warm and my muscles relaxed.

I still do standing therapy, and I still don't like it. I don't like the horrible (not fashionable) but necessary boots. It's like going skiing without the fun and the freedom. I'm hooked into the boots, and then my feet are put onto a pedestal, which is much like putting on ski boots and stepping into skis. Then a belt is put around my butt to help to hold me in place with the machine. The physio lifts me to a standing position (only after all the physio on the bed of course, otherwise it'd be impossible.) and I stand for as long as I can 'stand' it. It's good for my blood circulation, my bones, posture and spine. While I'm vertical, my arms are manoeuvred much the way they are when I was lying down for regular physio. Ideally, I would do this every day, but I'm too busy with other things, because remember, everything takes longer for me to do than a person who has four working limbs. However, without these sessions, my muscles would shorten and it would eventually become impossible even to have my arms lifted to wash, or my legs moved to put on shoes – and without a change of shoes, I would truly despair.

These therapies hurt like hell, but as always, whether swimming, physio or standing therapy, it feels like I've done some good afterwards.

According to doctors, I'm a weird case. I will never recover the use of my limbs or speak, but I am doing far better with a good attitude than the doctors ever expected. I never step back or look back. The way I look at it, although I may only be inching forward, I'm going in the right direction.

Food: always moist.

I suspect my eating is a particularly curious experience to watch. Since I cannot develop the full power to chew, my food needs to be somewhat soft and cut into small pieces; food with a tougher texture like beef must be cut into very tiny pieces. But make no mistake, I can eat beef, and juicy hamburgers, and lovely cakes.

The amount of food that goes into my mouth should be of a specific quantity: not too big a bite, not too small. It needs to be that way because my tongue cannot push the food around in the mouth the way everybody else's does unconsciously. My meal cannot be too dry or too hard either. Like most Finns, I like coffee, which is a good thing because I get to have most of my food dunked in a warm cup of it.

Even some twenty years since the stroke, I'm still in the process of learning how to eat. Now and then, I still give assistants scary moments when a little piece of food slips down my throat unintentionally and I start to choke. It's a matter of practise, practise, practise, and mealtimes are always an opportunity to improve my skills.

Perspective: always positive.

You could say that life has been unfair to me, stripping me of the control of my body. Well, I don´t have time to think about that. I want to live my life, not just to survive, but also to thrive as I did before the stroke. It requires that I accept things as they are and take any situation and mould it into the right shape for me. Sometimes, I have to learn a new skill and a different way to communicate. My new life is not ordinary, but then again, I never planned to live an ordinary life. It's all in the way you see your circumstances, to make your experience a good one.

So, I'm writing and speaking to the world, quite an unexpected turn in my life. I'm sharing with people all across the globe, saying that no situation is impossible to overcome. Every situation has a good opportunity behind it. Life is to be lived and it is amazing.

Enough about me.

Henning is often told he's an angel (for marrying me). Or he's treated like a prince or some other romantic hero. He doesn't like it, but he's too thoughtful to say that to the person who is paying the compliment. I think he's wise, because he can see that a comment like that is really saying that I needed rescuing. Well, we both know I don't.

Henning and I talk as though we are on the same level. In fact, he addresses everyone in the same way, even officials and assistants. I like it, because it means he can relate to everyone. Of course, some people won't connect with him because they don't want to.

Henning rarely gets cross with anyone. He is Mr Patient, unless someone doesn't show up when s/he's supposed to, and doesn't call to give warning either. That really burns him. So, if you know you're supposed to be with Henning, be warned if he has been expecting you, and you're very late, that makes him very cross (although he probably won't say much about it when you do finally show up).

Family:

Of course, every life has high points and low points. The only low point in our marriage came even before we were married. That was the day we had the news we can't have a child because it's just too risky. But even that has a silver lining. One day, we'd like to adopt a needy child from the Caribbean, or somewhere else where we have a connection. We've got too much love to keep to ourselves and although we can't give birth, we can make raising a child a blessing to ourselves and someone else.

And so on it goes: as long as we can communicate.

My family has described me as having the courage to reach out to the world. Well, when you are locked-in, you value every opportunity to communicate. I will share with anyone, if sharing will help someone's situation.

How do we get and give the best life has to offer? The key is communication. For me, the only times I've been miserable have been when communication has broken down. Henning and I rarely have difficulty, and only then if communication has broken down. Mostly we 'talk' through everything and life is very steady. Anthropologists don't know precisely when humans began to communicate effectively; some would say we haven't managed it yet – especially not across the sexes!

Humanity has gone from drawing on walls to launching entire books as files across cyberspace, so that people all over the world can buy them. Today we can share the minutest bit of trivia (and we do!), or share profound memories and ideas with almost anyone, and even have our messages translated into other languages without the need for a personal translator. We can share intimate details or photographs, and have those privacies pirated or broadcast universally. And we can live very publically, confessing even our deepest fears, hopes and aspirations to the world, or remain anonymous, reclusive and private.

Blogging:

Before the stroke, I did not share my emotions, although I was always outspoken with my opinions. Who I am today is quite different, because although I am still content to share my opinion, I no longer hide my feelings. I release those too, for two reasons:

» Because I've learnt others can benefit when I share, including those who may be going through similar situations.

» Because holding in my deep emotions is not good for me.

After the stroke, the only thing I could do independently was to go onto the computer and write; to friends or to my journal. Admittedly, I was depressed after the stroke. What I didn't realise was that every word I wrote was therapy. I was seeking peace of mind; I didn't understand the value of sharing. When *In the Blink of an Eye* was published, and I got feedback from strangers, it was then I discovered how inspiring my story was.

Responses to my blog posts:

Mostly, people are generous and warm when they respond to my posts. If they are encouraged, I'm encouraged. But, believe it or not, there are a few who like to poke fun at a woman who has physical limitations. I get rude responses sometimes, being told to shut it, or why can't I put my fingers to better use! To those I say... nothing. I don't think about them or concern myself with them. You can't please all of the people all of the time, and their comments roll off me like water off a duck's back. We have to ignore the rude few to help the hopeful remainder.

The proof is in the pudding:

Recently, which is over twenty years since the stroke, I posted on the blog my mother's memory of all that happened *that night and the day after...* which was perhaps the longest, slowest stroke in history. Soon after the blog post went out, we had a family occasion. It was Anu's mother's birthday. You might remember the night of the stroke was Alli's fiftieth birthday, and Jukka drove like a madman to get to me at the Mikkeli hospital. This time it was January 2015, and after another party for her, all the guests left and the family remained and sat together: Isa and Äiti, Jukka, Anu and Sofia, Anu's parents, Henning and me. We began to chat casually. Everyone had read the blog post that I had just put out, and we began to talk about it. Anu's mother, Alli, was first to mention it.

"That night was a horror. When I heard what had happened I couldn't stop crying. It was such a tragedy. But, Kati, look at you now. You are a miracle. How you have walked in *Sisu*[3] is amazing. We never know what will happen to us, do we?"

"That was the worst night of my life," Marjatta began, "I was seeing my wonderful daughter slowly fade away, and the doctors were ignoring it. Couldn't they see? But you have made it through, Kati, life has treated you badly, but you have not complained. You have made it through."

The two ladies had started a flood. Suddenly, everybody was ready to speak, and to listen, all at the same time, about the horrors of my becoming paralysed. They were sharing, and crying, which for Finnish people are two miracles, while I sat speechless, at their expression of love, anger, pain and sadness. Then something happened that had never happened before, or since.

---

3. *Sisu* is a Finnish concept I will share with you in some detail on page 438

"I want to say that the worst night in the world was the night Kati lost her physical freedom." My dad was speaking about the incident, calmly and openly. Never before had he talked about his feelings.

He continued, "I wanted to die that next day, when I saw my beautiful daughter lying trapped and speechless in that hospital bed. I wanted to change places with her. I wanted to strangle that doctor who ignored her and acted superior. But Kati didn't die. None of us died. In fact we are better for this. We've gone on to live above all of the sadness."

There wasn't a dry eye in the room. Isa, never one to share his thoughts (with the occasional exception when he's had too much to drink), was sharing with the entire room his own pain. In a way, he spoke for all of us. He wouldn't stop and we didn't want him to.

"Do you remember how Eetu ran away from Kati when the wheelchair got too close? That cat was a terror in his own right!" Everyone was mesmerised, stunned that Risto Lepistö was sharing his feelings. "Well, we have survived that crazy cat, and Kati has made it through. Life goes on," he said.

Imagine this room full of people, usually reserved and private about their innermost feelings, telling one another their painful memories, now without bitterness, or even sadness. We had never before talked about those days after the stroke. The subject was the elephant in the room. But now, every soul was healing, finally at peace with what had happened.

Intimate secrets:

Book two, *Living Underwater*, is the material that is foremost in my mind right now. It is my full autobiography. My family is 100 per cent supportive of this project, and helpful. They've even come forward to be interviewed formally, so that I can present as accurate a picture as possible about my life, in order to help others. Anu is the quietest person in the family. When we interviewed her for the book, she shared something about an incident that happened in 2009, nearly ten years ago. When she visited Aruba with Jukka and Sofia, she had a private conversation with Terry, who told her about our intimate life and how I was unable to 'fulfil all his needs'. Anu was appalled that he would discuss with her, our intimate life, but she never said a word to me, because she didn't want to put a negative impression on someone I loved. Now, she decided to share the story, to make sure any detail that might be important would be exposed.

I'll tell you what this most exposes – love and respect within my family has no bounds. The quiet, demure and modest Anu, wise beyond her years and courteous and kind, held on to a secret and then risked sharing it, all in order to offer anything that might be useful to furthering my passion to help others.

Sharing:

Sharing your story helps others to understand theirs. When I share, others are stirred up to remember, consider and release pent up emotions, which is healthy for everyone. Henning has said he sees that when people meet me, they automatically reflect on their own lives.

When Henning and I started this process, we wanted to help others. Never in our wildest imaginings did we expect it would spark a miracle in our own family. Wow! When we do something for others, always, it reaps a reward for ourselves.

CHAPTER 35

Casa van der Hoeven

I'm going to share with you some stories about how we
live, to give you an idea of...

How we live.

People ask how Henning and I manage to live a relatively
balanced and normal life? Well, we flush all our preconceived
ideas of how things should be down the drain.

We recycle any social or peer pressure and make our
lifestyle fit our needs, instead of putting unnecessary stress
on ourselves to fit into a life that isn't practical for us. Our
life is routine, scheduled but never dull.

Although we may not be able to be spontaneous, we find
ways to entertain ourselves and bring a smile.

Sometimes I mess with Henning. He says I'm a control
freak. Really? Well, so is he – and I can prove it!

Above our dining table, we have a string of small lights
that hang from a fixture that is long and narrow. Each
light hangs from a separate cable and each cable can be
shortened or lengthened.

One day, Henning came home and as he was settling in, he noticed the lights were hanging at uneven distances from the main fixture, so he took care and attention to ensure each cable was the same length so that the bulbs were suspended the same distance from the fixture.

I wonder if he remembered he'd done the same thing the day before.

Any assistant of mine has to be willing to be my hands, so I can play a joke on Henkka every once in a while.

Last winter, we had a horrifying experience when we went sightseeing and were in a very high tower building. We were at the top of the building and had decided it was time to come down. I was ready to do so, because I really don't like heights. We got into the same lift we'd used to come up to the top. We pressed the button for the ground floor and waited, and waited. Nothing happened. I started to freak out a bit (which is a noisy and restless affair), so I'm glad no one other than our group was in the elevator. I began to think, this can't be happening! Everyone else, aware I hate heights, was quiet, I'm sure to try to keep the situation as calm as possible. Well, a few f*** words were running through my brain, and while of course I said nothing, I'm sure my family was well aware what was going through my head, more or less. There were crude words, but also horrifying images going around in my noggin.

First, Henkka tried to fix the elevator, but unfortunately there was no movement. I began to imagine how the whole lift could drop down like a rock. In fact, we were all getting nervous.

"Let's get out," someone said, so we all filed out. Hmm. Certainly we were not all going to take the stairs!

Henkka walked down the stairs to get the staff, who cleaned the threshold into the elevator and tested it, but again nothing happened. Henkka came back upstairs, thinking the door must be jammed somehow. We piled back into the increasing shrinking elevator, and waited. Then, all of a sudden we had a miracle – the elevator decided to cooperate! As we descended slowly but surely, you can perhaps imagine the relief we all felt.

Upon getting out on the ground floor, I swore I was done with tall buildings. These days I don't get much personal exercise. You know I've said already how much I love swimming? Well, it's been over a year since I've been able to swim in Mikkeli. The venue where I used to swim smoked me out after ten fabulous years. I used to take my own therapist, but a year ago I was told I could no longer do that. The therapist on hand is not compatible with my regime or handicap, and so I have had to give it up. A pity, but not worth dwelling on. As the expression goes, 'don't sweat the small stuff'.

Because I am paralysed, and don't get much casual exercise, I have to be selective about what calories I put into my mouth. Every calorie counts, not because I'm a world-class model who has to stay skinny, but because I'm a tetraplegic and calories are very hard to burn, so must be worth consuming.

I am very picky about food. Some foods I can eat, some I can't eat... and sometimes I just want what I want and will wait until I can have it. This means sometimes I don't eat when everybody else is eating. I love burgers. I don't overdo it, but when I really want something specific to eat, like a burger, I will forego the politeness of going along with what other people want and wait my turn to have what I want, even if that means going to a restaurant hours after other people have eaten.

And my friends understand; because when you have huge limits on your life, if you're patient and are surrounded by loved ones, no one will take offence at your eating peculiarities.

My mom's a great cook. In fact, I am very fortunate to still have my parents alive and well. They are close to each other, and to Henning and me.

I love watching them. Risto enjoys dry humour, a glass of wine, and lying back and allowing Marjatta to talk for them both. In spite of all the travels he's taken with me, he has his own dream destination, but has yet to go. Marjatta speaks with enthusiasm on any subject, but don't mess with her way of doing things. She has her set ways (I guess I get it from her), and sometimes even suggests I ought to organise differently to what I already do. It's all in good humour of course, and all because we are candidly honest with one another and love each other so much.

I sometimes wonder if it has been difficult for my mother since I got married, because she no longer is in charge of my life. But she tells me, and so does Henning, that she has totally deferred to him on the matters of my practical care. The only thing she's sensitive about is where we live.

One subject that is difficult to discuss is where Henning and I will eventually settle down. Finland is home, but one day we may find our journey leads us away from the north. That will be difficult for my family. But fulfilment is important as a couple, and we must go where our mission takes us. Ah, it would not be unacceptable to me if it turns out to be somewhere hot and sunny.

As we build the business, we must go where it is best. To stay in Finland may not be best for outreach into the community that receives our message.

Henning is the manager behind all that we do together. It's important that you know, in case you're thinking of taking your handicap public, that it is very hard work and a long haul to making progress. We don't say that to discourage you, but to say simply, it is worth it if you have your eyes wide open and are willing to be patient and to persevere, to gain a platform for your cause or disability.

*

We are breaking through in the media, through *Huffington Post* and other magazines, online and live presentations, to raise awareness and support for disabled, or less able, people. We are even helping in areas of research and development. Our mission is progressing. The first key is perseverance, the second, a positive attitude and the third is availability. To make inroads while everyone else is trying to make inroads, you need to plan, connect with other people, put in your effort, organise, be diligent and persist. It takes time, and a great deal of effort, but over time, you will be heard.

CHAPTER 36

Today's Inspirational Model

In Finland we have a concept that is very special that no one else in the world has. We have *sisu*. *Sisu* is a Finnish word that has no perfect translation. It is an ancient concept which was almost forgotten until Emilia Lahti bought it back to life through her university thesis and later the media. It is: determination, bravery, resilience, perseverance and fearless grit in the face of extreme adversity. It is what Finnish people have that protects them from being defeated (and what helped them win a war against mighty Russia in the last century). I'm sure other cultures have it too; they just don't have a name for it.

I remember right after the stroke, feeling as though I was floating powerless through space, my conscious mind gave up on life, yet my unconscious mind did not – that was *sisu*. Although my depression told me there was no reason left to live, my subconscious gave me the endurance to carry on. In the face of extreme adversity, my mother – and then I – had the coping mechanism, mindset, and capacity to keep going.

Another point when I could have given up was when I recognised there was not going to be a cure. But I did not give up. What gave me the strength to continue? *Sisu.* We humans can conquer anything. I've been told I'm a perfect example to demonstrate that the human spirit can overcome any obstacle. The power of my will, and the determination to achieve my purpose, has given me a full life. My approach is this: no matter what kind of situation we find ourselves in, we are blessed with choice; what attitude will we have towards life? Let's choose the *right* one. We can choose the *sisu* one.

Emilia Lahti, mother of *sisu*, first connected with me after I wrote *In the Blink of an Eye*. She has since nicknamed me Ambassador of Optimism. Well, I definitely have *sisu* and want to impart it to everyone, especially those who face a huge challenge in their lives. Strapped into my wheelchair, I have found that the biggest power I have resides deep inside myself. It isn't muscle power, or even brainpower, it's the power of my spirit: positivism, faith, passion for life and love. Sharing it makes my life full of purpose and gives me huge joy and delight.

And so, Henning and I have begun our outreach to those who need an inspirational message. We are both totally committed to it full time. I sit at my computer for eight hours a day, writing but also looking for ways to promote what I write. Since I've been married to Henning, my writing has transformed from hobby-writing to inspirational postings. The Internet invites the world to your doorstep, but to create and build a platform is time-consuming and requires meticulous exercise. I say this so no one feels discouraged when there isn't instant breakthrough. Just like overcoming challenges in our emotional or physical condition, we overcome the challenges to find our audience and inspire others. It's worth all the effort when that breakthrough comes.

The first recognition for our efforts came in 2014, when I was awarded the Finnish Young Achiever Award from the junior division of the Chamber of Commerce International, Finland. The Young Achiever is the world's most prestigious award; the junior division of the Chamber of Commerce International, Finland, is for those Finnish citizens who are performing between eighteen and forty years of age. The competition is the national branch of The Outstanding Young Persons Awards globally. *In the Blink of an Eye*, and my positive role modelling through blogging and guest appearances brought this attention, which in turn raised my profile. I've not done any of this work for personal notoriety, but with the award comes credibility and marketing by the Chamber of Commerce. It all helps us to get out our message of hope and inspiration. I'm living proof that we can rise above our circumstances and accomplish all we are born to achieve. With this same resilience, and positive attitude to life that I lead, we can affect thousands of others. That's why the jurors for the Young Achiever Award chose me.

Since then, I had an invitation from *Patient-Doctor Magazine* (Finland) and wrote for them for two years. Going from strength to strength, I have since had many more opportunities and platforms to share my story in order to help others live theirs.

For example, in the open world of the Internet I have engaged with many wonderful people. I met Emilia Lahti on line when Henning and I first began blogging. We became friends and wrote often. When she was planning a TEDx talk about *sisu*, she thought of us. She had familiarised herself with *In the Blink of an Eye* after she and I 'met' and read articles on locked-in syndrome too. She wanted to use my story in her talk. Amazing. That became a big step in the advancement of our international platform.

After I endured the stroke, my tongue felt tangled, tied around itself. In my head I was speaking clearly, but words came out slowly, slurred and then eventually not at all. I heard people talk, but I couldn't take part in their conversation. However, in 2005, with the help of a computer, I was enabled to write a book to share my story, which in turn raised my profile. Eventually, *In the Blink of an Eye* would lead to TEDx in 2014. You'd think that an immobile person who cannot speak would be unable to make public presentations, but nothing is impossible. With social media, TEDx and more, my voice is heard. I have much to be grateful for, beginning with my mother who said, "Wait a year and then we'll see," when I wanted to give up on life.

Speaking of using my voice, I'd like to pause, turn, and take a moment to offer my input to medical staff who treat patients like me, based on the experiences I've had. Some of my treatment was excellent, and some was extremely poor. I'm grateful to those who helped me, but to those who frustrated my efforts to get well, I have a few things to say, for the sake of others who will need your care.

When someone experiences a huge medical setback in their lives, you need to find a positive to give them something to aim for. Make no assumptions about the person you're dealing with and leave room for success. Allow for *sisu* in the lives of every patient. With enough encouragement, people can accomplish amazing feats. Enable them. Treat your patient; find and treat the cause of their medical issue, not the symptoms. Don't assume the person will be better off numbing the emotional pain and so medicate their brains. Instead, help them through it. It's more work but far more rewarding. Symptoms come and go, but if the condition is permanent, the person needs help to cope. Find remedies for the emotional pain and look for the positive in every experience. I remember when I couldn't sleep that sleeping pills were the quick fix on offer. Instead, I got a sweet Persian kitten, who slept on my pillow. She was the cure for my insomnia.

The human spirit can do so much more when empowered with hope. Inspire hope. You can be positive, open-minded and heal the spirit of a person who has had bad news. I remember I was able to move my arms, and I pushed a stuffed bear around my bed after the stroke. I might have done more if I'd been encouraged. Instead, the doctors discouraged me, putting these manoeuvres down to reflex, and saying, "there's no hope for change". False hope for a cure should not be given, but give the patient a hope for the future, nevertheless. Negativity and doom and gloom, actually do more harm to the person than the damage of the disease or condition. Try things, just in case they might work. It's worth the risk of failure, because it brings hope and gives the patient courage to try. Reaching to the stars may be impossible, but striving to achieve the best possible is so important. Every opportunity must be taken, just in case something changes, something works, or something brings light into the dark tunnel.

Encourage, observe and learn. When engaging with a mute, don't assume that they are stupid. Talk directly to them, not only to the spouse, parent or assistant. A patient will speak with their eyes, so look at them. You may feel sad, or pity for your patient, but don't let your shame or embarrassment cause you to ignore them. Don't avoid eye contact. It is the chief means of communication.

I may not be a medical expert, but I know what I've lived and I know what I needed at the crisis time, when I was overwhelmed with grief and needing rays of hope. You do not hurt a patient when you inspire them to hope for change, rather you can carry them through the shock and horror, and enable them to improve to their best at the same time.

Other platform breakthroughs have come through the relationships we've built. Since Emilia Lahti incorporated my life story in a presentation she gave in 2014 for TEDx, Turku, we were again invited to TEDx, this time to present. What an honour! When TEDx producer Johanna Molin asked us to take part, it felt right and Henning and I said, "Yes!" immediately. We were invited to be part of a team to present on the topic, 'Imagine if...' Hmm. How were we going to finish that sentence?

'Imagine if...' became 'Imagine if you had a stroke and you were no longer able to speak or move.' We prepared, auditioned and passed. Great!

As this was to be a live presentation, Henning had to be very much involved. He is my right hand, and with my condition, he is much more than that. He is literally my voice, my legs and the down-to-earth part of my brain. He helps me, and without him I would not be able to do all that I do. Truly, he is the other half of me.

Eventually, the date for the live show arrived; we were scheduled to present in Turku, over 300 kilometres from our home in Mikkeli. It was a December day in 2015, which I remember so well. Our excitement mounted as we drove the distance to Turku. But imagine this: when we arrived we were told, "You're first up!"

Well, such news was nerve-wracking for me, although Henning was as cool as a cucumber. There were four presentation groups in all, none of us were professional presenters, and so there were nerves all around; the other people preparing to present were as scared as I was, maybe even more.

When Henning and I got onto the stage I practically froze (as if I'm not frozen already). It's just as well I wasn't expected to speak personally, because if I hadn't already been struck dumb, this would have done it.

Henning sailed through, and fifteen minutes later, everybody in the auditorium, and those watching on air, knew about locked-in syndrome, and knew me. Wow! I've been sharing for years, blogging and encouraging people to keep a positive attitude no matter what, and to persevere in every challenge. In that fifteen minutes, hundreds in the auditorium and potentially millions around the world, got our message. In fifteen minutes, our message of hope touched lives near and far. I couldn't have been happier.

Not only that, Henning did so well, he eased the fears of everyone backstage and the rest of the show was as smooth as silk too. The whole adventure was a success for all involved. I wouldn't wish my circumstance on anyone, but that TEDx experience would not have happened to me without the stroke, and I wouldn't have experienced the elation of having my message reach the world.

Allow me to take time to say thank you publically to people who helped us to make the presentation smooth, and to create a great video from it too. Thanks to Enrique Tessieri, for the tips and presentation help; to Anna-Maria and Miikka, who added voice and polish to our video. What they did may seem small to them, but it's the little things that bring the big things into being, and so we thank them from our hearts. Thanks to Emilia, who hosted the programme, to Johanna who produced it, and to my assistants at the time, Emily and Miina, who were both present and so helpful. And I thank my dearest Henning, so annoyingly calm and wonderful on that day. You inspire me and make my life perfect. Thank you all.

You can decide for yourself how you think we did, but we had a fabulous time and a great deal of wonderful feedback. You can see the talk here:

https://youtu.be/eB1rgvwQ_T8

How many people get to do that?

For those who do not have access to open this link, below is my life system that I live by. It has been fine-tuned over the years, and is a nutshell in seven parts, to a fulfilled life:

» Positive attitude: come rain or shine, always have a positive attitude.

» Passion: whatever you do, put your heart into it and do it with passion. Get up, dress up, and show up: discipline will get you where you want to go.

» Determination: dream big and do not hold anything back. Keep your focus on the possibilities; aim high and stay humble.

» Perseverance: your dreams are waiting for you, so do not *ever* give up. At moments when the impossible challenges you, accept, adapt, and reinvent yourself, making the obstacles into stepping stones.

» Communication: speak your mind, express yourself, listen to others, so you understand. Share your thoughts and also your emotions.

» Humour: laughter is the best medicine. After love, humour is the best healer, not only for the body but also for the soul.

» Take action: be flexible, yet steady; firm but compassionate. The purpose of life is to live a meaningful life, so start being the person you want to be, and start living the life you want to live.

Do you know, since the stroke, what has been the biggest surprise of all? Every bit of my experience, one way or another, has come into play as we build our Inspirational Model platform. I've even had a few modelling gigs, which came together in 2017 at the Miss Wheelchair competition in Poland. What a highlight for me that was. I'll tell you straight off, I didn't win. I don't have the flexible facial muscles required to smile the way I used to as a model, and a model's smile is key to success. But boy, did we girls have fun! We were a huge inspiration to others as well. People who are wheelchair-bound and beautiful, are now better able to recognise their possibilities.

What do you get when you have twenty-four wheelchair-using women from all over the world in one room? A bundle of pure, and untamed, positive energy. We had seven days of hard work. It was a privilege to work with the other women, both for me to participate and for Henning to witness it. There was no animosity in the air; rather it was like a gathering of old friends.

However impressive that gala was, and it was very well-organised and beautifully presented, it was far from the best of what the whole event had to offer. At the end of the journey, an incredible joy overtook us all. Henning said to me he felt as if he was between angels and God himself. Throughout that journey, we did not see disability, colour or gender; what we did see was a collection of amazing human beings who do not let circumstances define who they are. We saw courage, strength, commitment and mutual respect. It was amazing.

Participating in the Miss Wheelchair world pageant opened a door for me that I thought was forever closed. A few months after the gala, I was approached by Nawal Benzaouia, the Founder and CEO of the Massiraa agency, who I met at the pageant in Warsaw. She wanted me to be part of her inclusive model agency, and I enthusiastically accepted. The first fashion show was in October 2018 in Colombo, Sri Lanka. Being on the catwalk felt unreal. My childhood dream became real, despite the circumstances.

One of the main subjects that I advocate for is better communication. Not only for communication devices for the disabled, but also better communication in general between all people. I was invited to represent the disabled people that cannot communicate in the traditional matter at a Sisulle Ääni (Sisu voice system project) meeting.

At the meeting, we met Heidi Majander, who is the initiator of the project. Heidi was making a documentary about voice systems and asked us to be a part of the movie. As the project progressed, we became more and more involved. In the process, the documentary started to develop around my life. The name of the film is; *Puhuva Katse,* which means, *Eyes Can Tell.* It won in the category of Best Documentary Short Film Award at the INDO-GLOBAL International Film Festival in Mumbai, India on July 2019.

The documentary has been on national television in Finland and has participated at various film festivals where it has been well received and gotten many appraisals.

Since my husband, Henning, and I have found our niche in this world, together we have forged many new relationships. Some of these have allowed our story to be shared around the world, and this has made a difference to many lives. Yes, it is exciting for us to see others inspired, and their lives changed for the better. Henning's idea to build my work as a new kind of model, an Inspirational Model, has captured people's imagination as to how they can make their lives better. I am so happy.

If you'd asked me twenty years ago if I thought I would ever be happy I'd say, "You've gotta be kidding." First, I worked hard to achieve my modelling goals, but I ended up paralysed. Next, I worked hard to get over it, and that led to a totally broken heart. When I stopped working and accepted my situation, when I really started to allow life to happen to me, guess what? I'm happier now than I've ever been. That includes even before I had the stroke.

I'm happy. Why? Because I've found true love? Yes, that helps. My husband is awesome and every day I'm grateful for him in my life. But it isn't just that we love each other that makes life wonderful, it's that we work together for a fit purpose, and we have a fulfilling reason to get up in the morning. That is what makes me happiest. Would modelling have done it for me? I suppose. But I was forced to take a long detour, which made me a better person. Along the way, I've found my reason to be alive: to take that determination, which is my key quality, and use it to share what I've learnt in my life in order to help other people benefit in theirs.

Life is full of surprises, some great, some terrible. But we've got to take the bad with the good, so that the good is really appreciated. We all need to find our purpose for being. Nothing happens without a reason. When we look for it, we'll find it. Or maybe we just need to be open to it when it happens, letting it come to us. I might have missed my reason, and that would have been the biggest tragedy of all.

Sometimes, wisdom tells us we need to give up, let go, and move on. I had to acknowledge a cure was not going to happen and allow the miracles in my life to take other forms, which they have. I totally accept my condition. I am connected to people all over the world. I have met and am married to a wonderful man who loves me just as I am, and I love him too. That's three miracles and there are others. We have to look for life and miracles, not just wait for them to happen.

Henning's grandfather, now passed away, gave a map to his grandson, and the clue to finding the greatest treasure of all ending with these words:

"... Be honest, be sincere and let the flow take you to where the world finds its beat... Just say how you feel, with no nonsense or deceit, and all your dreams will become real."

Kati and Henning

At the computer

The face of Sisu Finland 2015

TEDx Talk 2015

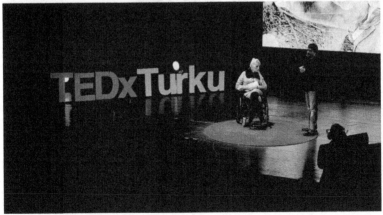

Photoshoot Mikkeli, Finland

Fashionshow Colombo,
Sri Lanka 2018

Miss Wheelchair World
Warsaw, Poland 2017

Filming documentary in London, UK 2017

Kati with her parents Risto and Marjatta 2018

Kati with her niece Sofia 2018

Kati and Henning

Kati with Happy

Kati with Alegria

Part 4: Riding the Tide

Give what you have
to find who you are
and
what you're made of.

Sarah Tun: summing up Kati's philosophy

WELCOME TO TODAY

Kati's World

Kati is profound. Working with her on this book has been both a privilege and an educational journey. My number one lesson has been: if she can overcome her circumstances, I can overcome mine.

When I began to share with others this project, and to introduce friends and colleagues to Kati's situation and personality, every single person looked shocked and saddened at first. But like Kati, I began to share how fulfilled she is, how delightful and insightful, and they relax.

"How can you interview her?" and I explain the spelling. Again, they grimace or are dumbstruck. But I say, "She's happy. She's well."

People show surprise when I say she's married. "Was she married before the stroke?" They are inevitably surprised and impressed that Henning met her only a few years ago, almost two decades after the stroke.

So now we're going to share some of the valuable life lessons that Kati has for us. These are gathered over two decades, culminating in some shared insights from both her husband, Henning, and herself. You've been on Kati's journey up until now. Welcome to 'today', where Kati offers inspiration and encouragement for your journey. Today is the first day of the rest of your life; may we each make the most of our day.

Sarah Tun

Overview of Kati's perspective

Not all that glitters is gold. The fact is that you don't need to be gold. Gold is just a symbol, and as a human being you are so much more than just a symbol.

The outer victories are the most celebrated, but we all know, or at least we all need to know, that the greatest and most important victories come from the difficult battles fought deep inside ourselves.

It's fall 1994, Los Angeles, California. I was living the best time of my life, living my childhood dream of being a professional model. Only God knows from where I got the crazy idea to become a model. There I was on the other side of the world, in the City of Angels, meeting celebrities like they were ordinary people. Working for big international campaigns, music videos, doing fashion shows, you name it. A crazy, hectic time, but still so wonderful that I would not change it for anything else.

After months of rehabilitation in Helsinki, diagnosed with locked-in syndrome (LIS), I wound up living with my parents, much like a baby, completely paralysed, completely dependent on them. Depression sunk in. Difficult times were ahead, but still I would not take antidepressants. I thought that I would have to face the music, sooner or later, so it might as well be sooner and get it over.

Kati on attitude

The main thing about your attitude is that it should be you. You should not put on an attitude that is fake, because an attitude like this will be weak and it will crumble when stronger winds hit your life. Take this advice: do not assume an attitude, and do not let an attitude become you, but let the attitude be a reflection of you. Remember – there is a thin line between being cool and being a fool.

Only real, everlasting disability in life, is a bad attitude. A good attitude is like fertiliser to the people around you, to help them flourish.

Smile and you will be happy.

Happily ever after is a state of mind.

There are three enemies of personal peace: regret over yesterday's mistakes, stressing over tomorrow's problems and ingratitude for today's blessings.

Kati on depending on an assistant

I am completely dependent on another person. I always need an assistant. I have assistants working with me for most of the day doing everything, from the biggest to the smallest of chores.

It's not easy to find a good assistant. It's not an intellectual job, but it is unusual and requires someone very special with the same view of life as the client. For the assistant, perhaps it is simply a job, but for me it is life. Finding an assistant with a balance between the two can be very difficult.

I have had some wonderful assistants, and to them I am very grateful.

I'm stubborn and I don't give up easily. Once or twice I have had to admit I was wasting my time and energy. It's happened when I am trying to spell; I can't give up when an assistant doesn't understand what I'm spelling.

No matter how challenging, I like to prove I can achieve. If someone says that I cannot do something, you can bet your ass I will do just that.

Some of my assistants have been like sisters to me. We can be very close. It's wonderful to build that much trust with someone on whom I am dependent.

Kati on depression

By defeating my depression, I evolved. When I was able to set aside fears and overcome life´s obstacles, I came out a winner.

When I knew that absolutely nothing could stop me anymore, I achieved something great, something unique, and that made me feel like a real winner.

You do have strength, you just need to realise it. Everything worth fighting for does not come easily, nor fast, and it is worth the effort – just wait.

To achieve your personal best in all fields of life you can't fear failure. Think big, and just keep doing everything you possibly can.

Kati on disability

Henning is my right hand; actually, he is more than that. Henning is my voice, my legs and the down-to-earth part of my brain. He helps me out with everything and without him, I would not be able to do all that I do. He is truly the other half of me.

Contrary to what many in society think, disabled people can do some things for themselves. People who are disabled may, in fact, have the most to offer to society. They have great insight because of their disability, which can translate to creative solutions for all. For this reason, I advocate for those who would seem to have no voice; I offer mine because they can identify with it. Once any of us have gained a platform, it is important we use it. We must not take for granted what we have. We must use our voices, and also our ears to listen to the voices of others. We learn and find solutions through communicating with others.

Kati on experience

Problems without solutions often have a way of solving themselves when you just put them aside in your mind and let your subconscious solve them for you.

Nothing is as expensive as experience. It can't be gained without having to pay the price.

It does not really matter how old you are; age is a state of mind and not a number. What matters is that are you willing to risk looking like a fool and follow your dreams no matter how stupid they might seem to other people.

I value greatly the second chance life has given me, and I don't plan to let it go to waste! Nowadays I don't value material things (well, not so much). Seriously, I really don't. Nor how famous someone is. I value the people in my life. Sure, material things are nice, but in the end it's the people that matter.

They say that you never know what you have until you lose it. This is not true, you know what you have, losing it is what makes you appreciate it.

Kati on fathers

A good father makes much difference in a child's life. He's a pillar of strength, support and discipline. A good father realises that his children are human, and that making mistakes is part of growing up. He shows his kids that everything has its value. He teaches his children to appreciate things. He accepts that his kids aren't exactly like him. He leads by example and, most importantly, a good father also illustrates the importance of affection by professing his love for their mother in front of them, and he won't fight with her in their presence. In all, he adheres to the values he'd like his children to follow.

Kati on fear

I was asked, have I been afraid at all? I cannot even imagine what I would be afraid of. Even when I was healthy, I went alone to LA and was in a pretty dangerous modelling world; I was not afraid one bit. One must dare to live. I have the same principle as someone else I once knew: "I'd rather live for a year as a lion than ten as a lamb."

If I'd not had the stroke, I would have never seen, learnt and experienced so many things.

Do not let your fears and weaknesses dictate your behaviour and decisions. Do not permit the fears or weaknesses of others to affect your behaviour and decisions. Fear is negativity sneaking in and taking control over one's life and the future. Fear does not permit people to live; sometimes it takes a life. Fear will wage war on all that is good, and destroy the future.

Kati on friendship

The stroke made me understand how very important friends and family are. My hospital room wall in Mikkeli, and also in rehab in Helsinki, were quite a sight – big walls covered with cards from corner to corner. I loved collecting the cards, and they reminded me of how many friends still thought of me, although I had disappeared from their circles. It was pretty comforting. The Christmas following the stroke, I wanted to show how important the people were and my appreciation to them for being there for me. So, I bought an unbelievable amount of presents for everybody.

I remember the first Christmas I was paralysed like it was yesterday. I remember sitting there in my wheelchair, overwhelmed with emotions, as everybody was going through their presents. Suddenly, a moment of rejoicing overtook me as I realised that *sharing* is the greatest thing in life. Sharing is the one thing that brings the most joy. Given everything that had happened to me, I was still able to share, and that made my life worth living.

No matter what one's situation, or condition, may be, sharing with others is the most meaningful thing we will ever do in our lives. I am not talking about sharing material things, but things like experience, knowledge, and history, and most importantly, thoughts, emotions, love, words... and shared moments.

Kati on hope

There are times when you must sail against the current to reach the calling of your heart. There are times that you must let go, and let the current take you to the blessing of being alive. We only understand so much, and sometimes we do not know what we really need to make our life complete.

Kati on life

Life is a pretty funky thing really. In order to understand and appreciate happiness, you have to experience first its sadness. All those grey shades of life as well. Life can be tough, so why not choose to make it more joyous? You can if you choose to.

Whatsoever you might be going through, it *can* be turned into your source of strength.

Life can be a wonderful journey if you keep your face to the sun and your back to the shadows. Cherish it, and savour it, as much as you can.

If you cannot get over your past, and you are only thinking of those nice memories of yesterday, then you can never move on and live a productive and meaningful life. You just have to forget them and move on.

An obstacle is whatever shows up, which we resist and don't welcome, or whatever we decide to use as an excuse to stop moving in the direction of our passion. In any case, something can only become an obstacle when, by our own decision, we choose to allow it to be.

The key to peace is to feel the pain and eventually let it go, for good. You must grieve the loss and feel all those feelings you have inside. Give yourself much time to grieve.

To achieve a truly peaceful heart, you should not try to bury the pain, but do what you have to in order to transform it. Claim your freedom through forgiveness of others.

Kati's Metaphor for Life

Life is a race, and the race is long, at the end it's a marathon you had against yourself. The victory will not be defined by how far you got, or how fast you did it, it will be defined by what you did along that marathon, and how many batons you passed on. It´s the journey, and not the outcome, that matters.

Kati on loneliness

Just like everything happens for a reason, so does every action produce a reaction. The rebel in me devoured the feelings of loneliness, and I grew strong, built up faith and hope, to always be positive and never give up. As I did this, I started to live, not just to survive. Life went on and on, and I found my ways to enjoy it. Then out of the blue... came love. Real Love. And I was ready for it.

Kati on love

Love is a never-ending fuel source. I recommend we use it to propel our lives forward; always forward, never backward. Love life, love people, love as much as you can with all your heart until it bursts... and then love some more.

I am sure that when you fell in love for the first time, you thought that love was this most beautiful and immense thing ever. But that first time was only puppy love. You'll discover there is so much more to love.

If you were in my shoes, still being able to share love in spite of a serious physical disability, you would know that love is as infinite and deep as the universe itself.

The natural state in which all humans should be living is in love, harmony and peace. We love with not only people, but also everything that surrounds us, living in harmony with all animals, plants and trees, at peace with our fellow man.

If all human beings would have the courage to open their hearts and love entirely, we would be able to do what may seem impossible.

Kati on marriage

Marriage is partnership for life, two people as one. It is a venture to create and be part of what is the most sacred to us as human beings: family.

Relationships require love and passion, but that is just the first level. For them to get stronger and go further, they require a certain kind of friendship, patience, understanding and commitment. To make a promise that should last a lifetime, getting married and starting a family, we need to understand that a relationship is an unselfish balancing act. This act is most of the time a fifty–fifty balancing act. It is an agreeable balancing act that sometimes can be sixty–forty, and other times, twenty–eighty.

Marriage also requires love, passion, friendship, patience, understanding and commitment. It involves sharing – giving, but also taking all of these – without an exact measurement. The right balance for a good marriage can be reached by acknowledging each person's stronger attributes and recognising each person's weaker characteristics.

Marriage is a house that you build, brick by brick. It is hard work. And that is when both partners are healthy and able to give of their best, their 100 per cent. When this is not the case, the balancing act of marriage takes on a whole different dimension, sometimes one hundred-zero. Perspectives of 'normal' do not apply in a relationship where one of the partners cannot give 100 per cent. Such relationships can be just as wonderful as any evenly balanced marriage. The proportion of each has to be adapted. What is the big deal about that? One of the greatest virtues of humankind is its ability to adapt.

Our household is just like any other in the sense that it is a balancing act. Two people are sharing their lives together.

Kati on negativity

Talking about problems is just like gossiping; do not waste your time with that. If you want to do something useful with your time, talk about solutions and improvements.

If you complain about your bad feelings, it does not change anything.

You cannot reach for anything if your hands are full of yesterday's junk.

Always recycle, recycle, and recycle, glass, metal and plastic, for the sake of our environment and our home planet. Also, recycle all the negative incidences, thoughts and emotions, and turn them into a positive effect on your life. For the sake of your life and your surroundings, such as family, friends and our home planet, recycle.

Kati on patience

If a brain injury does not teach you patience, I do not know what will. In my experience, patience comes gradually with experience.

Kati on physical intimacy

There's nothing more intimate in life than simply being understood. Eye contact is far more intimate than words. I should know.

After the stroke I was wondering, will I be intimate with someone ever again? I was afraid I would not. Well we know that fear proved to be useless.

I have never forgotten the first time after the stroke. I was *so* ashamed of my belly – it has a life of its own since no muscles work to hold it together – and I was so afraid. How would it all just happen? I went through every possible feeling on that night; from the shame to the big bang.

Well, everything went more than well in that department.

I have been intimate only with healthy men. Not because of prejudice but, think about it, I'm paralysed from the neck down, so I definitely must have a healthy partner or the intimacy part would remain a dream.

We all have a basic need for physical intimacy. Even me.

There are many kinds of intimacy, like, for instance, intellectual intimacy, which I definitely share with Henkka (among many other forms of intimacy).

One form of intimacy I certainly have with my assistants is physical intimacy. I don't mean that we have sex, but rather it's kind of physical, mental intimacy, between us. They wash and dress me. They do my hair and make-up, feed me, and cook for me. There is also a kind of mental intimacy all the time as well. I would think in some ways people can be even closer to an assistant than with a spouse, though not in my case.

Kati on privacy

I need someone with me most of the time. So, when I need privacy, I just blank out anyone else. Imagine taking a shower, but someone is with you, not some gorgeous male or female for a sexual encounter opted for by you, but someone washing every body part. How else could I put up with that level of physical invasion?

Kati on progress

We always want to be 'the best' but sometimes the best thing you can do is just to give up and move on, because you realise that you are just wasting your time and energy.

There is a saying, 'If you stand still you are moving backwards'. It may be so in a business environment, yet in physics that is not true. In reality, even if you stand still you are still moving forward. It's simple physics, where time always moves forward and with every breath you take, you move forward, and you move on.

I have learnt that there is no returning to your old self after trauma, even with a full recovery. It is certainly possible to live a great life, and to pursue realistic dreams based on being the best you can be. The process begins with accepting who and where you are right now.

I cannot pinpoint the exact moment when I found total acceptance of my situation. I probably just grew into it. I managed to understand that these were the cards that I had been dealt, and there was nothing else for me to do other than just to make the best of it.

Experiencing an obstacle can trigger our emotions, but if we control our emotions we can learn. As we focus on solving the problem rather than reacting to it, we can choose how we see things. Only then can we gain perspective on the situation. We cannot change the problem itself, but our perspective will alter how the obstacle appears. It is our choice to see any obstacle simply as a challenge to be overcome.

The surest way to a better life is to use better willpower.

I always say that positivity and zest for life are our most important assets.

Kati on raising social awareness

Communication is a two-way street: talking and listening.

I fought this battle and no matter how far I got, too many times I did not get a chance to speak. The main reason given is that event organisers believe a disabled person makes an audience feel uncomfortable and awkward. Instead, organisers prefer to bombard the audience with meaningless entertainment rather than important and significant training.

I urge all who have no voice to demand his/her right to speak and to share their thoughts.

Many in our society think that people with disabilities cannot do anything without help. They believe that the disabled should just sit in the corner and wait for others to have time to do something with them, and then go back to their corner. As a person who cannot move, more and more I want to do something to improve the quality of life for others and myself.

More and more I feel the need to defend myself and others like me, to get the rest of the world to understand how immensely important it is that we each have a voice, and ensure they understand what it really means when we cannot speak.

Too many people in our society have a passive-aggressive, dominating attitude towards the minority. This attitude is emphasised when a person is unable to speak. Such a person is considered to be the most useless person in society, even though they may be the one who is most likely to have a solution to a problem.

I defend all those who have no voice. It is their right, not only to their physical person, but to have a voice for their very identity.

Politics of Disability Care:

I never ever gave a thought for how uneven, and full of bumps, streets are. Now I know how hard the simplest trip can be for people in wheelchairs. Luckily I always have someone to push me. Or even two. Every architect should sit in a wheelchair and experience what the beautiful streets they design actually *feel* like or how those new buildings really work for those in a wheelchair.

The system works fine until something really goes wrong. And things only change when someone important or famous gets sick. The system also uses the fact that people don't stop caring about their loved ones and will pay ridiculous amounts of money for them. A little more help from the system would certainly have helped a lot in our family.

Kati on relationships

It's so much easier to criticise, and put blame on others, instead of taking responsibility and fight to love. Many people seem to know their rights very well, but they forget about their responsibilities.

Not everything is black and white. Not everything can be defined easily in a few words. In the end, success in all relationships, whether romantic, friendship, family or business partnerships, all comes down to communication.

Kati on self-image

I could have died on that awful evening; I did not. I was blessed with a higher purpose in life. The meaning of life is to turn a negative into positive. My destiny is to show others this, and to lead the way.

In medical terms, I have LIS, or locked-in syndrome. In spiritual terms, I have PWS – the 'power-of-will syndrome'. My soul is free to be whatever it wants to be.

Nobody and nothing can stop me from making my dreams come true, because it is impossible to stop a person who perseveres and never gives up. All the strength that I need is in the air that I breathe. I will take a big gasp and move on forward.

Let your strength be in your flexibility. Change the things that you can for the better.

Kati on self-pity

As children, we do not have control over our lives, yet as adults, we do. Step one is to stop ourselves floating on the seas of self-pity. Luck is random; it's like the weather that can't be controlled. However, destiny is a boat that can be sailed, a boat that does not sink unless you let it sink. The boat can survive all storms to reach a safe port. It can do all this if the captain has the will to do this; my friend, you are the captain.

Sometimes, as we sail through life, we are unexpectedly hit by a huge storm. After the initial turbulence of the episode, you may find some peace in the calm seas of self-pity, but do not deceive yourself; those calm seas are really the eye of the storm, and surviving in the middle of a storm is not the way to live. You have to pull yourself through it.

There have been times when I felt that people only visited me when they had nothing better to do. It shows itself when people say they'll come to see me, but then they don't come.

Live in the present. Do not linger in the past, playing over and over all those nice memories. We humans love to mull over why something happened, as if that 'why' matters.

Kati on senses

My values have definitely changed since the stroke. I have come to understand what really matters in life.

I still remember so very well during the first fall after the stroke, the plenty of colourful leaves in beautiful sunny autumn. When I saw them that year, it was like my eyes had been opened for the very first time. Never before had I taken the time even to notice their beauty or the brisk clear scent of fall that is truly unique. This goes for gorgeous summer flowers surrounded by green also. Finland really is so very beautiful.

Natural beauty and inner beauty; these are examples of what really matters.

Kati on sisu

Sisu is a Finnish construct generally meaning determination, bravery, and resilience. However, a full and proper translation into any other language is impossible. Emilia Lahti, the founder of sisu, talks about 'determination and resoluteness in the face of extreme adversity'.

Sisu transcends, it can be defined in a spiritual way, and it can be defined in a scientific way.

Sisu is the human spirit itself. Sisu is the light that floats out of the body only when its time on earth has expired. Sisu is the human spirit that defines all logic and breaks rules and barriers. Sisu is a power that all humans have, a power that can take us far beyond the visible horizon.

Sisu is a single-cell organism that can survive and thrive in the harshest conditions. It is at the beginning of life itself; sisu is evolution.

If a disaster was to occur, and all life on earth was swept away, a thousand years later there would be life roaming on this planet again. It is because of sisu; sisu always survives.

Sisu is in all of us. Sisu does not have an energy source, nor does it need it. Sisu is energy itself. Sisu is life.

I think that sisu is one of those things, like a certain instinct that humans seem to have lost as their brains developed. However, it is buried there, inside us, and we can still use it when we need it.

Sisu is always there. Although you cannot see it, it remains a light in your unconscious mind. Sisu keeps you alive when life is difficult, until you are ready to bounce back and start living and thriving again.

Sisu is apparent in the Finnish pride, when things are at their worst and we still do not give up, when we refuse to die. Sisu is our flexible strength. It is how we are able to adapt and still progress when everything is holding us back. Sisu is what makes an average person into an extraordinary person.

Sisu kept me alive until I was ready to accept my situation and to thrive.

Kati on success

If you don't go after what you want, you'll never get it. It's as simple as that. Life gives you what you settle for.

Never accept either success or failure as final. Never let victory make you arrogant and lazy; never let failure stop you from getting back up and giving life the best of yourself.

I'm very grateful that I didn't die, like so many other locked-in patients, but that I can educate people through writing blogs and articles with Henning, and giving speeches and making videos. I'm actually very surprised by how much people like those videos, and it gives me great satisfaction to know others enjoy them.

Let your strength be in your flexibility. Change the things that you can for the better.

If you are healthy, handsome or wealthy, you can get ahead easier in life without a doubt. Even if you are blessed that way, to reach your goals you must still make a move and go for them, because if you want to see things getting better, you do not wait for a person to bring you the solutions. You start by yourself.

A meaningful life is one that turns the negatives into positives.

Success should not come easy; success should be sweat and tears. Trust me, success is not about the top of the mountain; it is about the journey.

Kati on trauma

How to overcome trauma? How to think about and treat obstacles, and to triumph over them; we will come across obstacles in life repeatedly. What matters most is how we see and react to them.

We must keep our heads calm and think with reason without getting angry or sad, etc. This will determine how successful we will be at overcoming, or maybe even thriving, because of trauma. Very often we react emotionally and lose our perspective. Instead, we must not lose our heads.

If you lose your hope the game is lost.

Weak people are destroyed by crisis. Strong people survive a crisis. Flexible people find a way to transform a weakness into a strength and thrive.

What if your obstacle is intimidating and huge? It does not matter. What does matter is the present and that the obstacle exists. It will not go away by you feeling sorry for yourself. Instead of being upset, use the trauma to focus on the present. Don't look at the past, or the future. Instead, recognise your progress, no matter how small, or how slowly, it might happen. This difficult moment is temporary, just one moment of your entire life.

And don't allow yourself to get discouraged. Don't just stare at the obstacle, but see the opportunity within that obstacle.

In the process of dealing with an unexpected reality, we can create a far better reality. I've learnt to use my private turmoil to teach others. It matters less what happens to us in this life, and more what we do when it happens.

Accept the situation and move forward.

Kati on writing

The stroke left me feeling like I had no choices left. When the injury removed all career opportunities, my appreciation for literature grew. I had always loved writing, but was afraid really to pursue it. Creative writing felt too revealing for me, I hated to write about my feelings. I still do. What I hated the most became a dream come true. It was just like modelling for me, where I absolutely *hated* being in front of the camera, which led to some horrible pictures, but still, I wanted to pursue modelling. Now because of my limitations I am able to pursue the true passion of writing.

You can achieve anything if you just want it badly enough. In 2006, my autobiography was published in Finland and it sold out in two weeks. Now I am writing a second autobiography, this time in English.

Finding this writing outlet for my anger and frustration has also helped me to find compassion for others.

Kati's little snippets to remember

» Accept things that you cannot change and adapt.

» Enjoy the little things in life for they bring the big things into being.

» Not all that glitters is gold. The fact is that you don't need to be gold. Gold is just a symbol. And as a human being you are so much more than just a symbol.

» The outer victories are the most celebrated, but we all know – or at least we all need to know – that the greatest and most important victories come from the difficult battles fought deep inside ourselves.

» The closer you are to losing your life, the more alive you feel. Then you learn and understand to enjoy life to the fullest.

My name is Kati

My name is Kati van der Hoeven (Lepistö). Physically I am locked-in, but every single day my soul soars like no other.

AFTERWORD

by Sarah, Henning and Kati

Sarah

'Normal' is relative. Each of us has our own 'normal'. When we visit someone else's house, especially if it is overnight, we discover that person's 'normal'. Remember visiting your friend's house when you were a child? Other homes were fascinating to me; to discover that not everybody thought as we do, or did as we did, was a surprise on the first occasion, and a fascination on visitations to subsequent homes.

So too, with Kati and Henning.

Kati is stylish. Her home is as ordered, modern and stunning as she is. And why wouldn't it be?

Henning is as relaxed as he appears on first meeting him, and as attentive. Isn't it marvellous to learn people can be exactly as they seem?

One thing Kati has learnt to be, and a difference from the way she must have been as a dynamic young woman, is patient. When she is under the precise stretching of her physiotherapist, she gives herself time to release the tight, cramped muscles in her legs, arms, and hands. Though there is pain, and perhaps frustration too, she does not show it.

445

First, she is sat on the side of her bed facing a mirror, the therapist asking her to sit up straight. The spine needs some reminding as it likes to tilt Kati to the left. But moment by moment, three to four times a week, Kati sits until she can hold her position upright, not tilting and not falling backwards.

Then, positioned onto her back, the legs extended fully, they are lifted high and brought down straight. One leg at a time, each knee is bent and brought to her chest and held in position. Then, the knees are manoeuvred to the chest alternatively, as though she is walking up the side of a wall. It is a surprise to me that her legs are not dead weights, but rather are, to a degree, actively engaged in the process.

The arms – more stubborn to straighten – are extended from the side, one at a time, and the fingers too (the latter at a much lower pain threshold, as they exist in their own right in an otherwise permanently cramped state), are splayed one at a time, towards relief. And although she cannot lift her arms above her head, she can bring them back down, one at a time. I tell her she ought to play cricket – it's that sort of pitch. And she laughs.

Kati is not remarkable. She is a woman with a physical disability. But she has an attitude that won't quit, and she is a bright star in a universe full of all sorts of matter, some that shine, and some that do not. She has simply chosen to be light-hearted and a beacon to others in difficult circumstances who, instead of giving up, can simply decide, 'If she can do it, so can I.' In that, she is a remarkable role model and friend to anyone who wants to discover the key to living abundantly is not wealth, fame or power, but recognising our pre-ordained purpose and doing everything possible to achieve it, beginning with an attitude of determination, hope and love, and a never-ending faith in – all things are possible.

Henning

My wife is the other half of me.

If you are a narcissist, a selfish and self-centric person, if you need to play the role of victim or like the feeling of self-pity, then don't get involved with people with disabilities.

Sharing, giving and taking are still the ingredients of a successful marriage, but you must create your own equilibrium if you are not disabled. You don't have to feel like you're walking a tightrope, but you do need to recognise life will be different. Love happens, and there is still a way to ensure ecstasy can be reached. Trust me. But it will be a unique journey.

And if you do choose to go this route to love, shyness, shame or embarrassment can become your biggest enemies. One way to battle this is to develop a sense of humour that starts with learning to laugh at yourself and finding the humour in your situation. Even black humour can clean the soul, and it is freeing; it is better and truer than substance abuse.

Common sense and candour are your best friends, apart from your partner of course.

Kati

Our words that we keep saying to ourselves are extremely important. Are we aware of our unspoken thoughts? Our feelings follow those thoughts, and they will lead us to action. When I'm feeling low, I deliberately think happy thoughts and act happy, and I find myself feeling happy.

Some people chase happiness, while other people choose happiness. That makes the whole difference in our lives.

Happiness comes from the progressive realisation of a goal. My first goal was to survive. Now, having done that, it is to enable others to survive, against any odds.

Your body is a vessel: your mind is the sail, your dreams are the compass, and your spirit is the wind. Keep your spirit steady and strong; let it guide your soul to where it belongs, at the shores of real love and true happiness.

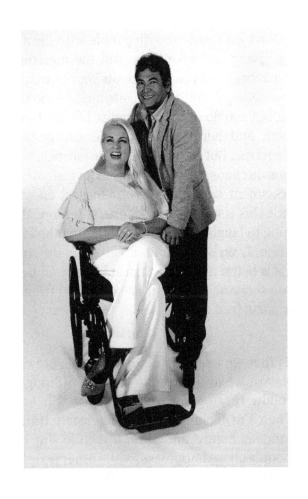

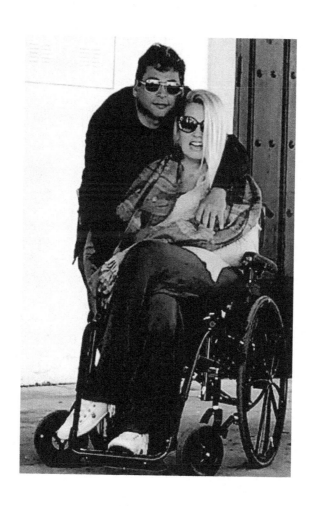

ACKNOWLEDGEMENTS

In our lives, we have people that make all the difference. People that lift us up when we are down, lend us their shoulder when we are sad, dance with us when we are happy.

I have had many people like that in my life. People that literally lifted me in and out of a wheelchair. Pushed me up steep hills and dried the tears from my eyes. People who helped me through depression and reminded me how to live, laugh and love again.

I will be forever grateful to these people in my life. They made the difference between me being a vegetable and being a woman. Because of them, I am living a blessed and meaningful life full of love and joy.

My husband, Henning van der Hoeven, who has been the never-tiring working force behind all that I do. Not only did he make all my dreams come true, but he believed in me even when I did not believe in myself. He took me to heights that I never thought I could reach. He is my hero, the wind beneath my wings.

My parents Marjatta and Risto for always believing in me and never giving up on me. For their everlasting love and unconditional support.

My brother Jukka and his wife Anu and daughter Sofia, for their love and constant support.

Irina, for sticking with me through thick and thin and being the definition of "best friend."

Jamie, for always being there despite the distance and always reminding me of who I am.

All the friends that always kept me in their mind and heart. You know who you are.

All the assistants/caregivers I have had through the years, I could not have made it this far without you all.

All my therapists, they helped me keep my body in shape and healthy.

The personnel of Mikkeli Social Services; "Essote - Etelä-Savon Sosiaali-ja Terveyspalvelut."

A special thanks to: Leena Jokiniemi, Sinikka Söderholm, Maija Rautio, Leeni Peltonen, Emilia Lahti, Ali Meehan, and Heidi Majander.

Sarah Tun (www.laruspress.com), who helped me to write this book and bring my story to the public.

Sarah Houldcroft (www.goldcrestbooks.com) for her guidance and helping me to publish my story.

CONTACT KATI

www.katilepisto.fi/en/

www.facebook.com/InspirationalModel

Made in the USA
Monee, IL
04 November 2020

46740911R00252